THE Face in THE Window

HAUNTING OHIO TALES

GHOSTS OF THE PAST SERIES

CHOSEN AND EDITED BY
CHRIS WOODYARD

AUTHOR OF THE *HAUNTED OHIO* SERIES

Kestrel
Publications

Also by Chris Woodyard

Haunted Ohio: Ghostly Tales from the Buckeye State
Haunted Ohio II: More Ghostly Tales from the Buckeye State
Haunted Ohio III: Still More Ghostly Tales from the Buckeye State
Haunted Ohio IV: Restless Spirits
Haunted Ohio V: 200 Years of Ghosts
Spooky Ohio: 13 Traditional Tales
Ghost Hunter's Guide to Haunted Ohio - Over 25 NEW, terrifying stories
The Wright Stuff: A Guide to Life in the Dayton Area
A Spot of Bother: Four Macabre Tales (Fiction)
The Face in the Window: Haunting Ohio Tales
The Headless Horror: More Haunting Ohio Tales
The Ghost Wore Black: Ghastly Tales from the Past
See the last page of the book for how to order your own copy of this book or other
books by Chris Woodyard

First Printing
Printed in the United States of America
Design and Typesetting by Rose Island Bookworks
Cover Art by Jessica Wiesel

Woodyard, Chris
The Face in the Window: Haunting Ohio Tales / Chris Woodyard
SUMMARY: A compilation of 19th- and early 20th-century newspaper and journal
articles on ghosts and hauntings with commentary and annotations by Chris
Woodyard.

ISBN 0-9628472-9-1

1. Ghosts
2. Ghost Stories
3. Ghosts—United States—Ohio
4. Ghosts—Ohio
5. Haunted Houses—United States—Ohio
6. Haunted Houses—Ohio
7. Ohio—History
398.25 W912H
070.593 Wo
Z1033.L73

Dedicated to

Curt Dalton of daytonhistorybooks.com,
researcher extraordinaire, who started the whole thing.

And to all the people in my life who love history.

Acknowledgments

Bucyrus Public Library, Reference Department

Joseph A. Citro

Curt Dalton, Dayton History Books Online

Ron Davidson, Archives Librarian, Sandusky Library

Natalie M. Fritz, The Heritage Center Library and Archives,
Clark County Historical Society

Sandy Grigsby, Reference Clerk,
Chillicothe and Ross County Public Library

Marsha Hamilton

Robin Heise, Local History Librarian, Greene County Room,
Xenia Community Library

Patrick Henry, Troy Local History Library

J.F. Hill, Local History Library, Greene County Room,
Xenia Community Library

Michelle Mellor and the Information Services Department
of the Public Library of Youngstown and Mahoning County

Tom Metzgar, Mid-Atlantic Karst Conservancy, (www.karst.org).

Marianne Neal

Nicholas A. Reiter

Ken Summers

Rich Wallace, Shelby County Historical Society

Local History Department, Toledo-Lucas County Public Library

Christina Walton, Genealogy Associate, Genealogy and Local History,
Wayne County Public Library

Sharon R. Watson, Local History & Genealogy Dept.,
Piqua Public Library

Jessica Wiesel

Marcia Weldy, Reference Library, Van Wert Brumbacker Library

Table of Contents

Foreword

By Joseph A. Citro

Vermont Folklorist and
Author of *Passing Strange, Lake Monsters, etc.*

Lately Chris Woodyard has been living in the past. She's been reading 19th and early 20th century newspapers and journals, trying to get an idea what Ohio—and by extension the rest of the country—was puzzling about more than a hundred years ago.

In those days even no-nonsense periodicals like *The New York Times* routinely published some highly mysterious stories. By studying such journalistic oddities it is possible to get a sense of what piqued our forbearers' curiosity long before the days of Robert Ripley, *Ghost Hunters*, and all the rest of the so-called "reality TV" boom.

Ghost stories. Murders. Madmen. Monsters. The entire dark spectrum of the weird is present in fading newsprint... but lost to most of us.

Here, with the critical eye of a historian, Chris has excavated the archives and has brought to light a wealth of strangeness: from pesky poltergeists to spontaneous etchings on window glass. From spook lights to petrified people. From familiar scenarios to some outrageously vexing vignettes I had never encountered before.

This is the sort of "documentation" researchers long for when trying to validate some modern tale of the bizarre, the outré, or the forbidden.

Chris has done a wonderful job of not only locating these "lost tales," but also putting them in historical context. She introduces the excerpts, summarizes, and analyzes, all with a clear mind and a delightful sense of humor.

She is ever aware that stories recorded in a diary, book, or newspaper are, in fact, "documented." But she never loses sight of the inescapable question: Is it true?

Ay, there's the rub!

Well, here is the evidence, often in the words of the original experiencer. So be prepared; each of us has some hard decisions to make about the kind of world we have inherited.

Maybe the simple fact that these marvelous reports are no less fascinating today means that, in over a hundred years, things haven't really changed all that much. A mystery is still a mystery. And, as Chris Woodyard repeatedly and ably demonstrates: Be it fact or fiction, there is no purer joy than a good story.

Introduction
A Scrapbook of Victorian Horrors

"I wants to make your flesh creep."
The Pickwick Papers, Charles Dickens

This is a book written by the dead. You can hear their voices, telling their stories in a whisper of ashes, but the writers are all dead and dust, sleeping peacefully in their ancient graveyards—unless their corpses turned to stone or were stolen by the Resurrection Men.

In my *Haunted Ohio* series, I took you along to the places I visited, gave you a sense of what I or other witnesses had seen and felt in those haunt-spots. In this book, the first of a series, I take you on a trip to the past where you will read the words of long-dead reporters, editors, and witnesses. These are ghosts risen from the grave.

We may think of the past as an idyllic, small-town place out of *The Music Man* or *Pollyanna*, where all is clean, cozy, and cheerful. That is not what you will find in this book. Here bodies are mangled horribly, gore is splashed from the murderer's axe, and headless bodies spout blood. The level of violence in the papers is staggering: husbands beat their wives bloody; men cut their throats; children are savaged by dogs or fall into cisterns; people become human torches when they knock over oil lamps. They are cut to pieces by trains or eaten by rats. It could be a nasty, verminous world. Victorian journalists were pioneers in "if it bleeds, it leads." Papers did not hesitate to print revolting details of deaths and accidents which spared neither the sufferings of the victims or their families.

It was also a world where ghosts still walked. Although it was a time of ferment and change with the arrival of automobiles, electricity, women's rights, factories, and advances in medicine, there was still a fascination with ghost stories, monsters, wonders and curiosities.

Why, you may ask, would I want to collect strange old stories from antique newspapers? Am I, as Washington Irving once wrote: "a literary ghoul, feeding in the charnel-house of decayed literature"?

These stories may be old, but they are anything but decayed. Unread for years, they're a trove of brand-new Fortean treasures and historical oddities for the connoisseur of ghosts and strange tales.

I started life as an historian and I have tried to keep my intrusions to a minimum because these historic tales need to be told in their own voices. I have done what I can to corroborate stories or to follow up when possible, but sometimes the archive does not have a crucial newspaper edition or, a century ago, the story just petered out with no resolution. I've also tried to provide some context, annotation and backstories because the past really is a different country and topical references can be obscure. After each story you'll find a citation for that story, the county where the story took place, and notes on the story or my comments.

I confess that I haven't tried to verify the truth of every single story. Some journalistic hoaxes are easy to spot. Other stories, often using names of real individuals are plausible enough to pass for truth. Newspapers also get the facts twisted.

I leave a more thorough documentation to future historians. In writing the *Haunted Ohio* series, I was aware I couldn't prove one syllable, no matter how carefully I quoted my witnesses. In this book, at this distance of time and space from the original events, regretfully I must concede that the most I can guarantee is a ripping yarn.

Think of me as a Victorian mud lark, fishing in the mudflats of a tide of old newspapers, plucking a bloodthirsty fiend here, a petrified corpse there, my attention diverted by a shiny spook light *there*.

Here in my parlor, full of stuffed birds under glass, with my scissors and glue pot and red morocco scrapbook stamped in gilt, I sit and listen to the voices of the dead rustling around me as I fashion my scrapbook of Victorian horrors.

Now open it, and meet the tales that would not die—the ghosts of the past....

Note on spelling and formatting:

I have kept most of the spelling as it was in the article except for obvious spelling errors. Punctuation was a little shaky at times, depending on the newspaper. I have not tried to regularize this or make it conform to any standard. Period newspapers often inserted headlines into the text of an article for emphasis and I have kept these intact. I have divided newspaper articles, which were often one long undivided column, into what I think are logical paragraphs for ease of reading. This is dense language and sometimes difficult to read. I have not censored any politically incorrect or bigoted remarks. The language is as it came from the pencil of the reporter. It should be understood that the sentiments expressed in these articles, no matter how odious or bigoted, are not my own, but those of the original journalist or newspaper in which they appeared.

The Face in the Window
Haunting Ohio Tales

1.

Snapshot of a Ghost

Spirit Photos, Women in White, and Haunted Bridges

The Modern Ghost.
In these days of the boasted triumphs of science, there is as much need
for a ghost editor on the staff of every well-conducted newspaper, as
there is at particular seasons for a snake editor. In spite of the fact that
many very beautiful things have been said and published on the decay
of superstitious beliefs, at the present day, the mysterious and the
unexplainable excite as much interest as they ever did. And while few
people will be found candid enough to admit that they believe in the
supernatural they will all confess to an uncanny feeling on the narra-
tion of some apparently well-authenticated tale of ghostly visitance.

Bradford [PA] Era 29 March 1888: p. 2

Fashions in ghosts change as predictably as skirt lengths. Ohio's earliest
European settlers fervently believed in ghosts, witches, and the Devil.
With death as their constant companion, how could they not?

The terrible weaponry of the Civil War may have created a short vogue
for headless ghosts. That war's unbearable losses encouraged the rise of
Spiritualism with its white-draped ladies and rappings. The country's many
widows were personified in the ghostly Women in Black. Some of these apparitions were even captured in spirit photographs, a genre made popular
and possible by advances in photographic technology and "special effects."

In the forward-thinking era of Business, Thrift, and Industry of the
1880s-90s, ghosts and the supernatural had no place. They were a remnant
of ancestral superstition, a quaint tale, as outmoded as a powdered wig or a
buckskin shirt. Witches, death omens, and hauntings were ridiculed as the
base superstitions of our pioneer forefathers.

Yet people still saw ghosts. Spiritualism, which might have died in the
materialism of the 1880s, lingered, fed by tragedy, eventually transmuted
into a parlor game of Ouija boards, spirit trumpets, and table tipping.

The Victorians were fond of feminine phantoms: vaporous Grey Ladies;
Women in White; and the Woman in Black—a Grim Reaper in weepers.
Moaning, chain-rattling spectres were still making the rounds. One thing
I find interesting in reading the 19th-century papers is that there are no
vanishing hitchhiker stories; no crybaby bridges, and no Hookman tales.

Ghost stories are generally told as reported by witnesses (possibly with some tongue-in-cheek comments) or presented frankly as fiction.

Despite these ghostly trends, 19th-century ghost stories are surprisingly timeless. People who die too soon, suicides, murder victims, the dead, restless until their bones are properly buried, ghosts who appear in photographs, women in white—these phantoms still haunt us today, linking us to the people—and the ghosts—of the past.

Let us begin with a story that could have come from a modern paranormal investigator's case files.

SNAP SHOT OF A GHOST
OHIO DOCTOR CLAIMS TO HAVE ACCOMPLISHED THE FEAT
AT BUCYRUS THE GHOST OF A SUICIDE HAS BEEN SEEN REPEATEDLY
EDITOR SEES THE APPARITION
WAS PRESENT WHEN PHOTOGRAPH OF SPOOK WAS TAKEN
HOUSE WHERE GHOST APPEARS WAS BUILT FOR BRIDAL COUPLE BUT IS UNINHABITED

Bucyrus, Ohio. Feb. 25. The entire northern part of Crawford County is trying to solve a mystery which surrounds a little cottage on the farm of Horace Burger, seven miles north of this city. The cottage, which was built as a bridal present to his daughter by Mr. Burger, is small but comfortable. It is only fifty feet from one of the most travelled roads in the county, with a pretty grove of native forest trees at the rear. In this wood, before the house was built, a wandering workman named J.G. Klinghart took his life by hanging himself.

After their wedding, the young couple took up their residence under the most auspicious circumstances. A week had not passed when their nights were disturbed by strange tappings on the windows and at the doors. Moans and groans came from nowhere in particular. Later on the figure of the suicide could be plainly seen about the house and woods, and though the windows and doors were securely fastened, he would enter the house and wander aimlessly from room to room, his coming being heralded by a dim phosphorescent light, a damp draught and weary, sighing groans.

The young couple supposed at first that some of their friends were making them the target of a practical joke, but two weeks of such a honeymoon convinced them that life at the old family home, amid friends, would be more congenial, and they gave over the cottage to the ghost.

Burger volunteered to prove the fallacy of their story and the next night went to sleep in the cottage. He was awakened suddenly about midnight by a cold breath and sitting bolt upright, he saw the well-known figure of Klinghardt wandering about the room. Burger threw a stick of wood at the apparition. Though his aim was true, the stick seemed to go through the misty form without result. Burger lighted a lamp, but the ghost had gone. He returned to bed and the ghost reappeared. This was enough, and he went home to acknowledge that he did not understand the matter.

LAUGHED AT THE FARMER

Smiles greeted his return, and his son volunteered for a night at the cottage. His experience was similar to that of the others. He had been present when Klinghardt had been cut from the tree, and is sure he recognized in the ghost the unfortunate man. Matthew Burger, though not a believer in the supernatural, could not explain the gruesome problem, though he was averse to talking of the matter because he knew that his statements would seem improbable to the community.

Joseph Oswald was not a believer in spirits, but was speedily convinced that such things were possible. A shot gun which was called into use was of no avail, and although close aim was taken at the wandering apparition, no damage was done except to the walls of the cottage.

Night after night a new candidate came forward to prove the foolishness of his neighbors, but none has either explained the problem or will consent to spend a second night in the place.

Parties have been made up to explode the fallacy, but they have invariably ended in making a larger number of mystified people, all of whom would gladly welcome proof that they were victims of hallucination rather than the observers of a real ghost in his weary journey from the grave to the scene of its departure from life.

John Wilford, George Burger, John Strohm, Philip Cramer, R.D. Whisler and Tony Herzer are all referred to as being able to corroborate the stories of the reality of the ghost.

So notorious had the affairs of the Burger neighborhood become that they attracted attention in the neighboring village of New Washington. Dr. Miller, who, with Editor Lantz of the village paper; J.B. Ledman, superintendent of the Sycamore schools, and Undertaker John Geiger had been present when the body of Klinghardt had been cut down, decided to investigate.

A SNAPSHOT AT MIDNIGHT

Speaking of the matter, Dr. Miller says that when he determined to investigate he kept the matter quiet, so as not to apprise anyone who might be the cause of the joke. He took along his camera, determined to get the only photograph of a real ghost ever taken. He waited until a few minutes before midnight and then went to the grove where the dead man had been found hanging. The doctor knew the way to the sapling and intended to go to it in the moonlight and from there to the grave. He had gone but a short distance when he perceived a form ahead of him leading the way. He was surprised, but not frightened. For a moment he forgot his camera, but just before reaching the woods, he remembered it and he quickly made an exposure. The photo shows plainly the apparition in the woods. The trip to the tree was continued under the supernatural guidance and also the visit to the grave. Being convinced that what he saw was a ghost and not desiring any further acquaintance, the doctor returned to his sleigh and went home.

He has expressed himself as firmly convinced that the Burgers and their friends are sincere in their belief and he cannot explain the matter. Other people have become interested and will make an investigation.
Hutchinson [KS] News 25 February 1903: p. 8 CRAWFORD COUNTY

Such as these young men from Clyde.

GHOST IS REAL
BUCYRUS YOUNG MEN VISIT CELEBRATED
"HAUNTED HOUSE" AND ARE CONVINCED.

Clyde, O., Feb. 23. Two Clyde young men had their courage completely quelled yesterday when they visited the haunted house near Bucyrus. Dean Richmond, assistant manager of the Clyde cutlery works, and Harry Rader, an employee, went to the haunted house to face the ghosts in their den. They went by way of Tiffin and New Washington, hiring a livery rig at the latter place.

They stayed there till last midnight, when they were glad to get away. They returned to Clyde today. Mr. Richmond told his friends here that at first they thought it was a fake, but a number of weird groans and unearthly sounds convinced them otherwise. They endured it for a time and then left.
The Stark County Democrat [Canton, OH] 24 February 1903, Weekly Edition: p. 7 CRAWFORD COUNTY

I have found only one small article describing the photo, but what I would give for the original!

> A New Washington physician has succeeded in getting a flash-light [flash] photograph of a genuine ghost. He deliberately entered a haunted house the other night and laid a neat trap into which the poor unsuspecting spirit walked. The snap-shot is a sort of x-ray affair, showing a skeleton clothed in nebulous flesh and slightly luminous drapery. It will undoubtedly make a very valuable acquisition to modern science.
> *The Stark County Democrat* [Canton, OH] 20 February 1903: p. 4
> CRAWFORD COUNTY

NOTE: This story simply seemed too good to be true. It appeared in a number of papers in 1903 including the *Salt Lake [UT] Tribune* 29 March 1903: p. 23 where the source is said to be the "Bucyrus correspondent of the *Chicago Inter-Ocean*" and the farmer's name is spelled Berger. The *Inter-Ocean* was a Chicago-based newspaper rather like today's *Wall Street Journal* or *New York Times*: meant as a source of news for wealthy business people. It's not a place you'd expect to find a joke story; however, the *Inter-Ocean* did run a number of ghost stories.. Although I haven't located the suicide, I've found a number of the witnesses in census reports. For example, P.F. Lantz was the editor of the *New Washington Herald*, a newspaper from the neighboring Crawford County community of New Washington. Dr. Burton R. Miller was originally from Tiffin and practiced in New Washington from 1897. He was for a time the Seneca County Coroner.

Despite exposures of fraudulent spirit photographers, there were those who still believed.

PHOTOGRAPHS OF GHOSTS
REMARKABLE RESULT OF FLASHLIGHT PICTURES OF MAN AND WIFE

"Have you ever seen the photograph of a ghost?" was the odd question propounded by a guest at the Aragon to his companions at dinner.

Those to whom the question was addressed replied that they had not only never seen the photograph of ghosts nor a ghost, and that they have never so much as heard of the snapshot man getting in his work on the spirit world.

"Well, I'm not in any sense of the word a Spiritualist," continued the man who had asked the question, "but I firmly believe that I have seen, in fact, that my wife has at home, photographs of sure-enough spirits of the dead. I am sorry I can't show you the pictures themselves, as they are, to me at least, intensely interesting.

"Several years ago we were in a small town in Ohio for a few months, having gone there so that I could take charge of a job of work in my line for which my bid had been accepted. The job kept me there most of the winter, and I took my family with me.

"During our stay there we boarded at the home of a prominent young business man and found it very pleasant. His father and mother, who were pretty well advanced in years and pretty well fixed financially, too, resided immediately across the street. It was from them that we first learned the family were firm believers in Spiritualism. In fact, the old man regarded himself as endowed in a rare degree with the faculties of a medium.

"After our discovery of the fact that they were Spiritualists they made strenuous efforts to convert both my wife and myself, but neither one of us entertaining the slightest sympathy with any sort of superstition, they made little headway in their efforts at conversion. However, they frequently made the statement that they would at some time produce such overwhelming evidence in favor of their faith that we would be obliged to acknowledge its sound basis in truth.

"On one occasion the father and son, the latter having a camera and the former promising to call up the spirit, agreed to take photographs of ghosts. We consented to be present at the experiment and my wife and I both sat for flashlight pictures. The pictures were developed, and beside my wife on the print from the plate was a marvelous likeness of her sister who had been dead about 10 years, and whom the Spiritualists had never seen or even heard of. The picture of the dead girl showed gray and rather misty, but each feature was distinct and the likeness was unmistakable.

"Beside me in the other picture was an excellent photograph of my father, appearing exactly as he used to in the last year of his life. I was simply dumfounded at the sight, for in this case, too, the likeness was too perfect to admit of any mistake, and of my father also the Spiritualists knew absolutely nothing.

"We have preserved the pictures and they are regarded as great curios in our family. I have never been able to find anyone who would give any sort of a satisfactory explanation of the phenomenon, and while it did not in any sense convert me to the doctrine of Spiritualism, it has made me infinitely more respectful in my attitude toward the faiths and opinions of others. The whole world is a mystery."

Cincinnati [OH] Enquirer 10 August 1905: p. 6 WARREN COUNTY

Two things about this next story struck me: the completely unnerving encounter with a dead man who "dropped through the floor" and the photograph of the empty chair of his brother-in-law.

SPIRIT PHOTOGRAPHER HAD EXPERIENCE WITH "SPOOK" THEN TOOK UP ART, HE SAYS

Did you ever have your picture taken with a "spook" looking over your shoulder into the camera? Possibly that happened and you didn't know it.

August Spies, photographer, who has operated a studio on W. Market St. for several years, claims that he has a picture of a spirit and to prove his claim, produces the picture of a bearded man taken by himself many years ago in Kenton. Looking over the shoulder of the man is a faint outline of a head which Spies is positive is a spirit.

Spies, to corroborate what he says is the only real spirit picture he has ever seen, told the story of how he became interested in spirit photography.

"I was but a young man and had just opened a studio in Kenton when a policeman was stabbed one night and brought to the office next door to my studio where he died.

"Three nights after that as I was leaving my studio I saw the same man standing and leaning against the door of the office in which he had died. I spoke to him and, when I received no answer, walked up to him, but before I could get there he dropped through the floor.

"That started me thinking and soon after that I was taken to my first spiritualist circle by a friend. At this meeting a voice called in German and I being the only one there who spoke that language, answered it. It was my grandfather from Germany whom I had never seen. He dissuaded me from making a trip to Germany which I had contemplated.

"It was not long after that when I was taken ill with pneumonia and I went to my sister's farm in Indiana to rest for a month. While there I took pictures of the entire family, both individual settings and groups. Everyone turned out splendid with the exception of the picture of my brother-in-law. The chair on which he had been sitting came out perfect in every detail and there was no flaw in the picture with the exception that there was not the slightest trace of the man.

"I tried in many ways to explain this, but was unable to do so until told at a spiritualist meeting by a spirit that these had been accomplished by the spirits so that it might force me to think of spiritualism. At the same meeting I was told by departed spirits that I had the faculty of photographing spirits and that I should attempt to do so.

"This I attempted to do, but it was not until about two months later that I got any results. While developing a plate of a dentist who had an office next to my studio I saw that it looked cloudy and said, 'Why, doc, you moved.' The doctor denied this and as the plate became clearer I realized I had at last photographed a spirit.

"Less than a week before my wife died we had a conversation in which she agreed to communicate with me in the studio should our beliefs about spirits in the after world be correct. Since then she has rung the bell which announces my visitors many times. One night I heard a plate fall and when I investigated in the morning I found it had fallen from practically an impossible place. Later at a circle my wife told me she had dropped it. She has called to me repeatedly here. I heard her natural voice one evening as I was dozing when she said 'Hello, August.'"

Spies also told of many fake spirit photographs he had seen and showed a large number he had collected. He told how he had exposed one photographer in Cleveland who exposed plates for one-half time before taking the picture of the person who wished the photograph.

Sandusky [OH] Star Journal 10 July 1920 HARDIN COUNTY

Unusually, this next story involves a haunting that is entirely auditory. I fully expected to find a follow-up story with a solution to the mystery, but it never came.

NOISES LIKE AN ARMY'S TREAD DISTINCTLY HEARD IN THE SANDUSKY COURT HOUSE
NO SOLDIERS ARE VISIBLE ANYWHERE AND THE THING REMAINS A DEEP MYSTERY

Sandusky, Ohio, February 1.

The facts concerning a mystery of a sensational character were divulged to-day to a representative of *The Enquirer*.

For some time past strange noises have been heard at irregular intervals about the Courthouse in this city, especially in that part of the building occupied by Recorder Schippel. The noises were similar to those made by a company of soldiers at drill, and seemed to emanate from the courtroom, directly above the Recorder's office. At various times during the day there could be distinctly heard the rhythmic tread of men as if executing intricate military maneuvers. When these noises were first heard, Recorder Schippel at once ascended to the courtroom to learn the cause. Court was in session, and he inquired if there had been any men marching across the floor. He was told that there had not, but he was at first inclined to

DISCREDIT HIS OWN SENSES,

But as others had heard the measured tread, he soon felt that he had not been deceived by his imagination.

The next day, and for several days thereafter, the peculiar noises were repeated. Sheriff McGill, Auditor McFall, Probate Judge Goodwin, Treasurer Arend, and others about the Courthouse were called into Recorder Schippel's rooms and heard the noises distinctly. They became much interested, and were very anxious to ascertain whence came the sounds. The upper portion of the Courthouse was carefully searched, but nothing was discovered that could have produced the sounds. Climatic conditions had nothing to do with the matter. The marching continued on rainy and sunshiny, blustering and still days alike. The invisible soldiers, it seems, start from the northeastern part of the building, and go diagonally across it, then countermarch, and wind up with an exhibition drill directly over the center of the main room occupied by the Recorder. Their footsteps could be heard receding and approaching, as plainly as could those of real soldiers on a drillroom floor. Every effort was exhausted by the county officials to fathom the mystery, but not the slightest clew could be obtained as to the source of the noises. Men were stationed in every room of the Courthouse to await the appearance of the

GHOSTLY VISITANT.

They saw nothing, but the marching continued all the same. The county officials said to-day that they were completely nonplussed. They felt some delicacy about having the story get out as involving them in an effort to find military spooks, but as the marching continues every day, and can be distinctly heard by anyone who chooses to go to the Courthouse, they feel that as long as the public is not denied the privilege of verifying the manifestations themselves, they will not be accused of having been imposed upon by tricksters.

Cincinnati [OH] Enquirer 2 February 1896: p. 9 ERIE COUNTY

CROWDS VISIT A "HAUNTED" BUILDING
MANY STORIES OF STRANGE MANIFESTATIONS
IN SANDUSKY'S COURTHOUSE

Sandusky, Ohio, February 5. The dispatch in *The Enquirer* in relation to the courthouse mystery here has aroused the curiosity of the residents of this city and vicinity to the highest pitch. Great crowds of people have visited the building, and nearly all of them who have had sufficient patience to remain there until the "spirit soldiers," as they are now called, choose to begin their march, have been amply rewarded by hearing their measured tread.

County Treasurer Arend said to-day that about 10 o'clock last night, whilst he was in his office attending to some of the unfinished business of the day, he distinctly heard cries and moans, as of some human being in distress. The family of the janitor lives in the courthouse, and Treasurer Arend supposed that the noises emanated from their rooms. The cries and wails continued for several minutes, and the Treasurer finally decided to ascertain the cause.

Just as he was about to leave his office to do so Mr. Levi Green, the janitor, opened the door and excitedly inquired

WHAT WAS THE MATTER.

He said that he and the members of his family had heard cries and moans, and knowing that the Treasurer was the only other person in the building, he quite naturally inferred that he had sustained some injury, or been taken suddenly sick.

Treasurer Arend and the janitor were dumfounded when it was found that the source of the cries was unknown to either of them. A thorough search of the building was at once made, from basement to cupola, but nothing was found that threw any light upon the mystery.

Ex-Probate Judge A.E. Merrill, in discussing the matter to-day remarked that during the period that he was on the Probate bench he frequently heard strange noises in the courthouse; that he was often startled by them, but that he had never been able to determine from whence they came. He used to hear what sounded like the steady tramp, tramp of feet, and, although on several occasions he made quiet personal investigations, he was never rewarded by the discovery of anything that could aid in the

SOLUTION OF THE MYSTERY.

Mr. Edward Gosser, ex-janitor at the courthouse, and now holding a similar position in the Federal Building here, told an Enquirer man to-day that when he and his family lived in the courthouse, they were frequently frightened and annoyed by manifestations of the kind that are now taking place in that building.

Ex-Recorder James Flynn was asked to-day if during his term of office he heard these noises, and he replied:

"Yes, I heard them frequently, and they used to make me very nervous at first. I don't pretend to say what causes them. They occur, however, and they give a man's nervous system a first-class jar, too."

Cincinnati [OH] Enquirer 6 February 1896: p. 9 ERIE COUNTY

Bridges, those symbols of passage from life to death, attract ghost stories: Crybaby Bridges, Screaming Mimi Bridges, Hookman Bridges, bridges haunted by suicides and ghostly brides...

THE MOANING BRIDGE OF HAMILTON

Hamilton (Ohio). Despite the fact that this is a busy little city of nearly 20,000 inhabitants, and one so beautifully located as to dispel any thoughts of uncanny nooks where spirits or spooks might linger, it is too evident that she boasts of a strange and unearthly mystery which is located almost in the heart of the city. This mystery is the outgrowth of a terrible love tragedy, which occurred on the reservoir several years ago. The reservoir is formed by back water from the Miami River, and its chief purpose is to supply the city with ice, a commodity largely used in Hamilton.

The reservoir is also the resort of lovers in the summer time, and their boats may be seen on any quiet summer evening floating gaily along. The Hamilton Club House stands at the head of the reservoir, and its boats are in constant demand among the young people during the summer months. The reservoir is spanned by several wagon bridges. One particularly, located far up the reservoir, is a constant object of interest, to say nothing of awe and superstition. It is constructed of heavy timbers and sets low on the banks, so that occupants of row-boats are compelled to "duck" their heads pretty low in order to pass under. This bridge is called "the moaning bridge of Hamilton." This is the story:

A young man of Hamilton fell desperately in love with one of the fair daughters of the place. His love was returned and the twain were very happy. They were seen in each other's company very often, so that Dame Rumor was not at fault in reporting that the two would soon become man and wife. They were fond of boating, and were often seen together on the reservoir in their natty skiff. But that relentless destroyer, consumption, came to play a part in this tale of love, and in a few months physicians informed the young man that his death was but a question of a few weeks. Naturally, the victim brooded over this very much. His wife-to-be was handsome, healthy, and vivacious. He could not have the heart to make her a widow. He would not do that.

The two took their accustomed boat-ride one beautiful summer evening. They rode up to the bridge. Here, so far as could ever be learned, the young man deliberately shot his sweetheart through the head, and then put a bullet in his own brain. The young lady did not die immediately, it is thought, and her head fell over one side of the boat, her golden tresses floating in the water. The boat was caught by an eddy and swung further under the bridge. A farmer passing over the bridge about that hour on the evening of the tragedy says he heard moans issuing from beneath the bridge and looked under it, but evidently did not see the boat. However, the boat slowly drifted down to the club-house. A crimson tide followed in its wake, the life-blood of the fair young girl. The next morning early the boat with its ghastly burden was found at the club-house steps. The young lover could not live on earth with his bride. He would take her with him.

So the bridge moans for the dual death. At eventide those who may row up the reservoir can hear the low moans as they float out from 'neath the bridge. Some say it is the wind; others that it is the grasses on the banks shaken by the winds. But the moaning can be heard—moaning like a human being in deep agony. It is also said that at times a streak of crimson appears on the water's surface between the fatal bridge and the club house. One or two have been so bold as to declare that they have since seen this phantom boat floating down the stream with its dead lovers: the young girl's golden locks trailing in the water, and the blood from the cruel wound flowing back in a crimson stream.

Cincinnati [OH] Enquirer 20 October 1889: p. 20 BUTLER COUNTY

NOTE: I believe that the reservoir mentioned is now under the L. J. Smith North End Athletic Field. There is still a Reservoir Street in Hamilton.

This next story is the sort of thing you couldn't sell as fiction—it would be too implausible. And yet....

A GHOST ON THE BRIDGE
THE DEPARTED SPIRIT THAT PATROLS
A TOLEDO BRIDGE AT MIDNIGHT

Toledo, Ohio, December 27. One of the Cherry Street bridge-tenders said to me the other day:

"*The Enquirer* has caused an 'l of a row around this bridge. Since it published an account of Meyers' ghost haunting it, thousands of people have haunted me with questions about it. I do not know whether it is Meyers' ghost or his son's, but there is some mighty strange goings on around the west end of this bridge. I have seen it myself, but, Lord knows, I don't know what it is. I never went near enough to find out."

I hunted up Detective Louie Trotter, who gave me a more detailed account of the affair than I had been able to get elsewhere. He said: "I have heard the new bridge was haunted, and I know the old one was. It was like this: Some of the boys who live on the East Side were going home

from duty one August morning in 1882. When we reached the first pier I was horrified to see the body of someone hanging there. It did not take us long to cut the corpse down and we found it was Pop Meyers, as he was familiarly called. His face was just as pleasant as if he were selling a pair of shoes to a customer. There was not the least sign of pain, and his wide-open eyes were looking rather expectantly up the river. He had evidently put on a new shirt, collar, and necktie, and was well dressed, except that he had no coat or shoes on. Well, we carried him home and found some letters which plainly indicated that his mind had left his body. His son, who had brought so much care on the old man's mind by his dissipation, begged us to give him the rope with which his father had hanged himself. 'I want it as a reminder,' he said, 'of my father.' Well, some way he obtained the rope, and with it, shortly afterward, ended his life at the identical spot, with the same rope. It was not long after this that the report got around that Meyers was walking the bridge at night, carrying a rope and looking longingly up the river. I investigated the affair and found it was true something was haunting the bridge. The ghost was dressed just as Meyers was on the morning that I cut him down. The old bridge was carried away, and the story was forgotten. The first night the new bridge was opened late wayfarers were badly frightened by a phantom walking slowly along in his bare feet, making no noise as he softly trod the planks. That's all I know about it. Officer Kruse states that many people have recently told me they had seen Meyers' ghost patrolling the bridge, rope in hand, after midnight."
Cincinnati [OH] Enquirer 28 December 1884: p. 13 LUCAS COUNTY

I sighed when I read this, thinking it was simply too symmetrical to be true. I remained a skeptic until the reference librarians at the Local History Department, Toledo-Lucas County Public Library found information on the Cherry Street Bridge and located Trotter and Kruse as police officers in the Toledo city directories. I wondered if Meyers was the man who built the Meyers/Myers Block on Adams Street in downtown Toledo, which held clothing and shoe stores. I could not locate the original story in the *Enquirer*. But then, I found this:

A most important question in insurance circles was decided to-day by Judge Commager. It involved the question whether an insurance company was liable to pay insurance on the death of a suicide. The case was that of Mrs. Joseph Meyers vs. The Homeopathic Mutual Life Insurance Company. Her husband was insured in the company for $5,000, but let his policy lapse. He settled by accepting a paid-up policy for $2,500, in which there was a clause, not known to him, and not in the original contract, that should he take his life with his own hand the policy was null and void. He took the policy, thinking it was the same as the original, and did not examine it. Shortly afterward, he hung himself from one of the piers in the Cherry Street Bridge. The company refused to pay the policy and suit was brought to collect it by the widow, who claimed that the company did not keep good faith in putting a clause in the second policy not in the first, and that Meyers did not take his life with his own hand, as he was insane at the time, and therefore not responsible. These facts were proven to the satisfaction of Judge and jury, and a verdict of $2,525 brought for plaintiff. This is the full amount of policy and interest to date. The insurance company will appeal from the decision.

Cincinnati [OH] Enquirer 12 December 1884: p. 5 LUCAS COUNTY

Now I had a first name and was able to find this next article, which confirms important details, although it shows how the date and location of the story was slightly distorted in the memory of Detective Trotter.

SUICIDE AT TOLEDO

Toledo, Ohio, November 13. Joseph Myers, aged about twenty-seven, and unmarried, came home from a protracted spree at two o'clock this morning, and soon after that committed suicide by hanging himself in the yard, where he was found at daylight. He was the son of Joseph Myers, who hung himself on the Cherry Street Bridge last August, and on this occasion he used the same rope with which his father had hung himself, and which he had kept in his trunk, evidently with some such purpose in view. Dissipation and probable remorse at the thought that he had helped bring about his father's death by his profligacy seemed to be the causes of his action.

Cincinnati [OH] Enquirer 14 November 1881: p. 1 LUCAS COUNTY

And if that weren't strange enough, Toledo apparently had a second haunted bridge:

AT MIDNIGHT
STRANGE DOINGS ARE WITNESSED ON A BRIDGE, SAY TOLEDOANS

Toledo, Ohio, May 4. "Is the Fassett Street Bridge across the Maumee River haunted?" Scores of people who cross the bridge between the hours of 11 p.m. and 1:30 a.m. are asking one another the question.

About 11 p.m. on certain nights, they say a mysterious-looking man dressed in black makes his appearance on the bridge. The man is tall, straight and dignified and rapid in his movements. No person has been able so far to get a full view of his face. The mysterious man suddenly makes his appearance in the center of the bridge as though he had come up through the flooring. He then passes over the foot path and after that all trace of him is lost until about 1:30 a.m., when he is seen for a moment in the center of the bridge and then vanishes in some mysterious manner as though he dropped into the river.

Some believe the strange figure may be a woman in disguise who is perhaps doing a little detective work on her own hook on the movements of a gay husband, while others are convinced that the mysterious stranger is a real ghost, the troubled spirit of some departed being. It is recalled that a well-dressed stranger was found dead on the bridge years ago, shortly after it was built, near the spot where the mysterious figure makes its nightly appearance and disappearance.

Cincinnati [OH] Enquirer 5 May 1902: p. 4 LUCAS COUNTY

I've always been particularly interested in stories of ghosts attached to objects (see the chapter "Possessed Possessions" in *Haunted Ohio IV: Restless Spirits*.) Rocking chairs are the number one haunted object; here are two others.

GUARDING HER ROSARY AND PRAYER BOOK, REMOVED TO A BARN IS SAID TO BE THE WOMAN'S GHOST

Sandusky, Ohio. February 4. The people in the vicinity of Mustcash are worked up over the report that the ghost of a devout Christian woman, recently deceased, may be seen each night between 11 and 12 entering an old barn near the house in which she died.

The decedent was a strict Catholic, and to her a prayer book and rosary, which she possessed, were sacred. It is believed by her friends that she stands guard over these church articles, which the purchasers of the old homestead recently removed from the house and placed on a high ledge in the barn.

Many residents of Mustcash are afraid to pass the barn after dark, and some have expressed an intent to move out of the neighbourhood. The Zick family has already made arrangements to move. Mrs. Chapman, who resides opposite the barn, claims to have seen the ghost last night.

Cincinnati [OH] Enquirer 5 February 1906: p. 4 HURON COUNTY

A RED SHIRT AND A GHOST

Findlay [Ohio] February 24.

The inmates of a North Main Street boarding house are greatly excited over what the boarders term spiritual manifestations, growing out of the following circumstances. A stonemason by the name of Colpitts boarded at the house for some time and about a month ago went to Toledo, where he met a violent death, by having a slab fall upon him in a stoneyard. In the room in the boarding house in this city which he occupied, he left a red flannel shirt when he went away. His former roommate, thinking the dead man would have no further use for the garment, appropriated it, and the other night put it on for a night dress.

About the time churchyards yawn and graves give up their dead, the boarding house people sprang from their beds in great alarm, caused by ear-piercing yells coming from the room occupied by the young man who had taken possession of the dead man's shirt. Between screams he explained that he had been visited by the spirit of the departed stonemason, who was violently angry because his garments had been used. Of course everybody laughed except the young man, who discarded the spirit-haunted dress, laid down and slept peacefully the rest of the night.

The next night, however, another young man who took no stock in the story, borrowed the shirt and putting it on, went to his bed. At about the same hour that the previous disturbance had startled the boarding house, the inmates were again aroused by shrieks and screams of the most terrifying character, and in a moment afterward the young man with the haunted shirt in his hand, dashed downstairs as if the devil was after him, and took refuge under a table in the kitchen. He too had been visited by the former owner of the red shirt, whose anger had been intensified by the second attempt to appropriate his intimate piece of apparel. In the mean-time, and pending the appearance of someone with courage sufficient to meet the enraged spirit of the dead stonemason, the red shirt has been hung in the garret, from whence, it is said, strange, uncanny sounds come nightly, and the boarding house will soon shut up shop.

The Atlanta [GA] Constitution 25 February 1889 HANCOCK COUNTY

Women in White have always been a ghost-story standard. This is an odd tale. I've seen other accounts that emphasize how many people witnessed the apparition in Miamisburg. If it was a hallucination, it was one on a grand scale.

A GENUINE OHIO GHOST.
DAYTON PEOPLE TURN OUT EN MASSE TO LAY IT,
BUT IT WILL NOT DOWN.

A thousand people surround the graveyard in Miamisburg town, near Dayton, Ohio, every night, to witness the antics of what appears to be a genuine ghost. There is no doubt about the existence of the apparition. Mayer Marshall, general collector, and hundreds of prominent citizens all testify to having seen it. Last night several hundred people armed with clubs and guns assaulted the spectre, which appears to be a woman in white. Clubs, bullets and shot tore the air in which the misty figure floated without disconcerting it in the least.

The people of the town turned out en masse yesterday and began exhuming bodies in the cemetery to get at her ghostship. The remains of the Vuss family, composed of three people, have already been exhumed. The town is visited daily by hundreds of strangers and none are disappointed as the apparition is always on duty promptly at 9 o'clock. The strange figure was at once recognized by the inhabitants of the town as a young lady supposed to have been murdered several years ago. Her attitude while drifting among the graves is one of deep thought, with head inclined forward and hands clasped behind.

Huntingdon [PA] Journal 11 April 1884: p. 2 MONTGOMERY COUNTY

NOTE: This graveyard used to be located on the grounds where the Miamisburg Library now stands. Supposedly all the bodies were moved, although a Victorian gentleman in a cast-iron casket was found in the 1980s when the library was expanded. The exhumation of the bodies during this ghost panic suggests some sort of vampire hunt.

GHOST PARADES CHURCH.
ELECTRICIAN IS STARTLED BY SILENT WOMAN
CLAD IN WHITE

Springfield, Oct. 14. That a ghost infests St. Bernard's Catholic Church is the belief of John Herzog, an electrician who has been wiring in the church for some weeks.

Alone in the auditorium he was startled one night this week to see a white figure of a woman silently walk down the center aisle. Herzog says his hair stood on end, as the ghost advanced toward the chancel where he was working, passed him, marched solemnly back through a side aisle, ascended the winding stair to the choir loft and was seen no more.

In connection with the story as to the church being haunted, members recall the mysterious burning of the great pipe organ three or four years ago.

Massillon [OH] Evening Independent 14 October 1909: p. 1 CLARK COUNTY

NOTE: St. Bernard's Catholic Church is still an active parish in Springfield. I would like to know more about that "mysterious burning" of the pipe organ. Was it arson? Bad wiring? Or a fire-spook?

While the Woman in White at St. Bernard's may have been a saintly spirit, this next white-clad wraith had a criminal record.

"THE WOMAN IN WHITE"
A GHOSTLY VISITANT HAUNTING
THE COUNTY JAIL

A few years ago Mrs. Lizzie McConnemara, better known as "Mrs. Mack," a widow, living down at the foot of Plum Street, was arrested by the United States authorities, and convicted of perjury in swearing to false pension papers, on which she drew money for the death of her husband, who was killed in battle, while at the same time she was married to a second husband. She made as good a defense as was possible, being supported in some of her statements by two female confederates, who were also convicted of perjury, and all three of the women were sentenced to one year in the Penitentiary.

After sentence was passed the women were given their old quarters in the County Jail to await the trip to Columbus. In the meantime "Mrs. Mack," who occupied cell No. 3, was taken seriously ill, and in a few days died in her cell. One of the witnesses for Mrs. Mack was Maggie Wilson, who occupied cell No. 4, between which and Mrs. Mack's quarters there is a barred window about eighteen inches square. The woman now in the laundry department of the jail, and who was there at the time spoken of, says that she has heard Maggie Wilson say time and again that she saw the face of a ghost looking from cell No. 3 into hers. No one believed her at the time, but recent developments have shaken the incredulity of the jail people who now are in a flutter of excitement in consequence of the disclosures made last Saturday and Sunday nights.

The fated cell, No. 3, is now occupied by Martha J. Irwin, who was arrested some six weeks ago on East Pearl Street on the charge of dealing in counterfeit money. Her companion is Miss Minnie Mayrose, charged with grand larceny. In the cell adjoining (No. 4) Mary Fallon is imprisoned. The story, as told by Mrs. Irwin to an *Enquirer* reporter yesterday afternoon, and which the Jail officials believe to be true, is as follows: Mrs. Irwin formerly occupied the cell immediately below No. 3 and while there she has been frequently awakened in the night by strange noises above her head, as if by muffled footsteps and knocks upon the cell door. A few days ago she was placed in cell No. 3, and given as a companion Miss Mayrose...

Last Sunday morning, just as the clock pointed to twenty minutes past one o'clock, a form clothed in white was seen to enter the barred window of the cell on the north side and walking with a slow and measured tread, passed the little cot on which Mrs. Irwin lay, approached the door leading into the corridor, and made three distinct raps. This done, the ghost turned and pacing to the window in which it made its entry—vanished. The terrified woman never closed her eyes until daylight dawned.

She told her experience to Captain Suge Taylor and his assistants, but the idea of a ghost was scouted as the child of her imagination. Sunday night Mrs. Irwin did not remove her clothes upon retiring, but reversing her pillow, so that she could watch the window through which the apparition came, she waited to see if the visit would be repeated. Her companion not being scared, as she was not awake when the ghost came Saturday night, was calmly sleeping, with her face turned to the east wall, and nearly opposite the cot of Mrs. Irwin.

At precisely the same hour as before (1:20 a.m.) the vision again burst upon the horrified eyes of the watcher, and with a rapidly gliding motion stepped upon the floor. The latch on the barred window snapped perfectly distinct as it passed from the sill. The floor creaked as the phantom feet first touched it, and then, as before, all was still, save the momentary rustle of a piece of paper which seemed to have been disturbed by the trailing white robes.

Again it passed between the cots, glided to the same door, rapped three times, and then stalked to the head of the bed on which the watcher lay, and striking the iron frame just above her head, stared with brilliant wide-open eyes into those of the now almost petrified figure crouching terror-stricken on her bed. It remained there several seconds, and then, as quickly as it came, was lost to view. The raps on the door awoke Miss Mayrose, who, covered with a cold sweat, lay with her head submerged in her blanket, afraid to look out into the darkness.

All that horrible night the women paced the floor of their gloomy quarters, afraid to lie down. Mary Fallon, in the adjoining cell, swears by all that's true that she has seen a weird face at the window of the same cell before Mrs. Irwin ever was placed in it, and while it was unoccupied.

The description of the face of the strange visitor tallies perfectly with the features of "Mrs. Mack," as she is remembered by old employees at the jail. Mrs. Irwin never knew Mrs. Mack, and had never heard of her imprisonment until her experience with the ghost was detailed to those who knew her, when the resemblance was remarked and commented on with amazement by those who listened to and believed the story of the ghost.

Mrs. Irwin, who is a woman of the keenest intelligence and who declares that she was never a believer in ghosts, told the reporter that while the apparition was at the head of her bed she wanted to ask it questions, but that her tongue refused its office. She could not move, but was compelled to gaze on the sight, spellbound with fear. Who can explain this mystery? For mystery it seems. The women have no motive for telling an untruth on such a subject and their stories all point to the same fact, that "something" is haunting the County Jail.

Cincinnati [OH] Enquirer 15 January 1878: p. 8 HAMILTON COUNTY

A little light relief from a Mother-in-Law's ghost:

OBJECTS TO GHOSTLY CALLER.
WOMAN ASSERTS DEAD MOTHER-IN-LAW VISITS AND ANNOYS HER.

Cincinnati, O. "It's bad enough to have a mother-in-law pecking at you in real life, but when that mother-in-law continues at the pecking job after she has passed into the spirit world it is time for action."

This is the opinion of Mrs. John O'Donnell, wife of an actor of that name living at 320 East Eighty-ninth Street, New York City, and is also the reason why she filed a suit for divorce.

Mrs. O'Donnell was Ora Dresselhaus, a Cincinnati chorus girl, when she met O'Donnell less than a year ago. They were married in New York City in February, 1908, but found they were not matched right to travel in double harness and separated soon after, the bride returning to her Cincinnati home. Though there were many miles between the husband and wife, and O'Donnell could no longer bother her, Mrs. O'Donnell says the spirits of his dead relatives bothered her to such an extent that she was obliged to seek rest in divorce.

"It's awful to wake up in the night to find the ghost of your mother-in-law or some other relative standing over your bed with a club in her hand ready to whale you over the head if you say a word," said Mrs. O'Donnell.

State Center [IA] Enterprise 27 August 1908 HAMILTON COUNTY

There are many tales of canal ghosts in Ohio. Most are ghosts of the workers who died of violence, disease, or alcohol while building the canals, but here is a tale of a ghostly lock-keeper.

A WEIRD TALE OF THE CANAL LOCKS
NEAR NAPOLEON

Napoleon, O. July 21. Nestled in a clump of trees, almost on the boundary line between Lucas and Henry counties, is a famous landmark on the Miami and Erie Canal, called Buckland's Locks, and around this spot is woven a weird tale of tragic mystery which has lately culminated in a series of the strangest happenings in the history of the canal. The stories hang on the alleged visitation to the spot of a ghostly apparition and a remarkable series of sights and sounds which have enveloped that portion of the canal in dense mystery. There is absolutely no explanation of the mysterious events, and the matter is attracting much attention.

Probate Judge James Donovan of this county furnished a correspondent with an interesting account of the mysterious happenings which ran somewhat as follows: Boatmen passing the spot after dark are startled by weird groans, near the shore, as though someone was in great agony. But instead of growing fainter the cries increase, until suddenly a misty figure rises apparently from the water just in front of the boat, as it pauses near the lock.

The form can be plainly seen and is that of an old man, who fumbles about the sluice gates ahead of the craft a moment. Then stepping back, he throws them open, and without a word, fades away. As the boat continues its course to pass through the locks, the bargemen to their amazement see that the gates are tightly closed, although they could have sworn that the mysterious man of the night had opened them for them a moment before. At the second lock the strange figure is again seen, and so on until the series is passed, each time repeating the performance.

The spot aside from its ghostly happenings has a weird history. The last keeper was an old man by the name of Bill Bellington, who was a well-known character in that vicinity in the latter part of the eighties. He was a heavy drinker, and one night came home considerably the worse for his potations. About midnight an alarm of fire was sounded from the building, but before help could arrive, it was a mass of flames. The next day the charred remains of a man were found which were identified as those of Bellington. It was supposed that he had been murdered by plunderers bent on securing a sum of money reported to be hidden in the house. The strange stories concerning the locks have continued for a number of years. It is claimed by some that the strange figure is that of Bellington.

Akron [OH] Daily Democrat 21 July 1902: p. 5 LUCAS/HENRY COUNTY

An uncanny Man in Black, in a Grim Reaper/Count Dracula cloak, with a touch of Spring-heeled Jack.

LEGLESS GHOST IS WALKING.
RESIDENTS OF SPRUCE STREET DESCRIBE STRANGE APPARITION WHICH HAUNTS LOCALITY

There is a real ghost in this city although the presence of the weird thing has been kept a secret for two or three days in order that a delegation of local sleuths could unearth the mysterious rendezvous of the unwelcome visitor.

Spruce Street, which heretofore has had the reputation of being one of the most quiet and peaceful thoroughfares in the city, threatens to share honors with Sleepy Hollow where the famous headless horseman was wont to chase poor Ichabod Crane up and down the hills near Tarrytown.

But the comparison stops here, for instead of the headless phantom which infested the Sleepy Hollow district, the good neighbors on the street say it is a legless man that dashes out of the yards and jumps across the road only to disappear in an orchard across the street.

Mrs. John Gehrke of 108 Spruce Street was the first of many residents to discover the "awful thing" last Thursday night about ten thirty o'clock and she flushed the ghost in the yard and was terrified when the thing which looks like a man dressed in a long black cape, skimmed over the ground across the road and disappeared in an old orchard which has the reputation of being spooky on account of a suicide which occurred there one winter's night.

Mrs. Eva Collier of 110 Spruce Street was the second party to witness the aeroplane antics of the spector, and although the story told by Mrs Gehrke was laughed at, the smiles from the lips of the doubting Thomases changed to looks of grave concern when Mrs. Collier described the unnatural flight which she witnessed.

Mrs. Ella Danforth of 120 Spruce Street was the third resident of the street to run across the night flyer and when her story was told among the neighbors, the cold chills began to creep along the spines of her listeners, and to add to her description of the ghostly thing, a young lad burst into the room and said he had seen the gruesome object the night before and had pursued it until it was lost in an old grape arbor near Woodford Avenue.

Needless to say there are few windows remaining open on Spruce Street these nights, and it is confidentially reported that several men on the street have failed to spend their evenings over in town since the apparition has cursed the street with its presence.

Elyria [OH] Republican 10 September 1908: p. 12 LORAIN COUNTY

NOTE: This creature sounds like the apparition known as Spring-heeled Jack who terrorized Victorian England with his uncanny appearance and his unearthly leaps. He falls into the Fortean Phantom Attacker category and there have been a few reports of similar entities from the United States and elsewhere. The definitive work on Spring-Heeled Jack is 'Spring-Heeled Jack,' Mike Dash, *Fortean Studies 3*, Steve Moore, ed., 1996: 7-125.

As many ghost articles end, we end this chapter with a question:
What was it?

GHOST VISITS THE CITY HOSPITAL
NURSES AND PATIENTS IN M WARD
PANIC-STRICKEN BY MYSTERIOUS APPARITION
LAST NIGHT

In sober earnest nurses and patients of M Ward of the City Hospital are discussing with bated breath an apparition that threw the entire ward into a panic at a late hour last night. The superstitiously inclined declare positively they saw a ghost, and the skeptics simply say they saw something they cannot explain.

The statement from all is that about 9:30 o'clock last night when about six electric lights were burning in the ward, casting fantastic shadows on wall and floor, a veiled figure suddenly appeared beside the bed of Lydia Work, a patient lying at the extreme south end of the ward. The woman sat up in her bed, gazed at the wraith dumbfounded, then with a shriek threw the sheet of her bed over her face and trembled in fear. With noiseless tread it next passed the bed of Catharine Yeager, who followed the example of Lydia Work and yelled at the top of her voice.

By this time the whole ward was astir. Miss Holt, the nurse in charge, started for the end of the ward where the commotion originated, and she, too, encountered the ghost. As she turned the mysterious figure had gained the door, and as the young woman with beating heart and heightened pulse gazed in open-mouthed astonishment it disappeared, waving its hands.

Miss Holt is a robust young woman, energetic and without a trace of hysteria in her disposition. Speaking on the subject last night she said: "Of course it's absurd to think there is anything supernatural about this thing, but nevertheless I cannot explain it. A dozen patients saw what I saw, a tall female figure robed in white with what appeared to be a veil over her face. All agree on this description but what it was none of us can tell. I know it's ridiculous to say it was a ghost, but what was it? All my patients were in their beds and were accounted for immediately and therefore could not have been walking in their sleep. I'm not afraid of dead people; hundreds have died in this ward, and I do not believe that, like Hamlet's father, they ever "revisited the glimpses of the moon." But I freely confess this thing gave me the creeps and I'd like to know what it was."

Cincinnati [OH] Enquirer 11 January 1904: p. 10 HAMILTON COUNTY

2.

The Face in the Window

Strange Images in the Glass

There are two signs, which appear to those spirits,
when they are attendant on man:
they see an old man of a whitish looking face...
they see also a face in the window...

– Emanuel Swedenborg –

It's a standard trope in horror films and fiction: the face appearing, suddenly, shockingly, at the window. And we've all heard the urban legends: the face of a terrified man etched into an Alabama courthouse window by lightning, the image of a man strangling his wife appearing on a tombstone at Carey, the Virgin Mary manifesting in a Florida window. Some call them examples of pareidolia or call them *acheiropoieta*: "images not made with hands" or, more simply, simulacra.

In 1871 something peculiar was happening in Sandusky. Faces—mystic, photographic portraits—began to appear on windows. They emerged overnight. They were invisible from the inside. They had a vague, misty quality as if a ghost with its face against the glass was peering from the window. Some windows had only one, others a dozen or more.

While it was the age of progress in industry and science, it was also the heyday of Spiritualism. All over America people were earnestly tipping tables, receiving messages rapped out by the dead, and watching ghostly figures emerge from mediums' cabinets. Some were simply credulous; others, like Sir William Crookes the distinguished English chemist, made it their scientific duty to study the spirit world in darkened rooms with the assistance of young lady mediums like Florence Cook, and write letters about these prodigies to Spiritualist papers.

There was a feeling among scientists and Spiritualists alike, that with hard work and perseverance, all could be revealed, including the mysteries of the World Beyond. It was an age of optimism—of miracles.

It was into this fevered atmosphere that the miraculous images of Sandusky came.

Charles Fort in his book *Wild Talents* discusses historic tales of images—crosses and death's heads—appearing in 1872 on window glass in Europe during the Franco-Prussian War and mentions reports of faces from Massachusetts, Milan, Sandusky, and Cincinnati. I have collected others from Indiana, Connecticut, Pennsylvania, California, and New York. Almost all of the articles say the same thing: that the faces are not sharply defined, cannot be seen by all viewers, and cannot be seen from the inside of the window. Fort suggests that the origin of these stories lies in the rise of spirit photography and wonders if the human imagination can affect a photographic plate.

Several of the following articles mention Daguerreotypes. The Daguerreotype photographic process was invented in 1839; in 1861 the first spirit photos were produced using the new medium by William Mumler, a Boston photographer. It must be remembered that until about 1860, besides drawings and paintings, images on glass—daguerreotypes and ambrotypes—were the only way to create portraits. Pictures on glass were etched, as it were, in the national consciousness.

I have to wonder if there was some kind of weather event—a volcanic eruption perhaps?—that caused a chemical reaction with window glass. If the images had appeared later in the year, they might have been linked to the Great Chicago Fire and the terrible Peshtigo fires, which were rumored to have been started by meteor falls. It was a year of mysteries, but the reports of these images are too numerous and too widespread to attribute them to a single mad spirit photographer.

The story opens with a salvo from the *New York Times*:

A GHOSTLY REVIVAL

Lovers of the marvellous will rejoice to learn that there is a prospect of a revival of the old-fashioned ghost in all its soul-thrilling and flesh-creeping perfection. Not long since the good people of Cincinnati were harrowed by the supernatural delineation of a deceased lady's face on one of the windows of her residence. As numbers of well-known citizens witnessed the phenomenon, and recorded their testimony in the public prints, only the most obstinate skeptic could doubt its existence. And now Sandusky, not to be outdone, favors us with a similar window-pane portrait, taken without aid of human hands, and presenting the additional attraction that the lady in this case is not only young and pretty, but alive; whereas the original of the Cincinnati phantasm was presumably ugly, and dead. So distinct is this last picture that, we are told, it is at once recognized as that of a young lady of New-Orleans, who occupied the room in the hotel to which the pictorial window belongs, and who was in the habit of looking through it for hours at a time.

In both of these cases, to be sure, the material scoffer may find a plausible physical explanation of the phenomenon. Granting that Cincinnati and Sandusky observation is entirely exact, it may be that the natural action of the light may produce in some way not yet understood, without the aid of chemicals, fortuitous photographs on the casual glass.

The New York Times 18 January 1871 ERIE/ HAMILTON COUNTY

NOTE: I have not yet been able to trace the face in the window from Cincinnati. In September of 1870, the *Cincinnati Enquirer* published a detailed story about the face of a dead woman that appeared in a window in Lawrence, Massachusetts. I wonder if someone at the *Times* assumed the phenomenon had taken place in Cincinnati. The young lady of New Orleans appears in the story below.

AN OPTICAL CURIOSITY

Yesterday morning crowds of people were gathered on Wayne Street, opposite the Lake House [in Sandusky], and seemed very intently engaged in looking at some object in one of the windows of that hotel. On inquiry we learned that the object of their gaze was an optical curiosity in the form of a lady's face, which had been photographically impressed upon one of the panes of glass in a window of the third story of the building. It appears that the room was occupied last summer by a family from New Orleans, and that the picture on the window pane is an exact likeness of a young lady, one of the members of that family. The photograph represents the lady in a sitting posture, looking out towards Water Street. A number of persons had seen the likeness, but supposed it to be a real lady in the room, and paid no particular attention to the matter, till Mr. Voltaire Scott [a local hotel owner] made the discovery that it was a photograph on the glass. Mr. Epler, of the Platt [photography] gallery, declares it to be a real photograph and a genuine curiosity. Looking from the inside of the room no outline can be discerned, nor is there any flaw in the glass—so that no doubt is left that the picture is the result of the chemical action of the light and moisture upon the glass. It is curious, at any rate. The picture is directly over the letter "E" in the word "Lake." *Sandusky Journal.*

The Defiance [OH] Democrat 11 February 1871: p. 1 ERIE COUNTY

Am I being cynical to suggest that this initial sighting was a prank? Was the young lady from New Orleans perhaps photographed during her stay and the photograph somehow transferred to the window? The Spiritualists would re-prove me for my lack of faith...

The *New York Times* weighed in again with a skeptical and condescending article, directed at Ohio's backwards denizens.

SPECTRAL FACES

In many of our Southern and Western States life is made pleasant by other conditions than those which prevail in our commonplace sea-board cities. Something of the freshness and simple faith of an earlier age still lingers in these localities, and one is not constantly shocked by the scoffing unbelief of communities which claim for themselves higher civilization. In this artless society of the border there still survive the most delightful of anachronisms. Sleeping beauties slumber through years and years in the most matter-of-fact way imaginable, prophetesses in every quarter make the direst revelations of coming wars and tempests to gaping and unquestioning auditors, and the old-fashioned divining-rod still guides baffled but undoubting seekers after buried treasures.

But the one point on which the remote rural districts are stringent is in the matter of spectral apparitions. The number of well-authenticated ghosts that have from time to time of late appeared in different parts of the country, is quite encouraging to lovers of the marvelous. Familiar spirits have attached themselves to little girls, and out of pure benevolence presented them with vast estates. To be sure, in the last notable case of this description at Memphis, the father of the fortunate young person so wondrously endowed, has had no great reason to be grateful for this spiritual benefaction. According to the last accounts the title-deeds of his promised property still remain in cloud land, and he has been beaten nearly to death for refusing to disclose their whereabouts to certain rapacious individuals envious of his good fortune. Then, again, Rev. Mr. Thrasher's ghost of Buchanan, Va.—a most excellent and promising spectre—has been pronounced by an investigating committee, a prosaic piece of mischief, concocted and carried out by his little daughter. This, however, we are glad to see the reverend gentleman sturdily denies, and with regard to this admirable apparition, we are left at least the consoling benefit of a doubt.

The latest spiritual manifestation in the West has taken the alluring shape of supernatural pictures unreasonably and unexpectedly appearing on window-panes. We are indebted to the correspondent of the *Chicago Times* for a very entertaining history of the course of this phenomenon at Milan, Ohio. He writes as one who has faith, and with a certain pre-

Raphaelite simplicity of grammar which we have more than once observed to be characteristic of the spirits and their earthly adherents...
The article quotes and ridicules the "Superhuman Photography" piece below and finishes:

> To the cynical mind the plausible inference would be that the good people of Milan had, with the aid of some ingenious photographer, put into practice a clever device to bring people from quite a distance with much accruing benefit to Milanese commerce. But we reject this worldly insinuation with disdain. We are content to take the pictures as they are, "looking some like daguerreotypes," and so to wonder and admire. But let us hope that these phantom painters will keep aloof from us. We have monsters enough to afflict us, and the last dread torment of spectral and fortuitous faces, with hairy eyes, nose, mouth, and whiskers, glaring suddenly from windows, may be spared to a community which is burdened with the Lincoln statue, and the more hideous reality of TWEED.

The New York Times 30 April 1871: p. 4 ERIE COUNTY

NOTE: This article is fascinating for its list of current paranormal phenomena. The "sleeping beauties" probably refers to Miss Susan C. Godsey of Tennessee who was said to have slept for 21 years, waking no more than 8 minutes at a time. She was examined by a committee of doctors who reported that the case was one of "collusion, misrepresentation and humbug" in the *Cincinnati Inquirer* of 12 and 20 October, 1870. I haven't found a specific "prophetess," although the word was sometimes used to describe female Spiritualists who preached while in a trance. The divining-rod is a dowsing-rod. The familiar spirits in Memphis refer to "Pink Lizzie," a ghostly little girl in a grave-stained pink dress who appeared to 13-year-old Clara Robertson at Brinkley Female College Feb. 21, 1871. The ghost made repeated appearances, telling of buried treasure. The ghost claimed to be Lizzie Davidson, daughter of the original owner of the Brinkley Female College building. There were séances, sealed jars, table-tipping, and trances—all too complicated for a mere note. I'll be writing about "Pink Lizzie" in a future book as well as telling the story of the Reverend Mr. Thrasher of Buchanan, Virginia and his poltergeist. The Lincoln statue was a controversial statue in Union Square showing Lincoln wearing a toga over his regular clothes. TWEED is William M. Tweed, "Boss Tweed," corrupt political boss of New York's Tammany Hall. The New York Times was bitterly opposed to Tweed, the hairy monster.

Now for the article with its "pre-Raphaelite simplicity of grammar" which the *Times* ridicules.

SUPERHUMAN PHOTOGRAPHY.
AN UNEXPLAINED MYSTERY – GHOSTLY PICTURES
ON HOUSE WINDOWS IN MILAN, OHIO.

Milan for the past two months has had a sensation, has been the center again of a good deal of talk and interest, owing to the fact that there has come upon the glass of certain windows there the appearance of pictures of human faces that look some like daguerreotypes that were taken twenty years ago, before the art was brought into its present high state of perfection.

The first appearance of the glass is a stony steel color interspersed with a dull ashen color. Or it has some of the appearance of water that has tar or crude oil mixed with it, and one can see the oily substance floating on the top of the water, giving it a variety of colors. When the discoloration of the glass is first noticed, there are no clearly defined outlines of the human face, but gradually, day by day, in the center of this discolored appearance, a face begins to take shape and form until it requires no sketch of the imagination in order to see the well-defined features of an individual who appears to be looking out of the window from the room within.

You go into the room and look out through the glass that has the picture upon it, and nothing can be seen. The glass is just as clear, apparently, as when it came from the maker's hands. Most of the rooms containing the windows having these pictures upon them are vacant ones, and having been for some time, although they have appeared upon the windows of rooms that are occupied.

The plainest picture is that of a middle-aged man upon the window of an old building at North Milan, across the Huron river. It was built for a hotel, and used for that purpose for a long time, but is falling into decay now, and is used as a dwelling house and occupied by a Mr. Horner. On the window of an unoccupied room, fronting east, is the picture, plain and well developed, so that one can see the hair, eyes, nose, mouth, and whiskers as clearly as in any of the old daguerreotypes that I have mentioned before. How this picture came here, or by what agency it was produced, no one can tell.

We cross the river and enter Milan proper, and fronting Andrews' hall look up to one of the windows, stepping back slowly in order to get the right angle, so that the light falls properly upon the glass we are looking at. Ah, we have it now, and we see a face that some say is Washington's. It is the well-defined picture of a man's head and shoulders. The head is covered with a military three-cornered hat, slightly shading a broad forehead, while the deep-set eyes, straight nose, firm mouth, square-set jaws, and smooth shaven face are plainly to be seen. How it came there, or by what agency it was produced, no one can tell.

Deacon Ashley, a member in good standing in the Presbyterian church, and a worthy man, keeps a jeweler's store on the south side of the square in Milan. One of these pictures commenced to show itself upon one of the upper windows of his store. The deacon protested, but day by day it continued to develop into the features of a negro woman. The deacon called in the services of soap and sand, but that would not eradicate it, and finally, despairing of disposing of it in any other way, he took paint and brush and hid it out of sight by painting the glass over, letting it remain so for a number of weeks, and then removing the paint from the glass, when he found that it was still there as plain as ever, and now he has come to the conclusion to let it alone, as he says it is growing plainer every day, so that one can see the ruffles around the border of the old negress' cap.

On two of the windows in the Exchange Hotel in Milan there are also two pictures, one of which resembles a Major Marsh, who died there soon after coming out of the army. The other picture on the Exchange hotel has three female figures in it, who seem to be sustaining a man in a reclining position, as though he had just escaped from the toils, vexations and sorrows of earth life, and was yet too weak and enfeebled to open his eyes and senses to the beauties and angel influences that surrounded him. People come from quite a distance to see these pictures, and almost everyone has a theory of his or her own in regard to the manner in which they are produced.

The Coshocton [OH] Democrat, 30 May 1871: p. 1 ERIE COUNTY

Taking a lead from the *Times*, other newspapers ridiculed the phenomenon.

REMARKABLE DEVELOPMENTS

The village of Milan, in Ohio, is a phantom-haunted locality. According to a correspondent who writes from that place nearly every second house in the village is developing into a weird sort of ghostly receptacle. Upon the window-panes of these houses faces are gradually appearing, having the effect of the old-fashioned daguerreotypes of the years past. Nobody can account for these visitations. They develop themselves on the glass gradually. First an eye, then a nose, then another eye, a mouth, and so on, until the whole face, sometimes bearded and sometimes smooth-shaven, becomes clearly visible to the beholder. Either the people of Milan, Ohio must be gifted with very strong imaginations, or else a marvel has arisen among them. None of the stupid townspeople think it advisable to remove the glasses and dispose of them. There's a fortune in those ghostly faces, if they only knew it.

The [VA] Petersburg Index 17 May 1871: p. 2 ERIE COUNTY

Like most flaps and crazes, this one spread beyond the bounds of the immediate area. Pictures were seen in Milan, Berlin Heights, Plymouth, Wadsworth, Sharon, and points south: Portsmouth, Cincinnati, and Kentucky.

PHANTOM PICTURES.

We recently gave an account of the weird faces that were said to have made their appearance on the windows of certain houses in Milan, Ohio. We clip the following article from a late number of the Sandusky Register:

"We have often heard the question why Sandusky and Milan only are the scenes of these strange phenomena. Our observations satisfy us that they are very general over the state, and, perhaps over the world. We discovered in North Fairfield, Huron County, Ohio, a few days ago, twelve of these pictures on one window of a sawmill. One of them, however, is a group of two persons—one a man with a hat on, the other a female, whose face occurs immediately in front of the man, both looking out of the window. Some of the others have the appearance of ancient philosophers, and some bear quite a strong resemblance to Washington in his old age.

Also in the house of the owner of the mill, on an upper window, there may be seen the picture of three persons looking out of the window, and there are several more on the windows of this house, to which it is not worthwhile to refer to especially. Also on an upper window on a large brick house there is a large pane of glass very strikingly stained, in which we can perceive two pictures...

Passing on from Fairfield to Plymouth, we discovered these pictures by the half dozen in town; one is of a cat in the post-office window—a lower window on the left side of the door as you pass it. This outline is so distinctly defined that no one can fail to see it. On a window of another house there is one of a horse; the head and breast only shown. This is also a clearly defined outline. There are, also, on other windows in the same buildings pictures of persons, which it requires no great stretch of fancy to see. We called the attention of several persons to these pictures; some can see them and others cannot.

Nobody can give a satisfactory solution to these phenomena. If it is natural photographing, as some suggest, why did they not occur in times past? Some maintain that the proportions of the constituents of glass are different from what they used to be, that the stain on the glass is the result of the sun on new glass. But these pictures occur on glass of ancient date.

Astronomers stated that over a year ago the atmosphere of the sun would expand during the summer of 1870, several millions of miles—that the effect on the earth would be very remarkable. If it is true that the atmosphere of the sun did expand last summer, it may be that the chemical effect of that luminary is different from what it used to be, and is the cause of the phenomena.

We believe that the best informed spiritual mediums say that spirits have nothing to do with the matter. But some humble ones say that it is the work of spirits; that they are paving the way to yet greater development; that the veil which has so long shrouded the future from man is about to be lifted; and that the new dispensation is being ushered in. We have neither theory nor belief about the matter, but look upon the phenomena as something very strange.

The Independent [Massillon, OH] 28 June 1871: p.1 ERIE, HURON COUNTY

NOTE: Let us pause for a breath of rationality. When a photographic studio no longer needed their old glass plates or a studio closed, the glass plates might be sold in bulk to a greenhouse or glazier. Windows in the early 1870s were usually made up of multiple small panes of glass or "lights" set in sash bars. Some sizes of glass photographic plates would be the ideal size for window panes. These glass negatives might still bear a faint image. Is it possible that a glazier in the Milan/Sandusky area had a large stock of these used glass photographic plates and had been installing them as window glass? One would think that the images would have been visible from the start, but perhaps something in the atmosphere or the weather "developed" the images, especially when viewed from an angle that allowed sunlight to reflect off the remaining silver. This might explain why viewers inside houses did not see the faint images, which were only visible at an oblique angle, such as from street level, looking upwards.

With so many sightings in these two communities, it is tempting to search for a practical explanation for this phenomenon. Perhaps the many images of George Washington are a clue. Some of the spectral images seem to correspond well to studio portraits and patriotic tableaux, popular at the time. Thanks to Marsha Hamilton for her clear explanation of this theory, which I find both intriguing and dampening to my sense of mystery.

The *New York Times* again:

SPECTRAL FACES

Scarcely in the memory of man have earthquakes been more general, tornados more frequent or more fierce, or floods more destructive. Never at any time have we had more wonderful seers prophesying evil to come. And, to complete our uneasiness, those unaccountable faces, which we had fondly hoped were indigenous to the window-panes of Milan, appear to be spreading themselves over the entire State of Ohio, and bid fair to convert every street in the country into a spectral art gallery.

Mr. E. W. Alexander writes to the Sandusky *Register* that on one window of a single saw-mill in North Fairfield, Huron County, Ohio, he has discovered no less than twelve of these pictures, representing every variety of sex, species, and condition of life. There are ancient philosophers and pretty women, there are horses and cats, and, as in Milan, there are many portraits of Washington in his old age. It is evident, therefore, that these ghostly photographers are at least patriotic, and that is some comfort.

Besides, there is "a group of two persons—one a man with a hat on— the other a female, whose face occurs immediately in front of the man, both looking out of the window." This is a combination which the most skillful of earthly artists might find some difficulty in reproducing with sufficient distinctness.

The New York Times 10 May 1871 HURON COUNTY

NOTE: E.W. Alexander was, as his obituary stated, a well-educated and eccentric character known as "The Sage of West Huron." He was a teacher, newspaper correspondent, "prophet," and phrenologist (see below for a description of phrenology). He died in 1925 at the age of 93.

And, as predicted by the *Times*, as the year wore on, more communities noticed faces in their windows. The following was a letter to the Editor of the *Orrville Crescent* from a correspondent in Wadsworth:

Wadsworth, O., Oct 6, 1871.

Ed. Crescent: I have not got a murder for you yet, but something of a different type of the sensational:

The little village of Sharon, five miles north of us, is fearfully agitated over pictures that are appearing upon the window panes in the residence of Mr. Philander Chandler, near the above mentioned village; they are commonly called Spirit Pictures and have not, as yet, been explained.

The rumor that there was one of these pictures appearing on Mr. Chandler's window, was enough to set people running there from all directions, and of course this place furnished its full quota. Some of the easily impressed aver that they can see a man's face distinctly, but the majority of the people that see it declare that it takes a fearful stretch of imagination to see anything like a human face. Mr. Clark of the *Enterprise* says that he trampled down all the shrubbery in the yard, and then failed to see it. But, there is something on the glass, sure, and a peculiarity of it is that from the inside of the room, nothing can be seen, and also, water fails to remove it. What is it?

Orrville [OH] Crescent 10 October 1871: p. 3 MEDINA COUNTY

The author then goes on to suggest that notorious Spiritualist Victoria Woodhull is the only person who could possibly explain the weird pictures, poking much fun at her "spirit guide" Demosthenes and her association with the "gushing Tilton," editor and abolitionist Theodore Tilton, who wrote a fulsome biography of Woodhull.

NOTE: Victoria Woodhull was Victoria Claflin Woodhull, born in Homer, Ohio. She was a spiritualist, claimed to be a healer and have the Greek orator Demosthenes as a spirit guide. Demosthenes told her that she would someday "rule her people" so she ran as the Equal Rights Party candidate for President on a ticket that included women's suffrage, the legalization of prostitution, and free love. She lost by a landslide. The "gushing Tilton" was also the husband of a woman who had an affair with the popular preacher Henry Ward Beecher. Woodhull exposed Beecher's adultery and was jailed for violating obscenity statutes and tried for libel. Philander Chandler and his wife Susan were both educated at Oberlin, a college noted for its liberal views.

The mirth continued with a letter published a week later.

Wadsworth, O., Oct. 9th 1871.

Mr. Editor Have you heard of the *Spirit pictures* appearing on window lights in Sharon and Wadsworth? A week ago a gentleman of Scientific pretensions and myself made it our business to visit a house five miles north-west of this place where it was purported that peculiar strange look designs, had within a short time appeared in brilliant rainbow colors on window glass; one pain [sic] was claimed to present the portrait of Prof. Peck (formerly of Oberlin, O.) who died in the West Indies four years ago; other panes clusters of foliage, &c.

We got there in the afternoon when the sun was well to the west and immediately went to work i.e. to look wise and strike attitudes in front of the suspected windows and ask learned questions of the occupants of the house.

We very carefully examined some beautiful and curious effects on the lower windows and then called for Prof. Peck, he was pointed out to us on an upper window, at first we could see nothing but the mass of different colors, after some pointing out and explaining we began to trace features so faint that it required great imagination on our part. Some people are quicker to recognize a portrait of this kind than others—different persons came up while we were trying to get the impression on our mind and at once saw the picture of a man, but no two saw it alike, one could see the head and neck of a man with smooth face and chin, another could see a vignette picture of a man with enormous whiskers, and still another the whole figure of a man.

The impression we got resembles the picture of Mike Sullivan, the pugilist, who was so beautifully pummeled by Morrissy on Long Island some years ago. As we have never seen Mr. Peck in the flesh we are not positive that this is a true portrait of him, if it is, he must have had an awful looking mug.

The proprietor of this house kindly offered to show us something on a window at another house. We proceeded to the place, the shutters that obscured the window were opened, a landscape was pointed out with water in the foreground, an irregular line of battle just beyond a gentle slope, and dense forest in the background. This, unlike the others, was on the surface of the glass; by a little exertion one of the party raised the window and crawled in, by way of experiment he wet his fingers with spittle and rubbed the surface of the glass, and no line of battle was ever annihilated quicker than that.

On one of the bar room windows of the National Hotel here in town, another curious design has appeared—a picture of a human head in profile; it don't require a great deal of imagination to trace the outlines of this figure. With the very limited knowledge I have of the science of Phrenology I would pronounce this a very peculiar head, the locality of amativeness and philoprogenitiveness extend out like a large tumor and reverence rims up like a haystack.

A month ago the Spiritual effects were scarce but now they are plenty.

If my opinion were asked how they are produced I should say it is a peculiar freak of the atmosphere on a soft quality of glass. OMEGA
Orrville [OH] Crescent 17 October 1871: p. 2 MEDINA COUNTY

NOTE: Professor Peck was Dr. Henry E. Peck, Professor of Sacred Rhetoric and Adjunct Professor of Mental and Moral Philosophy at Oberlin College until 1865. He was an Abolitionist and was considered very eccentric by his colleagues—perhaps the sort of person to appear in a "spirit picture"! I think that Sullivan was a bare-knuckles boxer James (not Mike) "Yankee" Sullivan. He was beaten by John Morrissey in 37 rounds in 1853 to make Morrissey the American boxing champion. Phrenology is a now-discredited "science" that said that character could be told from the shape and size of the head and the bumps on the head. Areas of the brain had specific functions and those areas might be felt as bumps. This writer is using the jargon of that medical specialty (amativeness: physical love and sexual attraction; philoprogenitiveness: producing many children) to comic effect.

The window pictures were also written up in the Spiritualist newspaper *Banner of Light* in 1874 by Hudson Tuttle, born in Berlin Heights, Ohio, who took a distinctly Spiritualistic view of the faces.

Tuttle begins by musing on the theories to account for the faces: that there is some chemical change in the glass, that an iridescent surface creates images "as clouds sometimes take the form of animals." He rejects the notion that they are human hoaxes "as the structure of the glass itself is changed, and there is nothing on its surface that can be rubbed or washed off."

He goes on to investigate a picture in his home town of Berlin Heights:

WINDOW PANE SPECTERS
THE FACE OF A PIONEER APPEARS ON
MR. LAUGHLIN'S WINDOW—IT APPEARS
ACCORDING TO THE PROMISE MADE
PREVIOUS TO DEATH.

Recently I heard that one of these pictures had appeared on the window in the residence of Mr. Milton Laughlin, of Berlin [Heights, OH], and it was represented as being so vivid and unmistakable that my curiosity was aroused... So dim, shadowy, and uncertain were the best of the Milan pictures that it seemed that if the ghostly dead had broken the quietude of their slumbers... to paint each other's portraits, they too, had better been asleep. A cloudy pane in which one person saw a "perfect" likeness of a prominent man, another thought a remarkable picture of a dog, and the writer failed to detect more than a cloudiness, which imagination could torture into no form, terrestrial nor celestial.

I expected to find nothing more in the window of Mr. Laughlin, and confess to being greatly surprised when the reality was better than reported. We were received by Mr. L. in a cordial manner and found several others present, examining the picture, among whom was Mr. H. Hoak, the well-known agriculturalist, enthusiastic as usual, and unabashed by ghostly paintings or ghosts themselves. There it was, on the lower right hand corner pane of the lower window! Mr. Laughlin adjusted the lamp and when we gained the right angle all exclaimed, it is Mr. Tucker! There were the exceedingly characteristic features, the sharp nose, the small and contracted mouth, the thick white beard, the short and snowy hair. Not on the glass as a picture, but as an intangible shadow behind the glass, looking in upon us!

That glass in the day time is the clearest in the window, for it is washed and scrubbed and rinsed to wash away, if possible, the picture. But when night throws a black back-ground against it, the light shines on the before-invisible face. It is not drawn with sharp lines and light and shade well defined... It resembles a dim daguerreotype... only in one position can the picture be seen....

On repairing to the sitting room, Mrs. Laughlin narrated the circumstances connected with the appearance... Mr. Hardin A. Tucker was well and favorably known in this vicinity as one of the pioneer inhabitants, and an upright, honest, intelligent man. He accepted the doctrines of Spiritualism, and was as usual with him, when he had come to a conclusion, fixed and unswerving in his belief. Shortly previous to his death, in conversation with Mrs. L., who is opposed to what she honestly considers a delusion into which many good people are misled, he said that it was useless for them to argue longer, but as he should soon discover the truthfulness of his belief, and if he found it possible he would return and compel her to believe.

Said Mrs. Laughlin, "As I was sitting in the kitchen one evening, in last April, alone, a sudden impulse made me look up at the window. There I saw the face of Mr. Tucker, looking in at me. I was terribly frightened, and yet I continued to look. I should think I steadily looked at him for half an hour. When I moved it grew indistinct, and I gained courage to take the lamp and leave the room...."

In the great hereafter do the pledges and obligations made in this life press on the soul until redeemed! Are we to believe that the spirit of Mr. H. could not depart from this weary earth in peace until he had fulfilled his promise, and finding no other method... fastened his shadowy features on the window glass? If so, then the souls of the dead are good chemists, and possess some subtle photographic knowledge unknown to us....
Sandusky [OH] Daily Register, 24 December 1873 ERIE COUNTY

And there the matter rested for the spectral faces in the Lake counties. I do wonder what it is about the area. In *Haunted Ohio V: 200 Years of Ghosts*, I told the story of a daring attempt to free Confederate prisoners from the camp on Johnson's Island and a mysterious sequel. In the Sandusky home of Captain Henry Haines, the hero of that episode, the Captain's ghostly face appeared in 1896, in a mirror in the room where he died. It seems to have been the same sort of image as materialized on the windows of Sandusky and Milan. Today in those towns the strange case of the faces in the window seems to have been completely forgotten.

Not all images on glass held a benign Spiritualist message of survival. Some were interpreted as a warning, as in this much later (1888) story from Eaton.

ON A WINDOW:
STRANGE FACE SEEN AT OLD MAN CHRISTMAN'S HOME, RECALLING THE CIRCUMSTANCES OF HIS HORRIBLE MURDER TWO YEARS AGO, AND THE LYNCHING OF WILLIAM MUSSEL.

Special Dispatch to *The Enquirer*.

Eaton, Ohio December 13. The murder of Daniel Christman, an old and wealthy farmer, two miles west of here, two years ago the 7th of this month and the lynching of William Mussel for the commission of the crime, a full account of which appeared in *The Enquirer* at the time, has been recalled to the minds of this community during the past two days by the mysterious and significant appearance of

A FACE UPON A WINDOW-GLASS.

In the house in which Christman resided at the time of the murder, and which is occupied by his widow and daughter. The affair has assumed a very sensational shape and hundreds of people are visiting the house and looking at the picture. The most sceptical see something that resembles the features of a man: the majority can see a very strong resemblance to Christman and some recognize it immediately as the countenance of old man Christman.

Old Mrs. Christman and her daughter say that they have seen it since last March, and it has filed them with such pleasure that they have avoided making it known to the public, from the fact that they did not want to be bothered with the people coming to see it.

THE PICTURE

Can only be seen from the outside of the house. Upon examination of the glass it is found to be perfectly clear, and in looking out through the glass nothing is seen. The glass has been in the window for nine years. There has been considerable lawing going on over the affairs of the estate, and as the Christman women lean strongly to the Spiritual belief, they take the singular appearance as a warning to their persecutors to desist. They do not seem the least disturbed about the matter and look upon it as a manifestation of disapproval by the old man over the way the business is being conducted. The affair is

A FEAST FOR CRANKS.

And it is liable to unhinge a few of them. It is surprising to hear the way people who have heretofore been looked upon as rational people talk about it and hear them express their views. The people seem as hungry to hear and talk about it as they were to hear about the murder and lynching. *Cincinnati [OH] Enquirer* 14 December 1888: p. 5 PREBLE COUNTY

NOTE: William Mussel had worked for Christman, but had moved to Indiana. When he returned to Ohio after leaving his wife, the Christmans took him in. He repaid them by killing Daniel Christman Dec. 7, 1886 with several blows from an axe. When Mrs. Christman didn't give him enough money, he cut her down with the axe and set the house on fire to cover his crime. Mrs. Christman recovered consciousness, smothered the fire on her bed, made her dying husband comfortable, and then walked a quarter mile to a neighbor's for help. Christman died that night. After two weeks, Mussel was found in Indiana and brought back to face trial. A committee of some of Eaton's most prominent citizens decided Mussel should die and a mob stormed the jail. Mussel was taken from his cell and strung up from the electric light tower, December 22, 1886.

This next tale is extraordinarily difficult to categorize: It has a threatening image in the glass of a window, poltergeist-like phenomena, mysterious noises, a phantom horseman, and a giant screaming white bird, which reminds me of the Mothman sightings at Point Pleasant, about 15 miles south of Pomeroy.

GHOSTLY PHANTOMS.
THE STRANGE FACE IN THE WINDOW.
A YOUNG LADY INJURED BY A FLYING
PIECE OF WOOD.
STARTLING SPIRITUAL MANIFESTATIONS
AT IRWIN CREEK.

Pomeroy, Ohio, May 5. Your correspondent has been furnished the following particulars of one of the strangest affairs that ever occurred in this section:

The neighbourhood of Irwin Creek, Meigs County, has been greatly excited in consequence of the discovery of startling ghostly phantoms and strange spiritual manifestations. The family of William Marshall, shortly after moving to that locality, began to notice unusual freaks in the way of mysterious voices and singular cries of distress. But little attention, however, was paid to any of these strange phenomena, until one evening Mrs. Marshall, an elderly lady, went to the front part of the house, and, as she stood gazing through the window to the public highway, there appeared a figure before the glass. At the sight of the object Mrs. Marshall screamed and fell back in terror, shouting that a man on the outside had made motions to strike her.

Several of the family instantly rushed out of the door, but failed to discover anything, though it was impossible for an individual to have secreted himself or got out of sight. The window being approached a second time by another member of the family the same occurrence was repeated and one of the sons instantly recognized the countenance of an enemy, with whom he had had a quarrel a few days previous and who had threatened his life. The features and expressions were plainly visible, and remained so for a long time, and the picture gave the impression that the owner's temper was in a terrible state of rage.

The family became intensely frightened. The next night the same likeness reappeared on the glass, and the attention of friends was directed to it until the whole neighbourhood witnessed the spectacle with great curiosity. But the most singular part of the affair came to light a short time afterward, when it was revealed that the individual whose face was shown in the window had devised a plot by which to kill the eldest son of the Marshall family, but the discovery of the face at the window put the latter on his guard, and prevented the tragical occurrence.

A few nights after the appearance of the face in the window strange noises were heard in different portions of the house, and the Marshalls became greatly alarmed for their safety. These noises grew more demonstrative, and bricks fell from the ceiling, doors slammed, and fire-brands were flung around in various directions. A young lady member of the household was considerably injured by a flying piece of wood that came from some unknown source and struck her on the leg, inflicting quite a painful wound.

The second son also had one of the most singular adventures while returning from Athens, Ohio, about twelve o'clock at night. When within one-and-a-half miles of home and while he was emerging from the edge of a forest, suddenly he heard the clatter of hoofs, and immediately there sprang across the road in front of him a huge, snow-white horse bearing a rider whose color was a fiery red, and making frightful bounds over the earth, they disappeared in a twinkling. The sight of this phantom horse and rider almost drove young Marshall wild with fright, and on reaching his relatives he was as pale as death, trembling and speechless.

The next morning, in company with some friends, young Marshall returned to the spot and measured the distance between the horse's footprints, showing the jump across the roadway to be fifty feet clear.

Occasionally the family would be disturbed by the most unearthly yells of dogs coming from underneath the house, although there was evidently not a canine about the building. A cat, which was the sole animal about the premises when the noisy demonstrations began, instantly fled and was found at a friend's house, miles away. On being returned to its native place it appeared worse frightened than before and ran from sight, and was never seen afterward.

Still another horrible spectre appeared to the family. Late one dark night an unusually bright light shone into the front part of the Marshall dwelling and a strange sound startled the sleepers. Springing from their couches they saw a huge white bird with monstrous outstretched wings moving to and fro in front of the building, and at intervals screaming hideously.

This huge-winged monster continued its movements for the space of half an hour and the members of the family, appalled with terror hied themselves to the darkest nooks and corners, some of them refusing to come out until long after broad daylight. Neighbors aver that they heard the bird scream also, but supposed it to be some large, wild animal.

The next day the Marshall family hastily gathered up all their goods and earthly possessions and disappeared from the neighborhood and not a single individual in that vicinity has yet been acquainted with their whereabouts.

The house they occupied is deserted and lonely, and no one can be found who will venture to take possession of it. The people of that vicinity who have occasion to pass the building after night do so in haste and in great fear, some of them declaring that even yet the same noisy demons and frightful apparitions can still be seen there.

Cincinnati [OH] Enquirer 6 May 1888: p. 20 MEIGS COUNTY

More benign, but still mystifying images filled a house in Cincinnati.

SPIRIT FINGERS DECORATE AN EAST END HOUSE WITH MYSTIFYING GHOSTLY DRAWINGS.

Carter Street lies in one of the earliest settled portions of Cincinnati... There is but one occupied dwelling on the street, and this is likely to become vacant soon. The few residences erected on Carter Street since the Queen City was young have been left to decay, probably because of the fact that the east sidewalk of Carter Street is the margin of an extremely cheerless view, a graveyard and a condemned graveyard at that—a city of the dead in ruins, far more spook suggestive than the modern well-kept cemetery.

Her friends have often commented upon the fact that Mrs. Mary J. Karnes, the sole Carter Street resident, was a brave woman to live so near the long disused graveyard, but the cheery-natured widow continued to reside there, in her own little home, after her husband's death, and reared her children to manhood and womanhood without experiencing any fear of her entombed neighbors.

Three weeks ago, however, all this peacefulness changed. One morning Mrs. Karnes noticed a plainly outlined letter *A* on her lamp chimney. No one had stirred in the house during the night, and no one could account for the appearance of the letter. Every night since then various pictures and letters have appeared upon some glass article in the house, the pictures representing a woman holding a rope, a steamship seemingly fastened in an iceberg, &c. These pictures are sometimes visible for an hour, then disappear, to return during the night.

The news of the work of the mysterious artist has penetrated the surrounding villages and throngs of visitors daily try to solve the mystery, and many go away from the cottage firmly believing that the artist comes from some tomb across the street. Mrs. Karnes is well known and esteemed throughout all the East End suburb....

Cincinnati [OH] Enquirer 28 December, 1896: p. 8 HAMILTON COUNTY

Sometimes owners of anomalous images just didn't want to be bothered and broke or painted over the "ghost."

THAT GHOST

Last week, there was much interest awakened in town over a "ghost," which stood within the window in the rear end of the Club house. The latter structure stands on Olive Street, but below from Center, the culvert that crosses Rachel Creek, the "ghost" could be seen.

It was the figure of a woman dressed in a dark bluish dress with white collar and dark belt about the waist. The figure could be seen from the neck down to the knees. She stood with her back toward the window, and on a passing glance, a person would most swear that a woman was standing behind the large pane of glass. It was, indeed, a most interesting curiosity, and attracted many people Thursday and Friday; and long and varied were the discussions as to the cause of it. On close inspection, a person could see no figure whatever. The glass was clear and apparently without blemish. The cause of the phenomenon was doubtless some slight curves or waves in the glass, which reflected the light in such gradations of shade and color as to give resemblance of a woman's form.

It was worth going a long distance to see, and was really as wonderful a curiosity as nine-tenths of the remarkable attractions billeted in guide books for the allurement of pilgrims. On Saturday, the window was painted and the remarkable curiosity blotted from existence. It was really a shame that this phenomenon was destroyed, for it occasioned no one any harm, and was very interesting to all lovers of the curious manifestations of natural laws. It was a bigger thing than the entire Club House.

Ironton [OH] Register 8 July 1880 LAWRENCE COUNTY

This sympathetic interest in the fate of the Ironton window "ghost" is ironic, considering that, eight years earlier, the Ironton papers had lambasted the people of Portsmouth for not appreciating a window-pane image of the late Mrs. Mollie Sullivan/Mollie Stuart that caused a sensation.

A WONDERFUL PHENOMENON

Our readers will remember the notice of the death of Mrs. Mollie Sullivan in our last issue [Mrs. Sullivan, 38, died Oct. 3, 1872 at her Fourth Street residence. To judge by comments in other articles, she had a reputation as a prostitute or kept woman.] On last Saturday, a lady living near the house lately occupied by the deceased woman, discovered the outlines of a human face in a window pane of an upper apartment where Mrs. Sullivan was wont to sit. The news rapidly spread, and so great was the crowd on Saturday afternoon and Sunday, that the owner of the house, Mr. Thomas, crushed the pane with a missile to keep the visitors away.

Before the destruction of the glass it was subjected to thorough and repeated scrubbings, and was perfectly transparent; no chemical coating could be discovered, which disproves the assertion that the woman had a negative taken on the pane and placed in the sash before her demise. It is without doubt one of the wonderful phenomena, either of light or electricity, imprinted on the window while the woman sat looking out. It is to be regretted that the glass was not preserved for examination, instead of being destroyed.

Portsmouth [OH] Times 5 October 1872: p. 3 SCIOTO COUNTY

Soon, the papers added a sinister twist.

GHASTLY PHENOMENON
THE FACE OF A DEAD WOMAN COMES BACK TO
HAUNT HER MURDERER

The *Vanceburg Kentuckian* prints the following story:

There formerly lived in [Portsmouth] a woman who kept a house of prostitution, and her name was Mollie Stuart. She, like other women of her stripe, had her "man," and his name was Sullivan. Well, a week or two ago her man fell out with her and tapped her on the head, from the effects of which she died in about 4 days. And since that time the strangest part of the whole transaction has transpired, and that is that on the panes of one of the windows in the house which she formerly occupied is to be seen, at all times, an apparition, or something for which we know no better name, in the form of Mollie Stuart....

Waterloo [IA] Courier 7 November 1872: p. 1 SCIOTO COUNTY

The reporter from the *Cincinnati Enquirer* went up a ladder to see the mysterious image for himself:

PANIC IN PORTSMOUTH, OHIO
HOW THE PROPHECY OF A LIVING CYPRIAN WAS
FULFILLED AFTER HER DEATH

Portsmouth, Ohio, October 5, 1872.

"Have you seen the ghostess?" is the question you are asked at every corner and crossing in the city. Here a group of men sit on the stone steps of All Saints or are gathered together on the sidewalk, the topic of conversation, the ghost. Little children, hurrying to the Sabbath-school, their faces blanched with fear, their lessons unlearned, talking in undertones of the wonderful thing that they have all heard of, and all have seen. Old women hurry down the streets in the burning sun: mothers, with babes in their arms, the cripple on his crutches, the aristocrat in his carriage, the man of business with his quick pace, the doctor, the lawyer, men, women and children of the different nationalities, the professional sport, the women of the town, all hurrying to the spot where thousand-tongued rumor has located the picture of her who was taken from the house last Friday and consigned to the dust from which she was taken.

Mollie Sullivan, or as she was better known, Mollie Stuart, lived on North Fourth Street, four doors below Jefferson, in a two-story frame dwelling, keeping what the keno gentlemen denominate a "sporting house." The house stands in a little yard about twenty feet front, the end fronting the street. A window in the second story in the side of the building looks out on Fourth Street. Here the woman would sit for hours at a time looking out... For the past three weeks she had felt that her end was approaching and during the early part of the week when a friend said, "Mollie, we will miss you when you are gone," she replied that they should see her again. "I will come back and look out of the window again," said she, "after I am dead."

Yesterday, Saturday afternoon, a lady whose residence is near, rushed breathlessly into the house exclaiming, "Mollie is looking out of the window upstairs." No credence was given the report, but as the news was communicated, many came to see the wonderful and unexplainable what-is-it?... Your correspondent, not to be outdone by others, was soon on the ground, and there on the middle pane of glass, of the lower row of panes in the bottom sash, was a distinct negative of the dead woman.

I am not one of those superstitious beings who rush into print with a long list of names to bear out the assertion that I have discovered something supernatural, and so I decided to convince myself that there was nothing deceptive in what I seemed to see. Mounting a ladder I reached the window. The room was vacated; no pictures adorned the walls to cast a reflection; no extraneous matter was on the surface of the glass. Thrusting my hand through a broken pane, I placed it over the negative: it still remained. Next, the glass was scrubbed on each side, the sash taken down, but the negative remained on the transparent pane. There was the rounded face, the full forehead, the short black hair, the modeled bust of the dead woman; and there it will remain until the glass is destroyed.

This Sunday forenoon I again visited the house. The window was undisturbed, but the image of the dead woman was still silently looking out into the dim invisibility of the Unknown, heedless of the hundreds that block the streets, sidewalks and neighboring yards. It requires no eagle eyes to see it there, just as she sat. Some crossed themselves as they approached the house. Some would come jesting, laughing at the idle rumor, stand gazing in awe at it a moment, and then retrace their steps, wondering why it was...

Persons visit the place prepared to discredit it anyhow, are the most puzzled of all. Various are the reasons given. Superstition leads all. The vast majority say that it is but the fulfillment of a dying woman's prophecy. One says the evil spirit placed it there; the moralist claims that the Almighty put it where it is to warn others of her mode of life, and prepare them for a reformation. Another says that her picture was negative in the grease and dirt on the surface of the glass by atmospheric pressures; some say that one of the freaks of electricity caused it. In the absence of any well-known reason, I think some strong reaction going on in the rays of light made a negative of the woman at a single sitting, and the woman may have discovered it herself before she died. Scientific men would do well to secure this pane of glass.

INCOGNITO.

Cincinnati [OH] Enquirer 9 October 1872: p. 4 SCIOTO COUNTY

NOTE: A Cyprian was a fancy name for a wanton person or prostitute. The image is described as having short black hair. Women's hair was usually worn long at this time. If Mollie was ill or had in fact been hit by her pimp, her hair might have been cut.

There was a good deal of animosity between the towns of Portsmouth and Ironton. The Ironton Register poked fun at the mysterious Portsmouth face of a woman "of extensive reputation."

The article chided the people in that "city of bogles" for disowning their ghost and quoting the poet Dryden: "true visions through transparent horn arise" to proclaim the ghost a true one since it passed through a "transparent medium" and "there it stuck, though profane hands took out the glass, deluged it with acids and other chemicals...Nothing but a spirit could have stood the tests and all the acids in the world can't make a simon-pure spirit wince."

The article went on to sneer at the people of Portsmouth for "ascribing this spiritual manifestation to the photographic art of a streak of lightning. Local pride ought to inspire a worthier course. Not every town can hope to have a visitor from the spirit land entrench itself in a pane of glass and hold its positions against acids, a subsidized press and a sacrilegious multitude." Finally, the piece commiserates with the spirit whose pane of glass was smashed.

"Alas, poor Ghost! You should go next time where you will be better appreciated. Portsmouth can't bear the open shame of taking her spirits in a glass-not much; she prefers a pint flask or half gallon jug down the cellar, or up a dark alley" and suggests entering into one of those liquor vessels: "and everybody will give thee a hearty welcome. Then, the editors will exclaim, 'That is a true spirit, indeed!'"

Ironton [OH] Register 17 October 1872 SCIOTO COUNTY

When we look back at the scoffing accounts of the faces in the windows, it becomes apparent why no scientists thought the strange phenomenon was worthy of study. Only the Spiritualists seemed to take the matter seriously and they were an easy target of ridicule. Were the faces mere illusions? Did they appear only in panes made from photographic glass plates? Or were there actually portraits in the glass: images rejected as impossible; melting away in the harsh sunlight of science like faces etched in frost on the window-pane?

What we cannot understand, we mock. Perhaps in the same spirit as the fearful boy whistles past the graveyard, the chroniclers of the faces described them in terms of crackpots and crackpottery like phrenology and Spiritualism, to trivialize those ghostly faces in the glass—so startling, so iridescent, and so haunting.

3.

That Hellbound Train

Headless Conductors and Train Wreck Horrors

The engine with murderous blood was damp
And was brilliantly lit with a brimstone lamp;
An imp, for fuel, was shoveling bones,
While the furnace rang with a thousand groans

– The Hellbound Train –
Traditional folksong

The era of steam was an era of death on the rails. With thousands of steam engines moving passengers and freight between towns large and small, fatalities among trainmen were second only to coal miners. Newspapers are full of horrific rail accidents. Engineers and brakemen were scalded to death by the steam. Firemen were roasted alive by white-hot heaps of coals. Wooden cars lit by oil lamps and heated by wood stoves meant that when a crash occurred, trapped passengers often burnt to death. Other gruesome news reports tell of railroad workers crushed to death, cut in half, or decapitated by railroad cars or wheels, like the "headless conductor" ghost at the Moonville Tunnel. (*Haunted Ohio* and *Haunted Ohio IV*.)

My own great-grandfather was killed in 1910 by "projecting freight," which struck his head as he worked as a fireman on the Erie line. He died at Black Hill, near the Ohio State Reformatory at Mansfield. I still have the contents of the dead man's pockets, but he has never returned.

Railroad accidents were a popular source of ghost stories, as in this classic "headless conductor" tale.

WELSH'S HEADLESS BODY
IS WHAT IS DRIVING MEN FROM A FREIGHT RUN
THE APPARITION OF A CONDUCTOR
RAISING A SENSATION.

Trainmen on the Lake Erie & Western railroad, between Findlay and Fostoria are greatly disturbed over what they claim is the ghost of a dead freight conductor, who was killed one night last November, about eight miles east of this city, by his train breaking into two sections, and then coming together suddenly throwing the conductor from the car on which he was standing to the track below, where he was beheaded by the wheels before the train could be controlled. The accident occurred near the village of Arcadia, at a point where dense woods almost form an arch above the track, and here it is that the ghost of Jimmie Welsh, the mutilated conductor makes its appearance nearly every night, as the midnight passenger train from Sandusky going west reaches the spot where he met his fate on that gloomy, autumnal night less than three months ago.

The engineer and other officials of the train assert that scarcely a night passes but what a headless apparition can be seen coming out of these woods, as the train nears the scene of the accident, carrying in its bloodless hand, something that looks like a lantern, which it waves backward and forward in a measureless sort of a manner as though searching for some lost object. The trainmen have no sort of doubt but it is the ghost of Jimmie Welsh, hunting for its lost head. The phantom is plainly visible until the engine with a scream of terror, voicing the feelings of the engineer, endeavours to escape from the horrible sight, when it turns and walking into the woods slowly fades away into a blue mist.

Two crews have already abandoned this road on account of this ghastly vision and have been transferred to other divisions of the road: and the present engineer in charge of the train was so badly frightened when he reached this city last night that it was with great difficulty he was persuaded to remain on his engine until relieved at Lima. He said to the Blade correspondent that he would not make the run again for all the money Senator Calvin S. Brice, the president of the road, possessed. The conductor and brakemen on the train confirmed the engineer's story and said they saw the ghost nearly every night, always seemingly engaged in the hopeless task of hunting for its head. On bright moonlight nights the apparition is not so plainly outlined as when the nights are dark and rainy, as has been the rule in the past. On such occasions the phantom conductor comes out clear and distinct having all the semblance of a man minus his head, while the lantern in his hand gives out a fitful, uncanny sort of illumination that freezes the blood in the veins of the boldest railroader on the line.

No other train is annoyed by this ghostly form, but this is explained by the fact that no other train passes the spot where Jimmie Welsh was killed, at the time of night when he was decapitated by the cruel wheels of his train. The matter has thoroughly alarmed all the employees of this division of the road, and unless the spirit of the dead conductor is appeased in some way it will be difficult to get men to make the midnight run from Sandusky to Lima.

The Lima [OH] Daily News 15 January 1890: p. 4 HANCOCK COUNTY

The next day, as if to counteract official company denials of the tale, there appeared this story:

RAILROAD SUPERSTITIONS

Talking with an old railroad man this morning about the sensation in last night's Times concerning the headless body of Welsh, he remarked there was nothing strange in it.

"Railroad men frequently encounter such experiences. I remember of hearing D. & M [Detroit & Mackinac] engineers tell about how engineer Ed. Lawlor who was killed in a head end collision near Swanders [Shelby County], used to climb in the engine when it would pass the point where the collision occurred and ride a mile or so and then suddenly disappear. If you could get with Jim Foley, Lawlor's fireman or in fact any of the old D. & M. men, they would tell you of the wonderful apparition."

John Miller, an old passenger engineer, who lived here, and was killed in a collision at Barkelow's curve, some years ago, used to declare that the ghost of Lawlor would get on his engine, and that he had frequently held a conversation with the spook.

The Lima [OH] Daily News 16 January 1890: p. 4 SHELBY COUNTY

In *Haunted Ohio IV: Restless Spirits*, I wrote about the terrible fiery train wreck at Republic, in Seneca County, and a phantom train seen there in recent years. The headlines for one of the first contemporary reports of the tragedy read "The Cars Take Fire and the Impaled Passengers Burn to Death, Unable to Escape or Be Rescued." Some news reports showed gruesome photos of the badly burned bodies. They also compared the tragedy to "the Ashtabula horror of the winter of 1877," otherwise known as the Ashtabula Bridge Disaster. (See *Haunted Ohio V: 200 Years of Ghosts*, "Fire and Ice.")

I had thought that my recent story of a phantom train seen at Republic was the only ghost story associated with the tragedy, but then I found this article from a few months after the crash. Something began to haunt the site almost immediately.

GHOST STOPPING TRAINS.
THE RAILROAD EMPLOYEES AT REPUBLIC, OHIO EXCITED OVER DANGER SIGNALS THAT ARE DISPLAYED NEAR THE LATE ACCIDENT BY UNSEEN HANDS.

Tiffin, O., March 3. The village of Republic has a ghost, which stops trains, and there is great excitement there. A few nights ago, when express

No. 5 (the same train that was wrecked January 4), was approaching the scene of that horrible disaster, the engineer saw a red light, the danger signal ahead, and applying the brakes and reversing the engine, the train came to a stand-still on almost the exact spot of the great wreck. Strange to say, when the train came to a stop, the light had disappeared, and could nowhere be seen. Before stopping, both the engineer and fireman noticed that the light appeared to be carried by a woman in white. Puzzled by the disappearance of the signal, the conductor walked over the track for some distance ahead, but could discover nothing.

The train then backed to Republic station, and the operator was questioned, but he assured them that no signal had been sent out. The train then proceeded on its way cautiously, the engineer keeping a sharp lookout, but nothing more was seen of the mysterious woman. This strange apparition has appeared on three occasions and has greatly excited trainmen. A posse has watched the place for several nights, but the ghost has not since appeared.

Jackson [Maquoketa, IA] Sentinel 10 March 1887: p. 2 SENECA COUNTY

Another classic railroad ghost tale is that of a phantom—usually a conductor with a red lantern—who stops a train wreck. In this case, the conductor's lantern was a spook light.

SPOOK LIGHT SAVED TRAIN.

In the spring of 1887, while I was engineer on the Fast Mail from Cleveland to Pittsburg (C. and P.R.R.), the following incident occurred: It had been raining steadily for three days and the hilly regions of Wellsville, Ohio, had a direct effect upon the hitherto small streams and creeks in converting them into raging torrents. My train was due at Wellsville at 1:23 a.m., and being 37 minutes late, I was running at full speed, about 55 miles per hour, and knew the track to be in good order and at this point free from probable obstructions of any kind.

My train was made up of four Pullman cars, three mail cars and a baggage car, all the Pullman cars being comfortably filled. We were approaching Wellsville when at a point about one mile from a stream known as Yellow Creek, just outside the city limits, I put my head out of the engine cab window to look for signals, when to my astonishment there was a red lantern swinging back and forth across the track, just in front of the engine, but, as it appeared to me, as high as the smokestack. I frantically closed the throttle, applied the brakes, and showered the rails with sand, which soon brought the train to a standstill. All this time the mysterious light was swaying to and fro just in front and above the engine. I stepped out onto the track, but there was no sign of a light of any kind, nor of any person, but it would have been quite impossible for any human being to have flagged the train, as above explained.

I walked ahead some 300 yards, and, not seeing any signal lights at the approach to the bridge, I knew something was wrong, and going a short distance further I found that the bridge had been swept away by the flooded stream, which almost covered the track.

What explanation can be given for this seemingly supernatural token, which saved scores of passengers from an untimely death and a watery grave?

Cincinnati [OH] Enquirer 10 February 1907: p. 3 COLUMBIANA COUNTY

NOTE: A Pullman car was a railroad sleeping car. A red lantern swung in a side-to-side arc was a signal for "stop."

It was not only the rails that were haunted, but train depots as well. The depot at Galion, for example, is famous for its haunted "coffin room." I wonder if the following depot still exists at the town of Westminster on the "eerie line?"

HAUNTED DEPOT.

Kenton, O., Sept. 13. The little village of Westminster, west of here, has a haunted depot and the inhabitants are frightened while the night operator is thinking of applying for a transfer or resigning his position. The village is on the Erie railroad and it is the Erie depot that has the ghost. Every night mysterious noises are heard and they appear to come from the garret of the place.

The noises sound like a heavy object being rolled across the floor, and this is not all, every once in a while an uncanny laugh breaks the monotony. The trainmen along the line have scouted the idea, and refused to believe the story until last night when the crew of a local freight heard the sounds and made a thorough exploration of the place, thinking that someone was putting up a job.

The origin could not be found, although the sounds could be clearly heard during the search. They discontinue promptly at daylight.

Akron [OH] Daily Democrat 13 September 1901: p. 7 ALLEN COUNTY

I find it intriguing when a ghost interacts with its surroundings, like this ghost climbing on a steam engine.

GHOST SAID TO HAVE WALKED UPON
A LOCOMOTIVE'S PILOT

Springfield, Ohio, January 1. It is stated on good authority that the Big Four trainmen seek the inside of the cars when passing under the bridge at the Deer Creek crossing, three miles east of London. Several men have been killed at the crossing, and a few days ago Engineer Combs, of Train No. 97, says he saw a ghost on the track.

The apparition was first discovered walking toward them and Combs opened the cylinder cock to frighten it away, but it walked up on the pilot of the engine and disappeared. It has been seen several times since then and the trainmen have become badly scared, it is said.

Cincinnati [OH] Enquirer 2 January 1896: p. 4 MADISON COUNTY

NOTE: The Big Four was the Cleveland, Cincinnati, Chicago and St. Louis Railway. The pilot is the projection at the front of the engine; it is also known as a "cow catcher." A cylinder cock is a device to expel condensed water from the steam system, under steam pressure, which is why all the old movies show steam shooting out from under the sides of the engine.

Like houses, machines can be haunted. Here's a tale of a persistent ghost on an engine about to be scrapped.

ENGINEER'S GHOST HAUNTS A LOCOMOTIVE
WHICH IS TO BE SOLD AS SCRAP.

Chillicothe, Ohio, December 14.

The remains of B.&O.S.-W. Engine 107 have been shipped to Cincinnati to be sold to the junk dealers. The engine had a remarkable history and has been regarded as a hoodoo for years.

About five years ago, just east of Roxabel [Roxabell, in Ross County], the engine exploded for some reason, which was never yet been disclosed, and the engineer, Robert Basim, was blown into an adjacent cornfield and instantly killed. The remains of the engine were gathered up and brought to this city, where they were placed in the "boneyard," along with other wrecks.

A short time later, the East End was terrified by the report that the engine was haunted. An engineer who had crossed the "Boneyard" after night declared that he had seen the old engineer sitting at the throttle as natural as life. Others saw the same ghastly sight, they claimed, and the terror finally became so great that people were afraid to pass the corner

near which the engine stood. Ever since it has been regarded as a hoodoo, although the ghost stories gradually died away. But those who lived near the place will never forget how intense the terror was for a time. Whether the ghost will accompany the engine to Cincinnati remains to be seen.
Cincinnati [OH] Enquirer 15 December 1898: p. 6 HAMILTON COUNTY

Some engines were believed to be hoodooed or bewitched or were called "man-killers." Like the lethal Engine 971.

AFRAID OF THE MAN-KILLER ON WHICH HE IS ENGINEER AND THREATENS TO QUIT RAILROADING

Akron, Ohio, May 1. The superstition among railway men that accidents never occur singly is strengthened by the remarkable experience of Engine 971, which pulls the Cleveland, Akron and Columbus accommodation train through this city.

This engine has had its deadly three in the last six weeks. Solon Miller, struck at a crossing at the edge of town by 971 and hurled to death, was buried six weeks ago.

Mrs. Frank Wiley, walking along the track with her husband three weeks ago Saturday night, fell before 971 and was horribly mangled.

William Norris, a milkman of this city, was the last victim, a few days ago. He was hurled nearly 100 yards by the engine.

Engineer John Simmons has applied for another engine, and says unless he gets it he will quit railroading forever.
Cincinnati [OH] Enquirer 2 May 1905: p. 6 SUMMIT COUNTY

NO WONDER THERE WAS A BAD WRECK WHEN THE "HOODOO" LOCOMOTIVE, WHICH AVERAGES A WRECK A MONTH, GOT BUSY ON FRIDAY THE THIRTEENTH OF THE MONTH, SOMETHING WAS BOUND TO LET GO PECULIAR MIX-UP ON D. AND I.

On Friday, the thirteenth of the month, C.H. & D. engine No. 450, the "hoodoo" locomotive took another spell and caused a bad wreck near Ironton, Ohio, in which large damage was caused and Engineer Gray badly hurt.

A double-header was pulling the grade at Tunnel No. 1 at 8 o'clock when the "hoodoo" engine, which was being assisted up the grade by another engine, suddenly left the track and rolled over an embankment, the whole train following and piling up in an indescribable mass. All the crew escaped by jumping. Engineer Harry Gray received a sprained wrist. The damage is heavy. Railroad men aver that old 450 averages a wreck a month, and all crews avoid going out on that engine if possible, sometimes alleging sickness and excuse.

Hamilton [OH] Sun 14 March 1903: p. 5 LAWRENCE COUNTY

The "Eerie Line" seems to have its own hoodoo. Here are two articles about a phantom train that came back—twice—to re-run its fatal journey. Ghostly legends often speak of ghosts that haunt on anniversaries of some tragedy, but you rarely find them in real life. The Phantom Train of River Styx is a ghastly exception.

HAUNTED.
RIVER STYX BRIDGE
FEARFUL SIGHTS WITNESSED AT THE PLACE
WHERE ENGINEER LOGAN LOST HIS LIFE
PHANTOM TRAIN DASHES DOWN STEEP GRADE
FRIGHTFUL WRECK RE-ENACTED EVERY NIGHT
STRANGE STORY

The ill-fated train, on which Engineer Alex. W. Logan lost his life, is said to haunt the bridge over the River Styx near Rittman.

It was at this place that he went to his heroic death last spring. The frightful wreck caused great excitement in this city. There were a large number of Akron people on No. 5 that morning. Local citizens recall the circumstances surrounding the brave sacrifice made by Engineer Logan, whose steady nerve saved the passengers behind him.

That which follows is taken from the *Wadsworth Banner* of Friday:

Several Rittman people are very much excited at what has occurred at the Styx bridge over the Erie at that place during the past week, and what they term was the appearance of a phantom train.

The first appearance of this awe-inspiring, marvellous apparition, was on Saturday night, and was witnessed by Dr. Faber and a companion. The doctor had been out east to visit a patient and was leisurely driving along about 11 o'clock when his attention was attracted by the noise of a swiftly moving train. He casually watched the train and saw the glaring headlight and dense clouds of smoke rolling up from the smokestack.

No particular attention was taken of the train, but just before it reached the bridge the shrill whistle of the engine caused the men to glance back. On came the train with the speed of the wind as it swept down the grade, throwing out great streaks of fire from the wheels. Just then was heard the "chuck, chuck" of the engine, as if she had been reversed. On further investigation a frightful sight met their gaze. The train was enveloped in great clouds of dust and steam and huge flames of fire shot up in every direction, and immense volumes of steam making a terrific noise shot up from the engine, and the noise of creaking timbers and breaking iron bars was plainly heard, but above all came the shrieks of those pinioned beneath the wreckage. The noise was plainly heard by a number of others. Spellbound at the sight before them Faber and his companion started immediately for the railroad, thinking that a frightful wreck had occurred. Imagine their surprise when they reached the bridge and found everything perfectly quiet, no sign of a wrecked train, and not even a ripple upon the placid surface of the Styx.

The men hurried to town and related their experience, but could not induce anyone else to visit this spot, so strong is the belief down there that this place is haunted or that some evil spirit lingers about this bridge. Near there the ill-fated train 5 jumped the track last spring and the engineer was killed, ever since which time many people have been afraid to pass over this stretch of track after night.

Akron Daily Democrat 28 October 1899: p. 3 WAYNE COUNTY

UNCANNY VISITANT
THE FORERUNNER OF SOME DIRE DISASTER.
RITTMAN PEOPLE ARE BORDERING ON NERVOUS PROSTRATION BECAUSE OF ANOTHER APPEARANCE OF THE PHANTOM TRAIN.

Again the Erie's phantom passenger train has been seen near Rittman, and the inhabitants of that town are now in a condition bordering on hysteria in consequence. The Erie's ghostly train is No. 5 that was wrecked two years ago on a trestle over the River Styx near Rittman. Engineer Alexander Logan lost his life trying to save his train. Its first appearance as a phantom train was a year ago. A week ago the phantom train was seen by three reputable citizens of Rittman, J.B. Ewing, Amos Goldner, and a man named Fielding were walking along the Erie tracks near the trestle when they were startled by a shrill whistle behind them. Turning, they beheld the headlight of a train bearing down upon them from the East. By the moon's light they could plainly see the great column of black smoke belching from the stack. The three decided it was Erie passenger No. 1 trying to make up time, by the way she was coming.

They all stepped a safe distance from the rails and waited for the train to pass. As it struck a slight curve in the track the men could plainly see that the locomotive pulled a baggage car, mail car, and three passenger coaches. Through the coach windows light from the interior was stealing. Shortly before the train reached the trestle it whistled again shrilly for brakes, and sparks began to fly from the wheels, as they ground upon the steel rain, locked by the brake application.

The men were wondering at the sudden stopping of the train, when it shot out on the trestle and plunged into the river. They plainly head the cracking of the trestle timbers, the hissing of escaping steam, and the shrieks and groans of the pinioned passengers. The astonished onlookers stood for a moment petrified, and then ran down over the embankment to the edge of the stream into which the train had plunged.

When they arrived upon the bank they were amazed to find that not a ripple disturbed the placid surface of the water. Looking up, they were surprised to find that the timbers of the trestle were stable and intact. The place was as quiet as death, and although the three men are possessed of an average amount of courage, they crept away from the haunted place with the cries of the dying in their ears, and hurried toward the town. These men might have doubted their own senses if it had not been for the fact that they were hailed by residents of houses nearby who had heard the noise of the wrecked train and asked if there had not been another wreck at the Styx Bridge.

The uncanny visitant has caused intense excitement among the residents of Rittman. The more credulous among them believe that the second appearance of the phantom presages some dire disaster to the village.

Akron [OH] Daily Democrat 23 April 1901: p. 5 WAYNE COUNTY

NOTE: See *Haunted Akron* by Jeri Holland and contributing editor, Ken Summers, who is writing a much-anticipated book on railroad ghosts. In *Haunted Akron* he tells the story of the River Styx wreck and its ghostly sequels and corrects some inaccurate legends that have grown up about the location.

4.

Rock, Fire, and Scissors
The Mysterious Poltergeist

"When you see a paragraph headed 'Extraordinary Occurrence,'
and you read how every night loud rapping is heard in some
part of the house, or how the rooms are being constantly set on fire,
or how all the sheets in the house are devoured by rats,
you may be quite sure that there is a young girl on the premises."

Dr. Samuel Wilks, M.D., F.R.S., *Diseases of the Nervous System*, 1878

The poltergeist may be paranormal, but is it a ghost? Poltergeists—the name means "noisy ghost" or "racketing spirit" in German—are noisy, destructive, maliciously random, and completely uncontrollable—the psychopathic toddlers of the spirit world. The pattern is consistent: a house with at least one child, usually entering adolescence, is suddenly terrorized by inexplicable phenomena: ghostly knockings, broken dishes, showers of stones, mysterious fires, objects that levitate, materialize, and dematerialize. Eventually the phenomena stop, typically after about six months at the most. Sometimes, as the events wane, someone will be caught faking an event and authorities will proclaim the mystery solved. It does no good to move; the family itself appears to be haunted. As ghost-hunter Harry Price said, "Ghosts haunt; poltergeists infest."

If you look closely, in most poltergeist cases the child/person who is the focal point feels powerless. There is an unresolved tension or stressful situation, perhaps even abuse, in the household. Poltergeist agents seem either able to project their rage to cause physical turmoil, sometimes to the point of bodily harm, or they create the phenomena in a dissociative state so they can, with all honesty, say that they were not responsible. They don't react well to authority figures—calling for an exorcism or consulting with the clergy usually makes things worse. I've seen intriguing new studies that show significant differences in the brains of "poltergeist vectors" as I call them. There have also been studies linking Borderline Personality Disorder diagnoses with poltergeist activity. Various hormonal shifts—adolescence; menstruation; and menopause—all seem to have some relation to poltergeist activity.

Dr. Hans Bender has done some detailed psychological studies of poltergeist agents and found that they "seem to be harboring extreme hostilities, which they are actively repressing from consciousness. Many appear to be crippled by a total inability to express these hostilities in a verbal...way...When confronted with their hostilities, these subjects tend to deny them or rationalize them away. Their anger is most often directed against parents or similar authority figures...The poltergeist, to use a crude metaphor, seems to be like a tea kettle blowing off the steam of excess repression." Keep the idea of denial in mind as you read some of these early cases.

SOURCE: *Miracles: A Parascientific Inquiry into Wondrous Phenomena*, D. Scott Rogo, (Chicago, IL: Contemporary Books, 1983) p. 155.

Let us start with some "normal" poltergeist cases. This tale's central character is the typical poltergeist vector: an adolescent girl aged about fourteen. As is often the way in a poltergeist infestation, there is an attempt to find a ghost responsible.

IT HAPPENED IN LIMA

An unsolved mystery: true, and as yet unexplainable. This story can be corroborated by either the *Times* or the *Gazette of Lima*, O., and happened eighteen or twenty years ago.

I was living on East Market Street at the time and had for my closest neighbors a fine and intelligent old German couple who had six children: two boys and four girls, one of the latter being dead. One of the girls, the baby of the family, aged about fourteen was a tall slender girl, around whom this story centers.

One day the mother returning home from shopping found the entire downstairs topsy-turvy. Pictures were gone from the wall, doylies and table covers missing from their accustomed places, even the heavy furniture moved about in the different rooms.

The above-mentioned articles were found in various hiding places shortly afterwards.

Taking the girl to task, she was surprised to learn that she had not been in the rooms disturbed.

Scolding and coaxing failed to change the girl's statement so the mother decided to drop the matter, thinking the girl in fear of punishment had lied.

The next day my mother ran over for a little neighborly chat and found the woman mixing dough preparatory to baking bread.

Leaving the pan set on the kitchen table she took my mother in the rooms that had been disturbed and after telling her of the strange occurrence they returned to the kitchen. Imagine their surprise to find the bread pan missing. The girl at this time was in a front room reading, and had no opportunity to get to the kitchen unseen. The pan was found under a bench in the pantry.

Shortly after this the girl was taken with a series of peculiar spells. Trembling all over she would become unconscious for a period of perhaps five minutes. Upon recovering she would be hysterical complaining that cats had been scratching her limbs. Upon examination the scratches would be visible often being of sufficient depth to allow blood to be seen. At the same time depredations were committed throughout the house of the same nature explained above.

As such things will, it became noised about and the house became the center of attraction.

One evening myself and four friends visited the house and in passing through the different rooms, I noticed particularly the position and condition of the house fixtures.

After conversing with the old folks for a short time the girl was suddenly stricken with a trancelike condition. I noted carefully that all the members of the family were about her endeavouring to give her relief. Upon her recovery we started to leave. Starting to pass through the two adjoining rooms: (the sitting room and parlor,) we found everything disarranged. Heavy pictures were removed from the wall and hid under beds. Bed clothing and wearing apparel were taken from their places and stuffed behind the piano which had been moved from one corner to another.

This condition prevailed for about three weeks. Not every day but just at least expected times. At the end of the three weeks, the family moved to a certain cemetery where the father and boys were employed.

At once the trouble ceased both at the old and the new home. A medium whom they consulted afterwards informed them that as they had lost one girl in the house from consumption, it was undoubtedly her spirit warning them to move owing to the damp cellar.

Several reporters from the daily paper investigated this condition, but I failed to ever see any explanation for the same in the press. If any of the readers were in Lima at the time mentioned they will remember this occasion which happened close to the bridge on Market Street.

C.H.D.

Dayton [OH] Daily News 20 January 1914 ALLEN COUNTY

NOTE: This was a submission in a ghost story contest sponsored by the *Dayton Daily News* in 1914. I like the twist at the end—where the medium speaks for the daughter who died of tuberculosis and who was trying to get them to move. The scratching on the skin may be a condition called dermographia or "skin writing," related to stigmata, where wounds, and sometimes words, mysteriously appear on the skin. I have not yet been able to corroborate this account with any Lima newspaper—which is a pity since it is such a vivid story.

GHOSTS IN OHIO
SPIRITS THAT REMOVE AND RESTORE
FINGER-RINGS, THROW THINGS ABOUT,
AND MYSTIFY PEOPLE GENERALLY

From the Dayton (Ohio) Journal, Jan. 28.

A story comes from the neighborhood of Salem which is not reported as a ghost story, but Spiritualists in the neighborhood rely upon the phenomena as a confirmation of their doctrines, notwithstanding the recent Katie King exposures. The circumstances as related are well authenticated and although most people of intelligence will reject them as fabrications or hallucinations, yet they are of interest.

The phenomena have been witnessed in a house occupied by James Oaks, on the State road, about a mile north of Salem, between that village and Phillipsburg. The premises are owned by Mr. Warren Cook. The house is a two-story brick, new and neat in appearance and is the last place that one would look for goblins. In fact, it is not regarded as a haunted house, but the phenomena, as stated, are regarded by many of the neighbors as spirit manifestations, and it is said that a daughter of Mr. Oaks, aged nine years, is a medium through whom the spirits desire to communicate, although she is as yet unconscious of her power.

One of the first manifestations was about as follows: The little daughter was presented a year or so ago with two finger-rings by an uncle who has since died. One day recently they disappeared from her fingers, and when questioned as to what had become of them, she said that a man had come and taken them off her hand. The story was, of course, disbelieved, and search was instituted for the missing articles, but without success.

Late in the day Mrs. Oaks directed her daughter to remove some dishes from the pantry to the table. While approaching the place where the dishes were, she was arrested on her way when she turned to her mother and said, "That man has brought my rings back," and sure enough they were placed one after another on her fingers. Mrs. Oaks could not see any person, but the daughter insisted that she could see a man plainly. This was not all that the accommodating spirit did. It removed the dishes from the table, as the girl had been directed to do, and then disappeared.

At other times the same figure will appear, invisible to all but the little girl and close the window shutters or open them if they are already closed, sometimes closing and opening them violently, and at others very gently.

The spirit, or whatever it may be, seems to have taken a special fancy to caring for the wardrobes of different members of the family, and it will lay out clothes, sometimes in order, and again promiscuously on the floor. Shoes have been removed from the feet of the children in the presence of the entire family without anyone being able to discover the agency. The shoes being replaced and bound in still harder knots, would again be removed by the same agency. Dishes, shoes, and articles of wearing apparel are thrown about the room and tables and chairs removed.

Spiritualists who have investigated the matter insist that the little girl is a medium and that the manifestations are from a spirit who desires to make communications through her. Many of the neighbors reject the whole story, while others, acquainted with Mr. Oaks' family, and knowing that they have no motive for fabricating such a story, are puzzled, and don't know what to make of it.

A son of Mr. Oaks, nineteen years of age, who believed that there was some human agency at the bottom of the singular proceedings, collected all his clothes, and putting them in his trunk, locked it up, and felt sure that it would not be disturbed. But next morning his surprise was great when he found every article removed from the trunk and lying on the floor.

The manifestations are said to take place either in day or night time, and at intervals of a week or more. Our information is derived from a reliable gentleman, who visited the family and heard the facts from them as they are related.

The New York Times 31 January 1875 MONTGOMERY

NOTE: This is the small town of Salem, near Dayton. Once again, there is a young "medium" in the house and the frequent poltergeist case theme of clothing and shoes being disturbed. There is also a comment about the house not looking like a haunted house, which we will hear in other cases. Katie King was an attractive female spirit, supposedly the daughter of a pirate, who materialized at séances from the 1840s onward. The exposure mentioned was of a young medium named Florence Cook who was caught flitting around the darkened séance room in her underwear. She or one of her confederates impersonated Katie King and there are photographs of the "ghost" in white robes, which look remarkably like Florence Cook.

I like how the author of the next story, from Gettysburg, in Darke County, sets the scene in a perfectly ordinary brick house in the country. There are a number of unusual features in this story: the messages, the blood, the headless apparition, the omens of death. It is curious how often the theme of torn or cut or stolen clothing recurs in poltergeist cases. I've read of the same events in cases from 12th-century England, 16th-century Scotland, and 19th-century Massachusetts. See the chapter, "A Family Bewitched," in this book for an astounding Ohio poltergeist case, where the destruction of the household's clothing was a prelude to the fragmentation of the family.

A GETTYSBURG GHOST

Why the mysterious and uncanny creatures which people ghostland should have chosen such an unghost-like haunt for their abode as a certain old farmhouse near Gettysburg, Darke County, is a mystery which a mere mortal may not solve.

The house is not isolated nor is there anything about its appearance which might suggest its connection with spirits not of earth. It must have been quite pretentious in its day and in its neighbourhood, for it is a well-built brick structure containing ten large rooms with a long hall running its entire length. It was built perhaps 75 years ago, and at the time our family first learned of it, it was owned and occupied by a wealthy farmer.

Quite suddenly, it seems, just a short time previous to the death of a young daughter, very strange and alarming incidents began to take place.

The first unearthly visitor from ghostland which presented itself was a headless figure of great height which paraded back and forth in front of the house every evening just after the lamps were lit. When approached it always disappeared into an old stone milk house which stood a short distance from the house.

On the whitewashed walls written in a mysterious hand were many hair raising inscriptions evidentially messages from the dark abodes intended for the occupants. The following is a fair sample: "I had intended to burn the barn but I feared if I did, God would bury me in my blood." But strangest of all this writing could neither be erased or white washed over though apparently done in ordinary lead pencil. This experiment was tried by the writer's grandparents when they later lived in this same house.

Finally the ghosts got so bold that they made daily as well as nightly visits playing such pranks as cutting the clothes off the line at midday and setting on fire the best silk dresses of the female members of the family.

The family became so alarmed by these weird antics that they stationed guards about the buildings. But still the mystery deepened and the ghost or ghosts somehow contrived to accomplish their strange feats. The guards too, came in for their share of attention for right into their midst, from nowhere it seems, would come flying shingles upon which were written all kinds of strange threats.

Finally the daughter and the old people died in quick succession and the rest of the family moved away. Then followed the rather difficult task of procuring a tenant. Some people a bit braver than their fellows were induced to try the place to teach them all they wanted to know concerning the mysterious powers of darkness. And they begged permission to move on.

Grandfather was quite sure he was not scared of ghosts and contracted to rent the farm for one year, vowing he'd stay the year. No sooner had they arrived in their new home, however, than things began to happen. Some of these could be explained, some couldn't. The climax came when one night about the hour of twelve a dreadful noise and unearthly shrieks in the big hall below stairs awakened the sleeping family. Grandfather wouldn't investigate because he said there were no ghosts and grandmother was afraid to.

Next morning the family were greeted by the rather gruesome sight of blood liberally sprinkled over the floor and walls of the hall.

It is needless to add that at the end of the year, grandfather too, moved on.

Dayton [OH] Daily News 28 January 1914 DARKE COUNTY

Ordinarily the objects moved and destroyed by a poltergeist are relatively small: kitchen crockery, pictures, linens, and clothing. This story's racketing spirit did some genuinely heavy lifting.

AN OHIO GHOST STORY
QUEER ANTICS IN A STAID QUAKER FAMILY'S PANTRY AND PARLOR

Correspondence Pittsburg Commercial

Martins Ferry, Ohio, June 27, 1877. A very curious phenomenon has just occurred in this community. The scene of action is about five miles in the country back of town, on a main road leading to Cadiz, at the house of Mr. William McComas, a wealthy farmer. The community around Mr. McComas are almost all Friends, Quakers, and are not in the habit of producing sudden excitements, hence their reports, together with those of well-known citizens of this place and Wheeling, stamp it with truth.

About 9 o'clock Monday morning Mrs. McComas heard a noise in the pantry, and on going in to learn the cause was surprised to see almost everything there falling from the shelves to the floor, and on replacing some cans of fruit saw they would not stay, but reeled about and fell to the floor. Being alarmed, she at once went and called the men from the fields where they were at work. On coming into the house they were struck with amazement with what was going on. The neighbors were sent for, many of whom came at once and saw sights such as to throw the most advanced spiritualistic medium far in the shade.

The cooking stove moved from one side of the room to the other. A large piano, weighing about 800 pounds, moved out from the wall half way across the parlor. Two clocks stationary upon mantels, fell off upon their faces on the floor. They were replaced and did not stop running, nor were they injured. A feather bed in one of the lower rooms raised itself high off the bedstead and rested on the floor, while a feather bed upstairs was carried from one room through another, down stairs, and rested on the hall floor. Pots filled with water were thrown off the stove. A sewing-machine was thrown almost across the room and rested upside down. Several large jars, containing butters of different kinds, and weighing about 40 pounds were turned upside down, and on being hastily tilted by the almost frantic people, were placed in a tub, where they remained but a moment, when they raised themselves out, emptying out their contents.

A tea canister, filled with tea, moved across the room in such a position as to empty itself and cover the floor with the tea as a farmer would cover the ground with grain; the drawers from the bureau would slowly move from their places out into the middle of the room; several large hams were repeatedly thrown from the hooks to the floor, books from the tables and book case were thrown all about the room, and, in fact, everything movable was during the day thrown out of place.

While the strange scene was transpiring the neighbors were flocking in, and passersby were filling up the house. More than 100 saw the affair, and all speak of it as something unheard of before. A part of the things in the pantry had in the meantime been replaced by Mrs. McComas, and while yet there explaining to a party of neighbors, everything she had replaced came tumbling down upon their heads. A batch of eight newly baked loaves of bread were torn into hundreds of pieces and cast about the room, several pieces of which were gathered up and sent to friends.

The phenomenon lasted all day Monday until night, was quiet throughout the night, but commenced action again early Tuesday morning, ceasing about noon. Hundreds of people have and are still visiting the scene of excitement. Hacks are running from Bridgeport out today. The question in our excited community is, what is it?

Dr. J.M. Todd, well known in Pittsburg or Bridgeport, went out, and "after a careful examination of all details and evidence" reports it as a mysterious and unaccountable truth.

Bristol Bucks Co. [PA] Gazette 5 July 1877: p. 2 BELMONT COUNTY

And, the sequel to the McComas affair, rounding up the usual suspects...

July 5 1877: Investigation of the mysterious happenings at the McComas residence indicate that strings were used and that there was nothing supernatural about the so-called "strange happenings." *Cadiz Year by Year, Gleanings from the Cadiz Republication Files 1868-1940,* Harry B. McConnell, (Cadiz, Ohio: Republican Printing Office, 1940)

NOTE: As usual, after this article, nothing more was heard from this very busy racketing spirit. I find it difficult to believe that "strings" produced the complete roster of effects listed.

These next two articles have some anomalous features for what seemed to be an ordinary stone- and corn-cob-throwing poltergeist tale. One is the strange little man seen by the children—a gremlin or a gnome out of a fairy tale. The other is a seemingly unrelated beautiful female spirit that startles a group of coon hunters. The article also points the finger at a 7-year-old boy of the family, who, pitifully, is terrified by his apparent psychokinetic abilities.

BUGABOO BUSINESS
DOINGS OF SPOOKS IN LOGAN COUNTY
SHOWERS OF CORN-COBS, CLUBS, STONES AND
OTHER MISSILES FLYING MYSTERIOUSLY
THROUGH THE AIR

Belle Center, Ohio, July 23. About three miles north-west of town there is a farm known as the Zahller Place, one of the oldest in the State, and owned by the heirs, one of whom occupies it. On last Friday afternoon the folks went blackberrying and two of the children went to a picnic nearby. About five o'clock the children returned, and they say as they came into the yard a man of small stature, bow-legged and very ragged, came out of the kitchen, walked past them, opened the garden gate and went in. He then jumped over the picket-fence into the barn-yard and disappeared in the barn. The children becoming frightened at his strange actions, went to a neighbor's house about half a mile distant and returned home in the evening. When their parents returned, they related their story. Mr. Zahller tracked the man through the garden and barn-yard by noticing three large-headed nails in the impression of his boot-heel. At the barn all traces were lost.

Now comes the mystery: Mrs. Zahller went to the barn-yard to milk; corn-cobs commenced falling near like someone was throwing at her. Mr. Zahller was standing nearby but didn't notice them. She asked him if he saw that. He answered no. Just then a large one hit near him, but he could not see where it came from. During Saturday the children were hit with corn-cobs, pieces of bark and small stones every time they attempted to go into the barn yard. Two of the family—one a boy of seven, and the other a young lady of eighteen—seemed to attract the most. When they came near the missiles were sure to fly. The boy, especially, was hurt about the face with small stones.

One of the neighbors, coming to witness the shower, was hit in the back by a wooden pin that had been used to fasten a large gate. A trace-chain that had been plowed up and was hung on a corner of the corn-crib, near the barn, also went sailing in the air in search of something to light on. Hundreds of people have been to see this sight since Saturday and all came away satisfied that they saw chips, small stones, corn-cobs, &c., falling near them, but unable to explain where they came from. One man says he saw corn-cobs start from the ground and soar over his head and light on the ground without the least noise. Another one says he was standing near a chicken house, the door of which was open, when some half dozen cobs came flying out. The house was searched, but nothing found...Some say the flying pieces are not noticed until they either strike them or fall on the ground nearby. The strangest thing is that they light as easy as a feather, no matter how large the article is. One man brought home a piece of an old walnut rail about a foot long and two by four inches thick. That, he says, he tried to aggravate the spirits, and said in a loud voice, "Don't throw anymore corn-cobs; throw a club this time." Just then this piece lit on his shoulder as easy as a feather and rolled to the ground. The whole neighborhood is excited, and watch the barn from morning until night, trying not to believe it, but at the same time convinced that they saw something, they know not what.

Cincinnati [OH] Enquirer 24 July 1880: p. 7 LOGAN COUNTY

STRANGE STORIES.
FURTHER PARTICULARS IN THE ZAHLER
SPOOK MYSTERY IN LOGAN COUNTY
A BEAUTIFUL FEMALE APPARITION WHICH
MYSTIFIES THE PEOPLE OF BELLE CENTER AND
ASTONISHES A PARTY OF COON-HUNTERS

Bellefontaine, Ohio, July 30. The peculiar manifestations of a ghostly character that have occurred of late in the Zahler homestead, near Belle Center, an account of which appeared in *The Enquirer* of Saturday, July 23d, still continue, and are causing considerable excitement and speculation; not only in that quiet little village, but here and throughout this entire section of country.

Your correspondent has been at considerable trouble to investigate the affair, and has culled the following particulars in addition to those already published. The little grotesque man who was seen just previous to the commencement of the phenomenon coming out of the Zahler farmhouse, had more the appearance of one of the demons as they appear in Hendrick Hudson's Crew in Rip Van Winkle than anything else. In fact he looked like a being of another age. He has never been seen since. The Zahler family consists of father, mother, and seven children, five boys and two girls, the oldest son being twenty-one years of age and the oldest daughter eighteen. The parents are intelligent Pennsylvania Germans, about forty-five years of age; the children are bright and active. That corn-cobs, sticks and other missiles fly through the air, sit up on end, and dance about, there cannot be the slightest doubt, or you will have to discredit the testimony of many respectable and veracious witnesses. One of the most reliable gentlemen residing in Belle Center, and who carries and exhibits a corn-cob which he will swear flew off the ground and struck him on the shoulder, without any human agency, tested the matter in various ways. He took a number of the cobs and marked them by cutting crosses, notches &c., upon them, and laid them near the barn alone. He then walked to the house and back, when those cobs began to raise up and fly through the air.

The peculiar thing about these manifestations is the fact that they are more distinct and better defined when one of the smaller children, a boy about seven years old, is present. The boy has become so frightened at his ghostly powers that it is almost impossible to get him to accompany anyone to the yard. All who have seen these occurrences positively assert that there is no fraud in the matter, and honestly believe that they are without human agency. They cannot, and do not, attempt to explain the matter, simply believing it to be one of those mysterious affairs that no man understands.

This is not the only mystery that affects the good people of Belle Center. They have been reveling in the luxury of a bona fide ghost—a ghost that walks in a lane and rides sometimes, too, as the sequel will show; a ghost that always appears in the form of a beautiful woman, and whom many people in this county say that they have seen. The strange part of the story is that this apparition was heard on one occasion to speak. No one ever got their hand on the spook, although many attempted it, as when they would approach and attempt to grasp it their hand only felt space and would go right through the form. Many reputable witnesses, among them an old, staid citizen of Bellefontaine, testify that this form has appeared to them, and even by their side in their vehicles, always in the form of a handsome female, clad in fleecy or cloudy white, with a halo around her head, but that on attempting to touch her they would only grasp space, and the ghostly visitant would vanish.

This apparition invariably appears in the road leading from Belle Center to Lisle's Mill, and has been dubbed the ghost of Lisle's lane. It has appeared to certain persons so often that they have got used to it, as it has always been friendly, and they, therefore, pay no attention to it. The time it was heard to speak was when a party of eight or ten coon-hunters were returning down the lane home. As they emerged from a corn-field they came upon a belated traveler in a buggy, and at the same time were aware of the approach of the well-known appearance. It immediately seemed to float into the buggy, where it seated itself on the vacant seat, paused a moment, and, as they rushed up, ejaculated, "Keno" and instantly vanished, leaving the traveler half dead from terror. These are strange facts but are vouched for by unimpeachable witnesses.

Cincinnati [OH] Enquirer 31 July 1880: p. 5 LOGAN COUNTY

NOTE: I don't know how unimpeachable those witnesses were. The strangest point is that a ghost would exclaim "Keno!" which is the name of a rather disreputable gambling game otherwise known as "Chinese Lottery."

Surprisingly, there are poltergeists that specialize in certain activities. One of these is the clothes-destroyer, as we saw from the Darke County story; another is the fire-spook, whom you'll meet at the end of this chapter; and the third is the "stone-throwing devil."

The first question that springs to mind about the hundreds of cases of stone-throwing poltergeists is, why stones? There is no answer to that question, but it is striking that, if these phenomena are all faked, as is invariably suggested, the poltergeists continue to do the same things over the centuries. It is strange that, while fashions in ghosts come and go, the patterns of poltergeist attacks do not change. A detailed eye-witness account of a stone-throwing poltergeist in New Hampshire in 1682 can be found in *Lithobolia: Or the Stone-Throwing Devil*, found at http://w3.salemstate.edu/~ebaker/chadweb/lithoweb.htm.

Poltergeists may spare a favored person, but they don't usually discriminate by gender as in this next story. It's unusual to find women and children the target and even more unusual to find serious injuries inflicted by these entities. The typical stone-throwing poltergeist scenario involves the missiles hitting softly, without harm to people, as in the Zahller corn-cobs that "light easy as a feather." (In fact, one psychic researcher, Adolphe d'Assier, in *Posthumous Humanity: A Study of Phantoms*, pp. 94-5, ingeniously suggests that all objects have their own "astral doubles" and that "in lieu of flinging stones, [poltergeists] fling their duplicates.")

THE HANOVER GHOST
A QUEER STORY OF A MYSTERIOUS BEING THAT HAUNTS THE OLD HILLERY FARM, NEAR HANOVER, LICKING COUNTY

The good people of Hanover, a village a few miles east of this city, are all torn up over the presence, in their midst, of a mysterious being or beings. It is reported that the farm of Mr. O.Z. Hillery, which adjoins the village is haunted, and that at divers different times the mysterious being has manifested its presence to the injury and terror of the inhabitants.

The *Advocate* reporter interviewed a Mr. B.C. Woodward, a man noted for his knowledge of the history of Licking County and his honesty about the mysterious matter:

"Mr. Woodward informed us that about three weeks since the recondite being first manifested itself in a very peculiar manner by hurling stones at defenceless women and children who came on the grounds, frequently, by the accuracy of its aim, injuring those at whom the stones were cast, but in no single instance were the stones ever hurled at a man. Thus the manifestations continued, increasing rather than diminishing, until Friday last, August 24, when the good people of Hanover, to the number of fourteen, rose up in their might, and armed with guns, pistols, knives and other weapons, repaired to the Hillery farm for the purpose of "laying" the ghost.

Weapons were a usual response when hunting ghosts and poltergeists, but then, incredibly, the hunting party brought along a group of women as *bait*.

> As it was a well-known fact that the ghost never manifested its presence to men, the services of seven ladies were called on to start his ghostship.
>
> The party had hardly arrived on the "haunted" ground, ere stones began flying about in every direction, and a Miss Fletcher was struck behind the ear by one of them and badly injured. As soon as one of the ladies would be struck by a stone, the men would make a rush in the direction from whence it came, but always failed to discover any trace of the bidden "stone thrower." All the ladies in the party were more or less injured, including Mrs. Fleming, who was badly hurt. But the most mysterious part of the affair is that not one of the fourteen men were in the least injured. Who can explain this mystery? The good people of Hanover would like to be enlightened.
>
> *Newark [OH] Daily Advocate* 27 August 1883: p. 4 LICKING COUNTY

Another stone-throwing poltergeist, and one that covers quite a large area, with that classic agent, an orphan girl:

STONES FALL ABOUT IN SHOWERS,
AND WEIRD KNOCKS COME AT NIGHT
STRANGE PHENOMENON ON A FARM
NEAR DEFIANCE
A HUMAN MAGNET IN THE PERSON OF
AN ORPHAN GIRL
THE HOUSE REPEATEDLY BOMBARDED
WITH BOULDERS

> Defiance, Ohio, November 19. Great excitement prevails about two miles west of here in the neighborhood of Mrs. William Bercaw's farm over a strange phenomenon. The weird tales told about the place have attracted much attention, and many people for miles have visited it and will vouch for the truth of this story. The Bercaw family consists of Mrs. Bercaw, her son Albert, and a fourteen-year-old girl who came to live with them from the Orphans' Home about two months ago.
>
> They were seated around the fire one evening about two weeks ago when the first storm of stones came, beating on the sides and top of the house, and breaking several panes of window glass. Albert made a diligent

search, but could not ascertain from whence they came. The stones continued to fall the whole night, and made such a noise the inmates.

COULD NOT SLEEP.

The girl seems to be the magnet of attraction in this phenomenon. Pieces of tile and brick, it is declared, are hurled at her whenever she leaves the house, and when she tries to enter it again they fall all around her.

When she is at one end of the room, the storm pelts against that side of the house with such force as to break the window panes and make large dents in the siding. When she goes to the other end the storm is centered there, and let her go where she will, her life seems to be in constant danger. She has not always been able to dodge the flying missiles, and has been cut about the head and face, but, strange to say, has not been seriously injured.

THE STONES VARY

From mere sand to a size that a strong man could not lift. Among many others a gentleman from this city visited the place. He was doubtful about the stories he had heard, remarking that he would believe it when he saw it, and not till then. He had scarcely finished the sentence when a large boulder fell just in front of him, barely missing his head.

It could not have come from any place but the sky, as there are no buildings close, behind which anyone could hide, and it was too large to have been thrown many feet. The gentleman came home feeling convinced that there was something ghost-like about the place. For more than a week the showers have come at regular intervals, covering a space of an acre of more, tearing off shingles and rolling to the foot of a hill on which the house was built.

The excitement and fear are made more intense by loud knocking on the door at a certain hour each night. During this time the door cannot be opened and

NOTHING CAN BE SEEN.

From the outside. When the door can be opened no one is there to answer the knock. Last Sunday the word first reached this city. People went in squads to the Bercaw farm and many report that there is surely something wrong there with the people of the place...

Every attempt to unearth the mystery has proved a failure. Guards have repeatedly watched to see who was knocking at the door or where the stones were coming from, but each time have been unsuccessful in discovering anything. The girl was taken to Sherwood yesterday, since which time all has been quiet on the farm of the Bercaws. But whether this change can be attributed to the girl or not is a question no one seems able to answer.

Cincinnati [OH] Enquirer 20 November 1892: p. 17 DEFIANCE COUNTY

FIRE SPOOKS

A subspecies of poltergeist is the fire spook or incendiary poltergeist. They are one of the strangest, most erratic, and most terrifying of paranormal entities. In one famous 1922 case, the "Fire Spook of Caledonia Mills," Mary Ellen, the 15-year-old adopted daughter of farmer Alex McDonald of Antigonish County, Nova Scotia seemed to be the focus for the mysterious fires that plagued the family. The case was investigated by Dr. Walter Prince of the American Institute for Scientific Research, who concluded that Mary Ellen was responsible for setting fires while in a dissociative state. Others believed that radio antennae in the neighborhood were sparking the fires.

These fiery mysteries may have some link to Spontaneous Human Combustion, where flammable objects near the fire are untouched and witnesses have said that the flames burn a bright blue. A case below specifically mentions hellish blue fire. There is also a class of religious relics, found mostly in Europe, of shirts and linens that show the marks of scorched hands—said to be produced by souls in Purgatory—not unlike the scorched garments in the Bush case below.

SPIRIT INCENDIARIES AT FINDLAY
THEY BURN UP BEDS AND CLOTHING IN A MOST MYSTERIOUS WAY

[Findlay, Ohio Spec. *Chicago Tribune*]

Six miles north-west of this city and two miles east of McComb, on the road leading from that village to Findlay, is a farm house from which the family was driven last Sunday by a series of fires as strange as they were unaccountable. The house was occupied by Samuel Miller and family, from whom the *Tribune* correspondent obtained the following particulars of the affair: The trouble began last Wednesday afternoon, when, without any apparent cause, a bed in one of the upper rooms caught fire, and in a few moments was completely consumed, without the flames communicating with a single other object in the apartment. No one had been in the chamber since morning, and there was no fire or light from which the bed could have caught. There was nothing left of the bed and its belongings but a little heap of ashes, but the door where the piece of furniture stood was not even scorched.

The next day, at about the same hour in the afternoon, a chest of clothing in quite another part of the house from the bedroom where the first fire took place, was discovered to be in flames, and despite all efforts to extinguish it, the same was soon in a pile of ashes. Yet not another thing in the room was injured in the slightest.

Friday afternoon at the usual hour the spirit of this same fire fiend took possession of another bedroom and destroyed a bed and bedding as quickly and as completely as on the occasion of its first visit, and with as little damage to the surroundings.

This was too much for the Miller family and they began preparations to remove Monday to other quarters, but Saturday afternoon a dress hanging in a closet full of clothing was burned in the same mysterious manner as the two beds and the chest, and not even the smell of smoke left upon the other garments. This decided the Millers upon an immediate removal, and bright and early Sunday morning they vacated the fire-haunted premises, which have since been in the hands of the spirit incendiaries and the curious multitude which the strange story has drawn to the spot.

There has been no recurrence of the mysterious fires since the house was abandoned, but whether this is because there is nothing left to burn but the walls or the spirits have been satisfied has not yet been discovered.
Cincinnati [OH] Enquirer 8 September 1889: p. 15 HANCOCK COUNTY

NOTE: The Miller family was an extensive one according to the 1880 census: Samuel Miller was 42; his wife Elizabeth/Eliza, 41. The children were Thomas, 20; Margaret, 17; William, 12; Mary, 11; Samuel, 8; Twins Ella and Edward, 4; Jacob, 2. By 1900 only Samuel and Elizabeth were at home with son Samuel, age 28, who was teaching school. Unfortunately there is no 1890 census, but we can assume that Samuel, age 17, the twins, age 13 and Jacob, age 9 would still have been at home, if alive and any one of them was of an age to have been the poltergeist vector. For that matter, Mrs. Miller, who would have been 50 in 1889, is also a candidate. See my theory about the burning of beds at the end of the chapter.

TORMENTED BY FIRE. THE QUEER STORY TOLD BY A GERMAN LABORER IN CLEVELAND

From the Cleveland (Ohio) Leader, April 28.

At No. 76 Lussenden Avenue live the family of John Bush, a hard-working German, employed at the Cleveland Rubber Works. The story, as learned by a *Leader* reporter, who visited the place yesterday, savors so much of the supernatural that he feels able simply to reproduce it without attempting any theory. The house, which stands in that portion of the Sixteenth Ward, between Giddings and Madison Avenues, largely inhabited by the employees of the mills and manufactories along the Cleveland and Pittsburgh Railway tracks, is small and unattractive in appearance, being but one story high, with an attic.

As the reporter approached it at dusk last evening the street in front and the yard were crowded with anxious-looking men, women, and children, who had been attracted from the neighborhood by the reports that they had heard of the mysterious appearance of fire at intervals within the house. Bush was found in the shed or back kitchen surrounded by another curious gathering, to whom he was relating a recent occurrence. The floor was covered with a couple of bed-ticks and articles of furniture, and, in the front room the wife and several other women were with the children, nine in all. The older of these sat about the room with fear in their white faces, while the younger toddled about in innocent play, unable to comprehend the unusual commotion. There was a heavy, unpleasant smell of smoke throughout the house, and various garments and articles of furniture showed marks of having been burned or scorched.

The man's statement, made in broken English, as best he could, is as follows:

Several months ago he moved from Amherst, where he had lived for 13 years, most of that time being employed as a switchman on the Lake Shore Road. Five or six years ago his house was destroyed by fire, the cause being, as was supposed, a defective flue.

His first home in this city was at No. 1177 Lincoln Avenue, where on Sunday, the 18th inst., the first remarkable appearance of flames occurred. Some clothes, a coat, vest, and dress, which hung upon the wall, suddenly began to smoke, sending forth a peculiarly sickening smell. This was followed in a moment by a dark blue blaze that leaped hungrily over the garments, and almost consumed them before the fire was extinguished by the astonished Bush. His wife said that matches in his pocket had ignited, but he was positive there were no matches there.

On the following day he went to work as usual, and when he came home was met by his wife, who was frantic with fear. During his absence the fire had appeared seven different times. In the first instance, the bed upon which one of the children lay sleeping took fire, reappearing twice after it had been put out. Being of a superstitious nature, she feared that some evil spirit hung over them and craved for the life of the youngest child. To appease the wrath of the unknown, whatever it was, she went out into the fields and cast to the winds all the money they had—some $30, (all but $10 of this was afterward found.)

The father decided to stay at home the following day and watch, calling in a friend to do the same. By this time the mystery was being noised about somewhat, and everybody that came in decided that the children had been playing with matches. There seemed no other explanation, but the youngsters stoutly denied this. Mr. J.B. McGee, living near, was called in to make an examination. He thought at first that it was an ignition of phosphorus, but upon hearing the story in detail, gave the solution up. Bush being a Catholic, appealed to Father Baker, of the Church of the Holy Family, who came to the place, but could shed no light on the subject. A second time, when Bush called on the priest, he told him the stories were all nonsense, and gave him to understand that he thought he was drunk.

Bush remained at the house on Lincoln Avenue until Tuesday, when he made up his mind to quit the place and move to the house on Lusseden Avenue, hoping thereby to shake off the mystery. On Friday the fire once more appeared, burning the straw in one of the beds. The straw in a barrel that stood in the shed was also burned in the same manner on Saturday, together with several coats that hung on the wall.

The family had by this time nearly become crazy. Many of their household goods and clothes had been destroyed, and some of the neighbors, filled with sympathy, came in and endeavoured to console them and pacify their fears as best they could. On Sunday, Mrs. Foland, a lady living on Giddings Avenue, dropped in to lend her aid in this direction. She took off her hat and laid it upon the table, where it had not remained five minutes when a large feather upon it was touched by the strange flame and nearly consumed. The reporter called upon Mrs. Foland who fully corroborated this statement and exhibited the hat as proof.

On Monday the fire appeared twice, each time destroying some clothes. Yesterday morning a child's dress that hung on a peg near the door smoked, blazed for a minute or two, and fell to the floor. These singular occurrences have been witnessed by neighbors who came in to watch out of curiosity, and there is no one living on the street but believes everything that is told. The reporter selected one man from the crowd that stood about while Bush was making his statement. He appeared intelligent, and ready to tell all he knew. Bush's story he pronounced true in every particular. He had himself seen a coat burn up in the mysterious manner described, but, like the rest, could offer no explanation whatever.

These are plain facts. There is no reason to doubt Bush's story, while there is good proof that he has told the truth. The suspense he has gone through seems to have nearly crazed him. No one can convince him there is not something supernatural in it. He insists that he has done nothing wrong to deserve this kind of persecution, and proposes to go to Amherst to-day for the testimonials of his former employers and others who knew him as to his good character, although he fails to show in what way they can aid him.

Lancaster [Pa] Daily Intelligencer 3 May 1880: p. 1 CUYAHOGA COUNTY

In a follow up story:

> The Bush family of Cleveland tell a strange story, and some folks
> believe them. They say their house is possessed by supernatural flames,
> which break out at unexpected times and places, consuming articles of
> clothing and even scorching persons. The blazes are very blue, suggesting
> a hellish origin, and disappear as strangely as they come. Partly burned
> garments are the best evidence the Bushes can produce in support of their
> word, but their motive for deception is not apparent.
> *Waukesha [WI] Freeman*, 3 June 1880: p. 3 CUYAHOGA COUNTY

IS IT WITCHCRAFT?
MYSTERIOUS FLAMES IN A CLEVELAND DWELLING
THEY LEAP UP IN CLOSETS AND CONSUME BEDDING
A FAMILY DESPOILED OF FURNITURE AND
CLOTHING AND DEMORALIZED WITH FEAR

Cleveland, Ohio, April 28. An extraordinary series of mysterious
fires has occasioned an unusual sensation in one of the outlying wards of
this city, and as yet no solution to their strange cause has been furnished.
Bedding and articles of domestic use have caught fire from no apparent
cause, and an entire family has not only been kept in constant terror of
flames, but has been subject to pecuniary loss that falls hard upon a man
who can ill afford to lose even so much as a dollar.

A short time ago there came to this city from North Amherst, a hard-
working and honest German named John Busch, whose principal worldly
goods were a "poor man's blessing" of eleven children. Two of these latter
were twins at their mother's breast. Busch had been in the employ of the
Lake Shore Railroad for a number of years, and had always had the reputation of an honest and steady-going fellow. He and his wife are devout
Roman Catholics, and are thoroughly superstitious. Shortly after Busch
removed to Cleveland his family began to be troubled by fires breaking
out in various parts of the house without any apparent cause. Busch was
living in a house on Lincoln Avenue, and, becoming imbued with the
belief that the place was haunted, he removed to 77 Lussenden Avenue,
where he thought he would find relief from the annoyance. The house on
Lincoln Avenue was a two-story frame dwelling which had been formerly
occupied as a bakery. Busch used the front parlor as a bed-room, and, the
house being small and his family very large, it was found necessary to put
three beds in the one room. The three beds were placed in rows about

three feet apart, the bed nearest the wall being placed against the door of a closet. A small child's crib occupied a place in one corner.

A little more than a week later Mr. and Mrs. Busch, several of the children, and a couple of friends were seated in this room quietly engaged in conversation when one of the party noticed a small stream of smoke issuing through a key-hole of the closet. The bed was immediately pulled away, when it was discovered that an old suit of clothes, the only garments in the closet, was on fire. The flames were already burning at a brisk rate, but were quickly extinguished. The family were at a loss to understand how the fire had started, as the closet had not been used for some time, and access to it was impossible except by the removal of the bed. This occurred on Sunday, April 18th. On Monday when Mrs. Busch, in going about her domestic duties, entered a pantry used for dishes, she was startled to see flames rising from the shelves. In a moment the paper which had been used for lining the shelves, was consumed, and nothing remained but the ashes, while the dishes were blackened with the smoke. Some relatives were summoned to the house by one of the children, and while they stood in the kitchen discussing the strange occurrence the child's crib in the front room began smoking, and upon their hastening to extinguish it a hole was found burned clear through the bed-tick.

Monday afternoon several fires occurred in the house, in different rooms. By this time the entire family had become thoroughly frightened, and Busch began looking about for another house. The news of the strange fires spread throughout the neighborhood, and created no end of excitement and discussion. Tuesday afternoon an entire mattress in the front room was consumed. A bunch of wadding that lay behind a door took fire. A kettle full of old rags blazed up, and its contents were suddenly consumed.

The terrified family moved out on the following morning, both husband and wife sharing the belief that the house was haunted. The new home on Lussenden Avenue was a story and a half frame building, and small. No beds were up on that night, and the whole family, wearied after the sleeplessness of the two previous nights, slept on the floor.

Thursday morning the work of putting the beds and arranging the household goods was begun. In the afternoon one of the children detected the odor of smoke, and upon rushing upstairs found one of the beds erected in the morning almost entirely consumed.

On Friday a hen's nest in an old barrel in the yard was burned.

Saturday, while Mrs. Busch was in the coal-shed adjoining the kitchen, she saw smoke rising from an old coat that was hanging on a nail. She says that the fire seemed to begin about the middle of the back. It was ruined before she could put the fire out.

The terror of the family increased day by day. The children were kept out of school to watch for fear the house would be burned. On Sunday a number of friends and relatives stayed during the day with the terrified people... Shortly after the bed caught fire, and was burned for a space of several feet before it could be extinguished. The stock of straw-beds was now exhausted, except one which on Monday met with the fate of the others.

To-day your correspondent visited the house and found the family in a pitiable state. The fire had absolutely burned all of their bedding except a couple of feather-pillows and a feather-tick. The mother was almost distracted, while the father acted like a man bereft of his senses. The most searching inquiry among neighbors and friends confirmed every statement made by Busch and his wife.

Your correspondent returned to his office in the city at noon, and was called to the telephone as soon as he entered. A friend out in the neighborhood telephoned from a manufacturing establishment nearby that he had just come from the house, and that the two pillows had just met the same mysterious fate as the other articles.

A rather strange feature of the mystery was called out by the declaration of an old German lady that if they would look in the feathers of the feather tick they would find a solid wreath of feathers, which was "the witch" that was causing the trouble. She said that if they would boil this "the witch" would be destroyed and they would suffer no more annoyance. Acting on her advice, they ripped open the tick, and, sure enough, there was a wreath of feathers several inches thick, forming a ring about ten inches in diameter. On Monday they gave it a vigorous boiling, but it did not prevent the return of the fires.

Mr. Busch has had to abandon his work to watch over his family, all of whose members are in constant dread of some serious calamity. Should the strange fires continue, your correspondent will forward further particulars.

Cincinnati [OH] Enquirer 29 April 1880: p. 4 CUYAHOGA COUNTY

At that, apparently, the fires ceased and the family survived, for in the 1900 census, Busch is listed as employed as a watchman on the railroad. The twins, Henry and Amadeus, who were just a year old when the fires began, are 21 and still living at home with at least two other siblings, 17 and 15. If you care to play Freudian analyst, perhaps Mrs. Busch, who was about 37 at the time of the fires and went on to have at least two other children, was exhausted by fulfilling her maternal and marital duties. The fires of passion burnt out, did her rage smolder?

The poltergeist burned all the bedding. No beds, no bedclothes, no "bedding," and no more babies? It's a theory.

NOTE: The "solid wreath of feathers" or feather crown, was a sign that the family had been bewitched. Boiling the crown was supposed to either bring the witch to the house so the curse could be removed or neutralize the evil powers of the witch.

For further reading on poltergeists, see: *Poltergeists: A History of Violent Ghostly Phenomena*, G.P. Maxwell-Stewart; *The Secret History of Poltergeists and Haunted Houses: From Pagan Folklore to Modern Manifestations*, Claude Lecouteux; *Poltergeists, An Introduction and Examination*, Sacheverell Sitwell; and *The Poltergeist*, William G. Roll (who studied the Columbus Tina Resch poltergeist case and wrote about it in *Unleashed: Of Poltergeists and Murder: The Curious Story of Tina Resch*, 2004.) Also G. Scott Rogo's *The Poltergeist Experience: Investigations into Ghostly Phenomena* and *On the Track of the Poltergeist*, and "An Investigation of Poltergeist and Other Phenomena Near Antigonish," by Dr. Walter Prince, *Journal of the American Society for Psychical Research* (March, 1922).

5.

The Death-Bed Promise:
Revenge Beyond the Grave in Coshocton

Promise me nothing. One day you will buy
Another ring, you know.
Then, if the dead walk in their sleep, must I
Come, shivering, back to say, "I told you so"?

– "A Woman's Last Word," Sarah Piatt –

W e all know that everybody in a small town knows everybody else's
business. It's one thing to whisper local gossip and tittle-tattle over
the back fence; it's another to see a neighbor's dirty laundry hung, not just in
public, but on the front page of the local newspaper. Uncovering this story
of a woman haunted by a broken death-bed promise was like watching a
train wreck—I couldn't look away from the paper-trail of sordid details that
sucked me into the lives of its dysfunctional cast of characters.

This story began with a snippet of an article in the *Van Wert Daily Bulletin*:

WRAITH HAUNTS WOMAN

Coshocton, O. July 26 – Walter Carnes and wife left their home
and are camping on the river bank for the rest of the summer because,
they declare, Mrs. Carnes is being haunted by the ghost of her former
husband, Simon Fisher. Five members of the family attest the truth of
the story.
Van Wert [OH] Daily Bulletin 26 July 1911: p. 1

Searching for the names from the Van Wert article, I was shocked to find
dozens of newspaper articles about the family's woes. As I read, I discovered a
startlingly frank saga of life, love, and lust, sweeping across decades and county lines; a small-town epic of jealousy and revenge from beyond the grave.

Let us start with the "ghost of her former husband, Simon Fisher" with
his obituary. The headline read: SIMON FISHER ENTERS REWARD,
a nicely ambiguous phrase, leaving open the question as to what the exact
nature of that reward might be.

After an illness of several years duration from a nervous disease, Simon Fisher, aged 70, died at his home on Main St. yesterday morning at 9 o'clock.

Mr. Fisher was a civil war veteran; he saw almost four years of active service in the war and was in Sherman's march to the sea. He was known as a soldier of unflinching valor and devotion to duty.

For the past several years Mr. Fisher had been unable to work at his trade of stone-mason because of his nervous affliction but his illness was not considered of a serious nature until the past ten days, when he grew rapidly worse.

The deceased is survived by a widow, Mrs. Linnie Fisher and five children, Mrs. Marang and Mrs. Martin of Newark, Dewey, Raymond, and Agnes Fisher of this city.

Funeral services will be from the late home on Main St. tomorrow afternoon, the Rev. C. C. Irwin officiating. Interment will take place in Oak Ridge cemetery.

Coshocton [OH] Daily Tribune 14 March 1911: p. 4 COSHOCTON COUNTY

From the records it appeared that Fisher had been married before: to Rachel, who died, aged 19, in 1870 and to English-born Anna who divorced him in 1889—for adultery. He married his wife Malinda Moore Middy, known as Linnie, who was 25 years younger, on July 20, 1892—the same day as Linnie was divorced from her first husband. There was reason for haste—the new bride was pregnant. Their first child was born in January of 1893. It does not appear that the marriage was a particularly happy one.

In 1902, the first marital stressors began to appear in the papers. Linnie's son, Ernest, from her first marriage, stole a gun and his stepfather bailed him out amid much legal wrangling. In 1903, in the space of a few months, a son, Raymond, was born and his sister "Midget" died of typhoid while two other children recovered from the deadly disease.

In July of 1908, 13-year-old Sarah Ethel stole money from her mother and took a train to Missouri, supposedly eloping with a lover. Four days later, 16-year-old daughter Bernice ran off to join the circus; a 1909 article reported on her snake-charming career.

1909 seems to have been the pivotal year for the Fisher family. In early August the papers reported that Linnie was in Roscoe with a Mr. Walter Carnes, visiting his mother. The photos of Carnes show him as tall and handsome, with dreamy, hooded eyes and a secret smile. He was 11 years younger than Linnie. No prizes for guessing what happened next. The newspapers did not beat around the bush.

SIMON FISHER A MODERN ENOCH ARDEN
SAYS HE FOUND ANOTHER MAN IN HIS PLACE
WHEN HE RETURNED FROM LONG JOURNEY

Have Walter Carnes, a married man of this city, and Mrs. Linnie Fisher, the wife of Simon Fisher, the woman who figured so prominently in probate court Friday, eloped?

The police were notified Sunday evening that Simon Fisher was on the war path and threatened the life of both his wife and Carnes. He met all out-going trains but saw no signs of the alleged elopers.

Mr. Fisher told an *Age* reporter Monday the full story of the trouble. He has been in Texas for the past several months and just returned Saturday night. When he reached home he said Carnes was there. A scene followed....

Fisher declares that he will kill Carnes at sight and will not be pacified for he says that he has only a few years to live at best and if he should be hung it would make little difference with him.

The elopers have not been heard from late this afternoon.

Coshocton [OH] Daily Age 15 August 1909: p. 5

The "Enoch Arden" of the headline refers to an 1864 poem by Alfred, Lord Tennyson. It tells the story of a sailor who is cast away and returns ten years later to find his wife happily remarried to a rival. (You've probably seen one of the movies based on this theme.) Arden never reveals his identity to his wife so as to not spoil her new happiness.

It wasn't a perfect analogy: several months in Texas aren't ten years on a desert island; nor did Fisher keep quiet as the next headline reads: SIMON FISHER APPLIES FOR A DIVORCE. Fisher charged Linnie with "extreme cruelty and gross neglect of duty."

Mr. Fisher claims that in May his wife beat him over the back with a chair and called him vile and vulgar names at various time. He claims that she stays out late at nights without his consent and that now she has abandoned him and gone away with another man."

Coshocton [OH] Daily Age 19 August 1909: p. 5

Fisher also charged his wife and Carnes with adultery, which was at that time a felony, sending the police in hot pursuit.

OFFICERS ARE AFTER ALLEGED AFFINITIES

Authorities by use of the telephone are trying to catch Mrs. Linnie Fisher and Walter Carnes before they leave the confines of Coshocton co. They are supposed to be near Warsaw Friday afternoon and the prospects are they will be in the hands of the law before night.

Simon Fisher, the husband, filed affidavit in a local court Thursday night, charging Carnes and Mrs. Fisher with statutory offense, and a deputy was sent to Roscoe to make the arrest, the pair alleged to have been at Carnes' home there. They had left.

Carnes has a wife and Mrs. Fisher a husband and children, but their romance has continued since the first of August, according to the affidavit. Authorities doubt if they have been out of the state.

Coshocton [OH] Daily Age 27 August 1909: p. 7

"Affinities" is such a charming word for such an ugly affair. Adultery was illegal and crossing state lines "for immoral purposes" would have compounded the felony.

Just a few days later, Linnie apparently decided to face the music and returned to Coshocton. She also filed a counter suit:

The defendant says that June 15, 1909, the husband told her he was going to Texas, that she could go to ____; that he would not live with her any longer. She declares that the property in contention was bought by her own earnings accrued by working and washing by the day. She claims that he repeatedly was cruel to her. She asks custody of their two children.

Coshocton [OH] Daily Times 31 August 1909: p. 1

Fisher shot back a notice requesting a divorce, custody of the minor children, a piece of land, and alimony. So far, it was all rather like a public soap opera, with mudslinging, charges and counter-charges. But then things took a darker turn.

NOT RESPONSIBLE FOR HIS WIFE'S RASH ACTIONS

Simon Fisher, whose wife, Linnie Fisher, attempted to commit suicide Monday afternoon, states that he was in no way responsible for her act. He states that her troubles all grew out of her friendship for Walter Carnes. Mr. Fisher says that Mrs. Fisher became angry Monday because he would not give her the bed room suit she wanted and that she kicked to pieces a picture of her, which he had had enlarged and which he would not have taken $25 for. He says that $125 of his money has already been squandered. "Few men who have been used as I have would take it as cool as I do," said he.

Coshocton [OH] Daily Age 22 September 1909: p. 5

Linnie's suicide attempt seems to have sobered all parties.

OLIVE BRANCH WAVES OVER FISHER HOME DOVE OF PEACE FLUTTERS IN AND DIVORCE PETITION IN PROBATE COURT IS DISMISSED.

The hatchet has been buried and all is once more peace and harmony in the family of Simon Fisher. Some months ago it will be remembered Simon applied for divorce from his wife Linnie Fisher...Not many weeks ago Linnie...following a fiery interview with Simon attempted to commit suicide in her lonely rooms in the Brower building on Hickory St. by swallowing a large quantity of morphine. Linnie, through the efforts of physicians, pulled through and then repentance set in and frequent interviews were arranged and as a result of these interviews Simon filed a motion in probate court Tuesday morning to have the divorce proceedings dismissed and Judge Ashman immediately dismissed the case....

Coshocton [OH] Daily Age 19 October 1909: p. 1

But, alas, the olive branch of peace withered quickly in the Fisher household.

LINNIE FISHER AND WALTER CARNES ARE LOCKED IN PRISON FOLLOWING WITHDRAWAL OF DIVORCE CASE, NIGHT POLICE FIND PLAINTIFF ENTERTAINING HER AFFINITY

Fickle fickle woman! Such a domestic mix-up. Linnie Fisher is again in jail.

The matrimonial sky of the Fisher family seemed to be cleared of all clouds when last Tuesday her husband Simon withdrew his petition for divorce and they departed hand-in-hand and presumably heart-to-heart. But bliss was fleeting.

That very evening she is said to have tired of Simon and to have sent him hence. It is said he "henced" to Canton and is now there nursing his broken heart.

Wednesday night the police stated they visited Mrs. Fisher's home and found her entertaining Walter Carnes, who had been the gay Lothario in her former troubles....

Linnie's probation officer was told of Carnes's presence in the city and he and three police officers surrounded the Fisher house on North Sixth Street late at night. They found Linnie and Carnes in bed. The two were placed under arrest and immediately taken to prison: Linnie being taken to the county jail and Carnes to the city prison. Both were charged with aiding and contributing to the delinquency and neglect of the three minor Fisher children who had been in the house.

Linnie is under a suspended sentence of a year in the work house at Columbus and it is very likely that she will take the trip for Judge Ashman has given her every chance, thinking that perhaps a little gentleness would do the woman more good and he has now come to the conclusion that she needs a little of the true bitter medicine."

Coshocton [OH] Daily Age 21 October 1909: p. 2

And just like that, the family was torn apart:

IN PRISON AND HER CHILDREN IN ORPHANS' HOME

The three younger children of Mr. and Mrs. Simon Fisher, Dewey 10 years old, Raymond 6, and Agnes 2, will be sent to the Canal Dover Children's Home Monday by Judge Ashman.

Mrs. Fisher and Walter Carnes were sent to the Columbus work-house this morning to work out a sentence of one year.

Coshocton [OH] Daily Tribune 23 October 1909: p. 1

After much pleading for leniency with the workhouse authorities by her attorney and her daughter Ethel, Linnie's sentence was shortened to just six weeks. She was released in December 1909.

Her husband, Simon Fisher, who has been weeping his heart away ever since his wife was sent away and declaring that if she was not released he would die of sorrow, is rejoicing.

Mrs. Fisher's 'affinity,' Walter Carnes, who was sent to the workhouse with the woman, is still there serving a sentence of a year. He will probably be released in six or seven months, with good behavior.

Mrs. Fisher's minor children are now in the Canal Dover Home.

Coshocton [OH] Daily Tribune 4 December 1909: p. 1

I found myself fervently hoping that the children made it home that year for Christmas.

Nothing was heard of the Fishers in the newspapers in the following year. Mrs. Walter Carnes, however, had had enough and filed for divorce a year after the fateful visit to Roscoe.

Then, unexpectedly, and after an illness of only ten days, Simon Fisher died on March 13, 1911. The dying man made his wife promise that after he was gone she would not marry Walter Carnes, nor even see him again. Linnie promised.

Death-bed promises were a serious matter, having an almost sacred binding force. They were not made lightly. That should have been the end of it.

But love—or obsession—never dies....

SPIRIT OF HER DEPARTED HUSBAND STALKS
THROUGH HOUSE AT MIDNIGHT
FOR SHE BROKE PROMISE
SIMON FISHER HAUNTS HIS WIFE, SAYS FAMILY
WIDOW OF LATE SIMON FISHER
SHADOW OF HER FORMER SELF
AND FAMILY HAS FEARS
HEAR STRANGE NOISES AND HAVE VISIONS OF MAN
WHO HATED WIFE'S AFFINITY
IS THE STOUT CLAIM OF FISHERS

The wrath of the spirit of the late Simon Fisher has been brought down upon the wife of Walter Carnes whose second husband was Fisher. Fisher secured a promise from his wife on his death-bed that she would never marry Carnes, whom he hated with a bitter hate; but just one month and three days after the death of Fisher the widow broke her promise and married Carnes. Since a month after the marriage the ghost of the late Mr. Fisher has haunted the little house on North Sixth Street in which Fisher and his wife lived but which is now occupied by Carnes and Fisher's widow. Mrs. Carnes has worried until she is but a shadow of her former self and little strands of silver have appeared in her hair. Although only 40 years old, Mrs. Carnes looks 50.

Simon Fisher when alive was a non-believer—had no religion. He and his wife quarreled and lived unhappily. Fisher was much older than his wife which partly explained the strained relations. Mrs. Fisher became enamored of Carnes and the two became fast friends. Fisher took a decided dislike to the younger man. At one time he became so enraged that he purchased a revolver and started out to find Carnes to shoot him.

DEATH-BED PROMISE

One day Fisher became suddenly ill and rapidly failed. Worry over his family troubles and physical disability soon sapped away his life blood and he died. A few minutes before his death he called his wife to his bedside and extracted from her the promise that she would never marry Carnes and would have nothing more to do with him. The promise was given.

Mr. Fisher was buried wearing a black suit and a white shirt and collar.

Just one month and three days after the death of her husband Mrs. Fisher was married to Carnes—on Easter Sunday last. They lived happily for a month when one night they were awakened by strange noises, as though someone were walking through the rooms of the restaurant in which the Carnes lived at the time. Mrs. Carnes and her husband became so frightened that they arose and lighted up the dining room of their restaurant and spent the rest of the night there.

A few weeks later the restaurant (now the Imperial) was sold by Mrs. Carnes and they moved into a house on North Sixth Street in which Mrs. Carnes and her former husband lived. The strange noises followed them there.

SEES THE SPIRIT

Ernest Middy, a son of Mrs. Carnes' by her first husband, Christ Middy, was lying on a couch in a downstairs room about two weeks ago when he was awakened by someone gently touching him on the shoulder. He awoke and was startled to see Simon Fisher standing by the couch. Before Middy could speak the shadowy form walked across the room to a door and entered the bedroom which was formerly used by Fisher. Middy, in an interview Tuesday, said that Fisher wore the same clothes he wore when buried. Middy declares that the vision was not an hallucination as he does not believe in spirits.

"I was born with a veil," said Middy. It is said that if the veil is kept that the child may see and talk with spirits. Middy however does not attach any importance to this.

Middy told the whole story to an *Age* reporter and is stout in his claim of its absolute veracity in every particular.

Other members of the family have heard strange noises in the house. One of Fisher's own children says that she heard sounds as though someone were walking through the house. Others have heard dresser drawers in an upstairs room rattle and doors have opened and closed. Investigation into the cause of these has never revealed anything.

DOGS HER STEPS

Mrs. Carnes has been followed around the house for hours by the spirit. She hears the footsteps but when glancing around she is unable to see anything. She will say but little about the strange occurrences but is worrying herself sick. Ever since the first strange noise was heard she has been ill and is rapidly losing flesh.

Mr. and Mrs. Carnes are now spending the summer in a camp to get away from the noises and the spirit's strange actions. The family fears that Mrs. Carnes may worry herself into a critical illness.

Mrs. Carnes was married three times. Her first husband was Christ Middy. By this marriage one son was born, Ernest, who with his wife lived with Mrs. Carnes. Her second husband was Fisher. They had five children all of whom are at home and all of whom have heard the noises. The third husband is Walter Carnes.

Coshocton [OH] Daily Age 25 July 1911: p. 1

When I first read this I thought that the apparition of her late husband was simply a projection of Linnie's guilty conscience—except that there were so many other witnesses....

In an article headed DEATHBED REQUEST VIOLATED; GHOSTS MAKE THINGS LIVELY, it was said that all five of the children were "showing the strain....A grown son and daughter each declare that on separate occasions they saw visions of Fisher. So vividly did he appear before one of them, and so penetrating the stern look in his eyes, that the child shrank back in horror and seemed to suffer a prolonged shock."

Warren [PA] Evening Mirror 27 July 1911: p. 1

Mr. and Mrs. Walter Carnes moved back into the house on North Sixth Street, three doors from the cemetery where three of her children and Simon Fisher were buried. And after the camping expedition in late July of 1911, there is nothing more in the papers about the ghost of Simon Fisher. Some ghosts simply wear out with time. Did Fisher's rage decay along with his body? Or did he find something better to do in the Afterlife?

Linnie and Walter seemed to live happily together. No scandals, no divorce suits, no suicide attempts, no children sent to the county home. Third time lucky? Perhaps they really were "affinities," a term the Spiritualists also used for "soul mates."

Walter Carnes died in April of 1922, age 44. There are no reports of him haunting his widow. Nor did she marry again. She died, aged 82 in February of 1949 and was buried at Oak Ridge Cemetery under a stone that reads "Mother, Linnie Fisher Carnes." Simon Fisher lies nearby. So, too, does Walter Carnes.

Which of her husbands do you suppose met her on the Other Side?

6.

Great Balls of Fire

Spook Lights and Mystery Lights

He saw a corpse candle moving before him along the road. It burned with a red flame, from which it was clear that it was not a woman who was doomed (a woman's candle is white), and the candle was small, indicating that a child was to die, for the size of corpse candles varies with the age of those whose death they foretell.

–*The Welsh Fairy Book*, W. Jenkyn Thomas, 1907–

Spook lights, corpse candles, will-o-the-wisps, jack-o-lanterns, *ignis fatuus*, ghost lights: they have many names, but always float just out of reach when the scientists try to study them. There are theories: swamp gas, natural gas leaks, earthquake lights caused by piezoelectric events when rocks scrape together under pressure, plasma formations, the souls of the dead carrying lanterns, markers for a safe path through the swamp or to a place where treasure is buried. But no one really knows....

Here are some of Ohio's most memorable historical spook lights.

One of the strangest features of spook lights is that sometimes they seem sentient. They can interact with humans and exhibit seemingly purposeful behavior, like this prophetic light near Barnesville, in Belmont County.

DAZZLING STAR
SEEN IN A MINE NEAR BARNESVILLE
AN OMEN WHICH THE WORKMEN DO NOT UNDERSTAND
SENDING DISMAY AMONG THEM WHILE AT WORK

Barnesville, Ohio. March 24 There are a number of coal miners in this place whose faith in ghosts and things supernatural has recently been made the stronger by personal experience with a mysterious visitation.

For several years the Fahner Brothers have operated a coal mine on the lands of Jehu Hayes, a short distance north of town, where from twenty to thirty men were employed digging the dusky diamonds.

93

The other day two of the miners were out in the main entry of the mine engaged in conversation about their work, when a bright ball of fire, in the shape of a star, suddenly appeared before them. In a moment the star became intensely brilliant and

FAIRLY DAZZLED THEIR EYES

Now it swayed back and forth, up and down, with great rapidity. Watching it for a time, one of the men started toward it with a view of investigation. As he approached the thing would move off. When he stopped it stopped. He followed it to the mouth of the entry, when it went out in the daylight and disappeared.

The men reported what they had seen to some of their companions, who ridiculed the idea and discredited their story. Among these was William Loeffler, the mine boss. The following day, however, Loeffler changed his tune. Just as he was entering the mine the fiery star appeared right in front of him. At one time it seemed that it would hit him square in the face and he raised his hand to strike it, but it darted off. He followed it to the end of the entry—a distance of two or three hundred yards—where it vanished for a moment, only to appear again in his rear. Sometimes it would hang in space, then dart to one side, and then the other, now lingering for a moment on the edge of a projecting piece of slate, and always moving off when an attempt was made to approach it. At different times

THE GLISTENING VISITOR

Appeared in the same manner and going through the same antics to the discomfiture of George Fahner and John Gallagher, and the latter three colored miners experienced a view of it, and were almost frightened out of their wits. They left the mine in a hurry, declaring that the place was haunted and they wouldn't work in it anymore. Finally Jas. Hines, whose son was crushed to death by falling slate in the mine a year ago, told the miners that the strange light was the spirit of his dead boy in the form of a star sent to warn them of the dangerous mine.

A day or two after Hines had imparted this information, Loeffler was acting as mule-driver when the star once more appeared. On this occasion he says he saw it just as he started with a train of loaded cars for the chute. It went through pretty much the same gyrations as on former occasions—darting from side to side, skimming along the roof, always keeping in advance and at one time

LINGERING FOR A MOMENT

On the point of one of the mule's ears. It would always disappear at the mouth of the entry when he went out, and meet him at the same place when entering the mine, and always disappearing at either end. A strange thing about its visits is that it never was seen in any of the several rooms leading from the main entry, and this fact was the cause of much theorizing among the miners, and it was generally conceded, and, indeed, accepted by all, that the mine entry was in danger, and they were having timely warning through this mysterious agency.

The climax came last week, however, and James Hines is now looked upon as a prophet. On Friday evening, the few men who had not been frightened from the mine had finished their day's work, and were on their way homeward. Loeffler remained behind to look after matters. Just as he was leaving the mine a hundred feet or more of the entry caved in, and Loeffler was partially buried. He saved his life by crawling through an aperture—none too soon, however, as a second slip of the hill completely closed it up. He escaped with a few severe bruises. The fall of the entry completely wrecked the mine, and operations are forever abandoned at that point.

ANOTHER PECULIAR PHASE

Of this story is that on the very day the mine fell in one year ago, at almost the exact hour, young Hines was killed in it. Was it his spirit in the form of a fiery star that warned the miners of their danger? If not, what was it?
Cincinnati [OH] Enquirer 25 March 1889: p. 1 BELMONT COUNTY

FLOATING BALL OF FIRE
A MOST MYSTERIOUS PHENOMENON
WHICH THE SUPERSTITIOUS REGARD AS
A HEAVENLY VISITANT
SOME OF THE PEOPLE VERY BADLY SCARED

St. Mary's, June 30 The whole country around Spencerville, a village fourteen miles north of this city, is torn up with feverish excitement over a strange and unnatural apparition which puts in an appearance regularly every night. The unwelcome phenomenon is seen near Conant, and the people there think it is a heavenly visitor. The mysterious object resembles a large ball of fire, and emits a very bright light. It is about two feet in diameter, and seems to be flat upon the bottom, with an oval shaped top, the color being blood red. At times the uncanny apparition may be seen floating a few feet above the ground, then suddenly shoots toward heaven.

The first appearance of the strange light was noticed about two years ago, but has been more frequently seen within the last two months. Some superstitious people, coming from a distance, are almost scared to death by the mysterious visitor suddenly looming up before them, then disappearing for a short time, before long to be seen again in the distance. Thousands of people watch the phenomenon nightly, and in the vicinity

where it generally puts in an appearance, the people are so terror-stricken that they are afraid of venturing to bed when night comes.
Xenia [OH] Daily Gazette 1 July 1891: p. 1 ALLEN COUNTY

Other balls of fire were observed at a brick yard in Celina in 1931 and at Van Wert in 1900 where the ball of fire rolled out of a forest onto the highway and "after dancing on airy legs..." evaporated in a ghostly blaze of blue. The object was delightfully described as "the curdling object." *Van Wert [OH] Times* 18 December 1900: p. 6 VAN WERT COUNTY

At Tiffin, a ball of fire was said to be "hurled in the house of Mr. Sheets every night. Even the police cannot solve the mystery." *Marion [OH] Daily Star* 23 September 1885: p. 4 SENECA COUNTY

The *Orrville Crescent* reported that "Near Fostoria, Thomas Sheets was mangled to pieces by reaper knives." Could it have been the same Mr. Sheets? *Orrville [OH] Crescent* 13 July 1886: p. 2 SENECA COUNTY

Something we forget, sitting in front of our blue-screen monitors in rooms lit by energy-saving bulbs, is how dark the countryside used to be. Electricity did not reach all parts of the country until the 1930s. Before that, people used candles, oil lamps, and natural gas to illuminate their houses. Out in the country, there were no street lamps and no flashlights, just the glow of a far-away city on the horizon or the twinkling light of a neighbor's lamp across the fields. Remembering that pervasive darkness makes the following two stories all the more mystifying.

TIMELY GHOST.
IT ONLY APPEARS ON THE THIRTEENTH
OF EACH MONTH

The residents of and near West Huron, O., are all stirred up over the appearance of a ghost in that locality. This is not an ordinary ghost, says the *Cleveland Plain Dealer*, a visitor from ethereal regions, robed in flowing white. It is different from any ever before seen.

In the first place, this ghost is supposed to be the visible spirit of a departed bachelor who had large sums of money while he was an occupant of a flesh and blood structure on this mundane sphere. The ghost is not to be seen every night [but] his visits are so regular that those who have a desire to view him may go to West Huron at the stated time and see him walk through board fences, disappear in haystacks and sink mysteriously into the ground or soar heavenward on fiery wings.

The ghost is always seen on the Woolverton farm, West Huron, between 11:30 and 12:30 on the thirteenth day of each and every month unless that day happens to fall on Sunday.

Farmer Dildine, who lives near West Huron, describes the ghost in glowing words. He says:

"I first saw him more than a year ago and exactly 13 years to the day after the death of the old rich bachelor. As I was passing down the hill at Slate Cut, I looked across the valley on to Woolverton's farm and there I saw a sight which baffles description... I saw a light kindle up suddenly, as of someone swinging a lantern. I paused to see what it meant. A weird glow, like an incandescent electric lamp, issued from the air or earth. Then there came to my view the form of a human being, but instead of being outlined in white it was invested with a bluish tinge—just as if you would look through a blue glass from the dark into a light room. This seemed to be the outside of the thing. Then the skeleton of the apparition appeared in dazzling brightness. The visitor seemed to be solid, and yet, he was not. The face of the thing, for I cannot better describe it, was intelligent looking, and the thing's feelings and emotions were plainly discernible. You could tell by its countenance what was transpiring within its phosphorescent self, as much as an ordinary man or woman's face shows sadness or pleasure. It beckoned for me to follow it, but I was afraid to do so."

Fort Wayne [IN] News 27 February 1899: p. 17 ERIE COUNTY

NOTE: This is an exceptionally mysterious apparition, almost like an alien visitation or a creature from *Close Encounters of the Third Kind*.

BOO! GHOSTLY MIDNIGHT ILLUMINATION OF A FARM HOUSE.
WHAT A FAMILY SAW ON RETURNING TO THEIR HOME FROM A RELIGIOUS REVIVAL MEETING
GOBLINS? BURGLARS? OR WHAT?

Plain City, O., March 26. Mrs. Nancy Reedy, widow, lives on her farm, four miles southwest of Plain City, on the London road, where her first husband, John Atkinson died nearly twenty years ago. Her son, William Atkinson, rents the farm, and with his wife and child and a farmhand, occupies the house with her. Mrs. Reedy has been spending two weeks with another married son in this place, and Sunday night William hitched the horses to the family carriage and brought his wife and child and Tuck Raynor, the hired man, to town to attend revival services at the

Universalist church. Before leaving home he drew down the window curtains in all the rooms, and was careful to fasten a favourite dog in the kitchen and lock all the outside doors.

It was half past eleven o'clock when the party returned home from the meeting, and when within half a mile of the dwelling, which stands about two hundred yards east of the road, the little boy exclaimed: "O, papa, our house is on fire!" Then they first observed that every visible window in the old fashioned, low frame building was ablaze with vivid light, and they drove hastily down the lane and into the door-yard, where they found the house dog cringing and whining in fear, and manifesting extreme pleasure at their coming.

All the windows, with the curtains drawn up, were yet streaming with light, but as Atkinson and Raynor sprang from the carriage, they observed the light in the north room window gradually dying out, and in a moment more, that part of the house was shrouded in darkness. Then the glare in the middle room windows began to waver and finally went out, and when all was darkness there, the lights began to lessen in the windows of the adjoining south room, or kitchen, and soon entirely disappeared.

As no one in the party had a match, Atkinson unlocked the north-side door and groped his way in darkness through the north and middle rooms to the kitchen, where he found matches and lighted a lamp. A thorough examination of every room in the house was then made, but no evidence was found that indicated the presence of nocturnal visitors during their absence. The curtains were all drawn down, save one in the kitchen window.

A pane of glass in the upper sash of this window had apparently been pushed out from the inside and was found lying, unbroken, on a pile of stones under the window, outside of the house. It is supposed that the dog made his exit from the room through this opening; but why he should have attempted escape at so high a point of egress, nobody attempts to explain. Indeed, the whole family are greatly excited and mystified by the affair; and it need hardly be said that when the men go out to the stable and care for the horses after dark the women go along too.

A *Press* reporter went to the Atkinson home yesterday morning and was told by Mrs. Reedy that, several years ago, when returning home with her family at a late hour from a visit with friends in Clarke County, the same ghastly lighting up of the house occurred as they approached, the lights suddenly disappearing as they drove in to the door-yard.

Sometime after that, a sister of Mrs. Reedy, while sleeping in the north room, awakened near midnight and saw by the dim light of a low-burning lamp a man's hand and arm lying beside her face on the pillow. She at once alarmed the inmates of the house, but the spectre arm and hand disappeared at her first outcry and the balance of the man could not be found. Still later than that, says Mrs. Reedy, a hired farm hand absolutely broke his engagement for her, on the grounds that the house was haunted and he could get no rest at night. Tuck Raynor, the present hired man, pronounces the case in which he has just figured to be clearly supernatural. Many others are of the same opinion, while there are some who would not believe that the visitation was ghostly if they had been there and clasped hands with the spooks. There is a mystery in it beyond the depths of common philosophy, anyway, and who shall solve it?

Newark [OH] Daily Advocate 26 March 1889: p. 3 MADISON COUNTY

NOTE: This is a very striking story, echoed in the 1904 Welsh religious revival where "stars" shone on rooftops and houses looked like they were on fire. Lights that switch off and on mysteriously, particularly when the power has been turned off, are still a major feature in reports of hauntings today. There are stories from Miami University's old Fisher Hall and several buildings at Kenyon College about light anomalies. (See "The Ghost of Fisher Hall" and "Shades of Purple: The Ghosts of Kenyon College" in *Haunted Ohio: Ghostly Tales from the Buckeye State.*)

Here is a trio of various kinds of spook lights:

GHOST STORY.
STRANGE OCCURRENCE DISTURBS THE QUIET OF MIDDLEPORT JUNCTION, O.

Pomeroy, O., Oct. 16 The few people who reside at Middleport Junction complain of a strange occurrence in that region which savors of the supernatural. On dark nights a light can be seen to appear suddenly at the edge of the Ohio river on the West Virginia shore, pause there for a short time and then begin slowly to ascend the hills on that side of the river until it reaches the summit, when it suddenly disappears. In the course of half an hour it will appear at the point where first seen and go over the same ground as at first. On a dark night it may be seen to do this for nearly a dozen times. The light can only be seen from the Ohio side.

Marion [OH] Daily Star 16 October 1895: p. 1 MEIGS COUNTY & WEST VIRGINIA

Xenia, O., as told in a telegram from that city, has developed the ghost of a man whose anatomical peculiarity is that, like that fabled race of men of strange lands who carried their heads under their arms, he is headless. Seen at night upon the streets in the mysterious hours of darkness, he disappears like a shot when approached. His mission seems to be to build phantom fires in the highways of the town, but when the morning comes there are no traces of fire visible there, [though] during the night, a bright light was to be seen.

Defiance [OH] Democrat 15 February 1873: p. 4 GREENE COUNTY

And, chilling in its simplicity:

WAS IT A SPOOK?

A few days since as Wm. Griffin and Ed. Benson were breaking a couple of colts west of town, a stream of white light some fifteen feet in length, emerged from the hollow in which Wm. Gilbreath was killed by a falling tree some two years since, and took a southwesterly course. When just in front of them, drew its two ends to the center, and busted, throwing fire in all directions. This was about three o'clock in the afternoon.

It is said that Wm. Gilbreath a few days before his death, by that fatal tree saw a similar light rise from the exact spot where he was afterwards killed, and took the same course and acted in like manner as that seen by Griffin and Benson.

Fairview correspondent of the Barnesville *Enterprise*.

The Ohio Democrat [New Philadelphia, OH] 13 January 1887: p. 4 GUERNSEY COUNTY

NOTE: William Gilbreath died February 20, 1885. On his tombstone is engraved: "Danger stands thick through all the ground/To push us to the tomb."

This spook light story has a whole host of paranormal elements: mysterious balls of fire, lost treasure, uncanny animals, and even a hint of what some may interpret as UFOs. In European folklore, spook lights and ball lightning are associated with finding lost treasure.

BLAZING RED BALL
HAS CAUSED TERROR IN MANY HEARTS
STRANGE ANIMAL HAS ALSO FRIGHTENED

NORTON PEOPLE
SPECTRAL APPARITIONS HAUNT THE LOCALITY
WHERE LIVED A WEALTHY MAN

There are those who believe in supernatural appearances and those who scoff at such things, but there are awesome happenings in Norton township, one mile south of Johnson's Corners, which silence the most sceptical when they have once seen the thing with their own eyes, for no explanation of the phenomena along natural lines has yet been suggested by those who have viewed this spectre.

Mysterious lights and strange animals figure in the hair-raising tales told by those who claim to have seen the things related and there are those residing in the vicinity whom it would take a great deal to entice from their homes alone after dark.

Those who have oftenest seen the unquiet spirit, as many are inclined to call the strange visitor, are Mr. John Breitenstein and his family, though Mr. Peter Shaffer and his family have also seen it and there are men who were formerly employed in Mr. Adam Kiehl's coal mine who could not be induced for love or money to enter the mine again....

A man named Shaneman lived in a little house across the road from the narrator, Mr. Breitenstein. Shaneman and his wife were believed to be quite rich, although they lived frugally. Right before his death, Mr. Shaneman sold some land in Barberton for a large sum.

Though every nook and cranny in the house was searched, $150 was all the money that could be found and it is said that from that day to this no trace of the fortune Shaneman was supposed to have possessed has been discovered. It was thought by many that the money was buried. Shaneman died very suddenly and there are those who say that the strange spectre about this place is the spirit of the old man trying to show where the money was hidden.

The supernatural strangeness began immediately after Shaneman's death, according to Mr. Breitenstein:

"The first time I saw anything supernatural was the night after Shaneman's death. Peter Shaffer, John Mong and myself were sitting up with the corpse. Mong was smoking, and Shaffer and I had been talking. All of a sudden Shaffer gave me a little nudge and directed my gaze to the ceiling at the corner of the room where the corpse lay when I saw a sight that fairly made my hair stand on end. What seemed a ball of fire had started from the corner of the room and was traveling slowly around the ceiling of the room.

"'Did you see it?' said Shaffer. 'Yes,' said I. 'Let's get out of here,' were Shaffer's next words, and we made for home as fast as we could.

"And since that time the strange light has haunted this vicinity with the most unpleasant regularity. I have seen it many times, as has every member of my family and many others. It is more often seen in the winter than at any other time, but I have seen it twice this summer, the last time only a few weeks ago, when the thing looked into my bedroom window making the room as light as day, waking me up with the glare.

"We see this strange light at many times and places. Sometimes it rises out of the fields behind the Shaneman house, other times it rests upon the roof of the house. One night not long after the death of Shaneman, I, with my family, the family of Peter Shaffer, and the other neighbors were sitting on the veranda of my home when suddenly a bright light as large as a street car lamp rose out of the fields behind the Shaneman house, came up the lane, passed my house where we were sitting and went on up past my barn. Everyone on the porch was silent, but as soon as the light disappeared, by a common impulse, all were on their feet making for the barn behind which it had disappeared, but nothing could be seen.

"Then my son Harry, who was married, moved into the house and he and his wife often saw the light. One night Harry came running over in breathless haste crying that our house was on fire. We rushed out to the back where a brilliant light was to be seen for a few moments, and then passed away into nothing.

"At one time we had an old apple tree which had blown down. One evening my son, Milton, came home late. He put up his horse and then came to the house. As he stepped into the door we saw that he was the color of death and whispered breathlessly, 'Oh, ma, come here!' My wife stepped to the door and there, playing about that old tree, were what seemed to be thousands of lights. They were about the size of candle flames and seemed to be of all colors of the rainbow. After a time they resolved themselves into balls of fire and rolled away down the orchard path.

"Peter Shaffer has told me of seeing the light many times and he isn't a man to lie," went on Mr. Breitenstein, "and this is the tale he told me: Shaffer, with his wife and two daughters were passing through the fields back of our house one night, bound for a neighbor's house. The women were walking ahead when suddenly Shaffer saw the mysterious light moving along beside him. Then one of the girls looked back and with a scream started to run and soon the entire family was running for dear life over the fields. They came to a fence, but stopped not for a moment and how they ever got over the fence not one was ever able to tell. When they reached the road the light disappeared."

But strange lights are not all that is said to be seen in this locality. The Misses Louise and Minnie Shaffer, when returning home late one night, are said to have seen a strange animal walking along in front of them, creeping between their feet, plainly visible, but of no substance, disappearing when they attempted to strike at it, but again walking with them a moment later. The girls took to their heels and arrived home almost dead with fright and now no money could hire them to go out late at night alone.

Mr. Shaffer also claims to have seen the strange animal and the tale of its appearance runs thus: It was just before the abandonment of Adam Kiehl's coal mine, and some coal was still being taken from the mine. It was about 4 o'clock in the afternoon when Shaffer saw someone going up the incline at the chutes and as he wanted to get some coal, he thought that would be a good time to go and order it. As he got near the mine, he saw the object hop up onto the platform on four feet.... As he approached he saw the object was not a man, but some kind of a grey animal [in other accounts it is described as looking like a wolf], which a moment later disappeared into the mine. He did not investigate, but made fast tracks for home.

A few days after this, Jean Cady, of Barberton and George Conrad, of Sherman, who were working in the mine, claim to have seen the strange animal in the mine, and their description of it coincides with that of Mr. Shaffer. They immediately took after it with picks. They would strike at it and it would fade into nothingness, but a moment later would be seen in another part of the mine. After a few fruitless attempts to approach it, the men became frightened, and Cady, it is said, quit work and could not be induced to enter the mine again.

This coal mine is just at the rear of Mr. Breitenstein's land. Mr. John Winkleman and family now reside in the Shaneman house and deny ever having seen anything supernatural; but Harry Breitenstein's family claim that there is a room in the house in which no one could sleep as the bed would be shaken by unseen forces. Another tenant's wife said she'd seen the light in her room one night.

In telling the story, Mr. Breitenstein said: "Folks may laugh if they will, but it is no laughing matter with us who live here and see it. What it is I do not know, but what I tell you I have seen, and this is gospel truth."

Akron [OH] Daily Democrat 8 August 1902: p. 1-2

The Stark County Democrat [Canton, OH] 12 August 1902: p. 8 SUMMIT COUNTY

THE SPOOK LIGHT OF ELMORE

The most famous "spook light" of them all is the mysterious light at Elmore. I first heard the story of the "spook light" of Elmore from Richard Gill, a folklorist, then living in Bowling Green, Ohio. He told it as "The Headless Motorcyclist of Elmore." I wrote about it in the first *Haunted Ohio* book, where it is the final story. The quick version goes like this: A young man returning from the First World War bought a motorcycle and went to see his fiancé. He found that she had married someone else in his absence. He roared off down the road on his motorcycle, rode off a bridge, under a barbed wire fence and was decapitated. Now if you blink your lights and honk your horn three times, you'll see his headlight running along the road until it vanishes in the middle of the bridge.

At least that is *one* of the versions.

Joel D. Rudinger of Firelands College, in his article "Folk Ogres of the Firelands: Narrative Variations of a North Central Ohio Community" [*Indiana Folklore, Journal of the Hoosier Folklore Society*, Vol. IX, No. 1 (1976) pp. 41-93] has done an extraordinary job of compiling several dozen variants of this story. The variants place the spook in multiple locations: Baybridge, Oak Harbor, Port Clinton, Catawba, Lakeside, Lindsey, Vermilion, Castalia, Fremont, Milan, Norwalk, and Elyria. (There are similar stories in Butler County, on the roads near Oxford.)

When I began researching this book, I found to my astonishment (and I can hear all you folklorists chuckling at my naiveté) that "my version" or Richard Gill's version were not the version as recorded in the newspapers of 1922 when people flocked to the area, trying to solve the mystery. There was no motorcycle, no wire fence, no decapitation, just a lonely stretch of road, a bridge, and a mysterious light. Here's what was being reported then:

"GHOST" LIGHT IS AGAIN ATTRACTION

Special to the *Star-Journal*

Oak Harbor, June 30 The ghost light, on what is called the Lindsey Rd. five miles southwest of Oak Harbor, is again receiving much attention and this road is the scene of watch parties almost every night.

The light resembles a full moon in shape and color and appears first over the center of a bridge over a small creek. It wavers there a moment and then travels to the west, disappearing near an abandoned house which is claimed to be haunted. Superstition has it that the light is the spirit of an old man who hung himself in this house many years ago. According to the story, the spirit in the form of this light, makes nightly visits to the scene of the dead. It appears at irregular periods during the night and may be seen on almost any clear night.

Thousands of persons from northwestern Ohio visited the place six years ago when interest in the light was sufficient to attract a scientist who vouchsafed the explanation that the light was caused by phosphorus which was present in the creek bed. Many are inclined to doubt this theory, however, as the light is visible only from the north and at a distance of more than 150 yards.

Those not inclined to accept either of the two theories are of the belief that it is caused by the reflection of automobile headlights from the south. The road, they say, is built almost on a straight line for miles so that the reflections of the lights are seen several minutes before any rays are visible. The travelling of the light to the west is supposed to be caused by automobiles turning off on a side road to reach Lindsey. A number of other explanations have been advanced but none has been accepted by everyone. *Sandusky [OH] Star Journal* 30 June 1922: p. 6 OTTAWA/SANDUSKY COUNTY

LIGHT STILL MYSTERY

Latest reports on the "spook light" on the Lindsey Rd., five miles southwest of Oak Harbor, tend to discredit the scientific theory that the light is caused by phosphorus from the creek bed, and also the theory that it is caused by the reflection of automobile headlights, and more credence is placed in the belief that the light is the spirit of the old man who is said to have hanged himself in the abandoned house beside the creek.

Farmers living near the creek say that the light can be seen at all seasons of the year, even during the winter when the creek is frozen over and covered with snow. This, according to chemists, spikes the first theory, as it would be impossible for the phosphorus to escape through the ice and snow to cause the light. This theory was never given much credence as it is said that the light is visible only from the north side of the creek. When someone approaches the bridge, the light is said to recede toward the south until the person gets some distance past the bridge, when the light goes out.

A local business man is reported to have chased the light in an automobile only to have the light burst into what is said to have looked like little balls of fire. Five others who were in the machine at the same time are said to have given the same story. Other than saying that the light could not have been caused by the reflection of automobile headlights, they were unable to account for the cause of the phenomenon. No other machine was sighted as they speeded father up the road, they said.

Other theories are being advanced, but are discredited almost instantly, due to flaws in reasoning which are readily discernible.

One of these theories is that someone is using a lantern to fool the people who come to see the light. This belief is scoffed at because of the many years that the light has been seen and its being visible at all seasons of the year. Nearly all agree that one would be unable to keep a secret of this kind so many years.

This leaves only the "ghost" theory as the only hope for the solution of the mystery, according to many people living in the vicinity of the creek. *Sandusky [OH] Star Journal* 3 July 1922: p. 5 OTTAWA/SANDUSKY COUNTY

STILL A MYSTERY

The "spook" light on the Lindsey Road is still a mystery, no further developments having been reported which would in any way account for the light's source except the belief that it is the spirit light of the suicide. Several autoists have chased the light, one reporting that when he drew near the light burst into little balls of fire. Another has reported that it grew in size and brilliance as he drew nearer until it fairly dazzled him and then went out so quickly as to leave the space about his auto in almost total darkness. Neither was able to explain the mystery. *Sandusky [OH] Star Journal* 7 July 1922: p. 6 OTTAWA/SANDUSKY COUNTY

WELL! WELL! HERE'S OL' FRIEND 'SPOOK' AGAIN

Oak Harbor, Sept. 10 (Special.) Courageous youths, unconvinced by the numerous theories as to the origin of the "Spook light" five miles southwest of Oak Harbor near the Lindsey Road, have been organizing ghost hunting parties in an effort to solve the mystery with the hope that the members of the parties may bask in the limelight of notoriety and be held up as heroes by their fellow townspeople.

Although many stories are current of the light's narrow escapes from being captured, all efforts thus far have proven futile and the light continues to appear over the bridge and makes its nightly visits to the abandoned hut where the superstitious say it visits the death scene of an old man, the spirit of whom the light is supposed to represent. It is claimed that the old man hanged himself in this hut many years ago.

One of the bands of youths who form the nightly watch party is reported to have surrounded the light after almost giving up in disgust after waiting three hours for its appearance. Under cover of the night's shadows they crept closer and closer and the light became brighter and brighter until they got within what seemed to be arm's reach when the light, seeming to be aware of human presence or hearing the voice of one of the party, burst open and broke into little balls of flame and disappeared. Before bursting it bobbed up and down as if seeking a way to retreat. Cornered, it flared up and became so bright it dazed the youths.

Returning to their home here with their clothes dishevelled and their eyes almost popping out of their heads, the dozen or more youths who made up the party promised to make another attempt to solve the mystery.

Meanwhile the light remains a mystery, no automobile having been found which could speed along the road fast enough to catch it. Fired at by hunters, it continues to bob up and down over the bridge and makes its nightly visits to the abandoned hut. Molesting no one, it seems to flare into a rage when a human approaches as if to blind those who trespass upon its domain. To the curious it is an ever increasing obstacle to their peace of mind.

If the youths do solve the mystery they will have done what chemists, spiritualists and town marshalls have failed to do. They are not bothered by remarks of the less romantic who say, "We shall see," and who watch their efforts in a skeptical way.

Citizens are watching their efforts and look to them as the one ray of hope left that the mystery may be solved.

Sandusky [OH] Register 12 September 1922 OTTAWA/SANDUSKY COUNTY

NOTE: Once again, a spook light seems to display intelligence or interact with observers.

SPOOK LIGHT MAKES SHIFT

Oak Harbor, Nov. 23

Port Clinton folk have been taking an active interest in the "spook light" on the Lindsey Rd., five miles southwest of Oak Harbor and eight youths from that place were immediately initiated into the mystery of the light. The spirit of the man who hung himself in the hut nearby, which the light is supposed to represent, did not seem to care as long as they watched from a distance but when they prowled around the bridge it moved out into a field. The youths then began prowling around the abandoned hut

and one ventured to open the door and throw a light inside. He did not go very far after opening the door for something hit him on the forehead and sent him staggering back to the support of his comrades. What he said in the excitement following is not clearly recalled by the other members of the party. Deputy Sheriff Eugene Carsten was a member of the party but his experience as a sleuth was not sufficient to solve the mystery.
Sandusky [OH] Register 24 November 1922: p. 9 OTTAWA/SANDUSKY COUNTY

And here the paper trail comes to an end. The mystery was not solved—has never been solved—although some believe that a distortion of auto headlights provides a logical explanation. I did my bit in perpetuating the legend of the Headless Motorcyclist, but am intrigued by the shift from a very traditional tale of the spirit of a dead man appearing as a ball of light to the dramatic tale of a motorcyclist we know today. Have I somehow colluded in creating a kind of "fakelore?" Or does folklore have its own standards of "truth?" For, truth-fully, if I hadn't uncovered these early spook light articles, I would, with a clear conscience, still be telling a tale of the mysterious light crossing the bridge as the headlight of the Headless Motorcylist of Elmore....

Perhaps the truth behind the story does not matter. As they have done for so many years, seekers will still go out to the bridge and wait—for a mystery, a marvel, to emerge from the darkness.

7.

The Awful Fate of a Mercer County Blasphemer

The Pinnacle of Prevaricating Perfection

Hoax stories can be an irritant when studying 19th-century newspapers, but sometimes you find a story of such peerless prevaricating perfection that you just have to stand and bare your head in reverence. Such a story is the following tale—that incomparable narrative:

PILLAR OF STONE.

AWFUL FATE OF A MERCER COUNTY BLASPHEMER.

A Bolt Descends and Roots Him to the Earth.

BIBLICAL MIRACLES ECLIPSED IN MODERN TIMES.

The Awful Image Still Stands, Glowing
with Heat, While Ghastly Blue
Flames Play About It.

August Gebauer, of Springfield, Witnesses
the Blood-Curdling Spectacle,
and Comes Home Helpless with
Horror at the Awful Sight.

Thousands Visit the Spot to See the
Human Petrified by God's Wrath—
The People Demand Excursions
to the Scene of the
Supernatural Tragedy.

The most awful event in Ohio's history—a weird and horrible manifestation of the omnipotence of an angry God, if it be true—occurred some days ago near Lima, Allen Co., O. Sylvester Redyan, a prominent farmer living within two miles of the town was struck dead in his field by a bolt of lightning and his

BODY TURNED IMMEDIATELY TO STONE.

He had just uttered a shocking blasphemy, and many believe that his fate was a direct visitation of God's wrath. The story, wired all over the state, was published in all the papers and awakened a storm of incredulity. Be its truth as it may, the *Globe Republic* presents this morning the testimony of two Springfield men who have just returned from the theatre of the superlatively frightful tragedy, and who

CORROBORATE THE ESSENTIAL FEATURES.

of the most horrible, terrifying occurrence of modern times.

Redyan was among the richest of Mercer County farmers. He was a brawny, black-browed, heavily-whiskered man of five and thirty years. He was in easy circumstances, and owned a fertile farm of several hundred acres. His family consisted of a wife and five children. Redyan, although generally respected, was a

COARSE, BRUTAL, DOMINEERING MAN,

and so addicted to profanity that his oaths were constant and frightful.

The fertility of Mercer County is well-known; but the prospects for abundant crops this fall have been almost if not wholly destroyed by a prolonged drought, the effects of which have been most noticeable in the wide and spreading cornfields. The stalks, once sturdy and brightest of living green, slowly

SHRIVELLED AND FADED

into the sere and yellow of an untimely decay, and the once branching blades hung limp and lifeless. This condition of things maddened Redyan, and moved him to utter the awful blasphemy that cost him his life and semblance to humanity. On the day in question, he and four of his hands were sitting in the entrance of a small cave in a mass of sandstone overlooking a forty acre field. The day was burning hot, and as Redyan looked out over the dreary waste of dying grain, his face

GREW DARK WITH PASSION

and discontent. It was then that he had an impassioned conversation with one of his hands named Phipps, a religious man and a firm believer in God and His goodness. Redyan denied the existence of a supreme being and averred that if He did exist He was a tyrant who deserved not to be. Phipps reproved him for his language, and bitter words resulted. Redyan finally rose to his feet, his face aflame with insane rage, and shaking his fist

WITH FURY AT THE SKY,

Shouted in ringing tones: "If Thou art a God descend and I will cut the heart from Thy body!"

The men shrank back appalled. For a single instant Redyan stood there, more like a brazen image than aught else, utterly powerless to move; then

THE HEAVENS BURST WIDE ASUNDER,

With a stunning shock, and a flaming bolt of fire descended, smiting and completely enveloping the blasphemous Sylvester Redyan, transfiguring him in the twinkling of an eye from mortal flesh and blood to a pillar of lifeless stone!

Sometime after the descent of the awful bolt, Redyan's hired help awoke to consciousness, to find themselves strewn about in various postures on the ground in the shade of the rocks—awoke to huddle closely together fairly frozen with horror after one glance at the frightful object!

STANDING ERECT AND RIGID

a few paces distant.

Benumbed though their senses were, they felt and knew that Redyan was lifeless. The form there, just within the cave entrance, could not be that of a living being. The only thing human about it was its shape. It bore Redyan's head, broad shoulders and massive chest. It was almost devoid of clothing, and was vested with a grayish, stony appearance. The defiant attitude was wholly gone; the clenched hand had been lowered, and the head was inclined slightly forward.

This much the men noted in their brief, fleeting glances.

"The hand of God has been laid upon him!" uttered Phipps, at length, his tones hollow and scarcely audible. "Come, boys, we must carry him to the house."

The men struggled to their feet. Their limbs almost

REFUSED TO SUPPORT THEM.

They hung back, as if loath to approach the horrible object.

"Come, boys," repeated Phipps, his own dread plainly revealed by his quavering tones, as his eyes swept over the haggard faces of his companions, "it has been an awful affair, but our duty is plain. We must not leave him here."

Reluctantly, the men advanced.

With each step toward the cave entrance the air seemed to grow hotter, as if exuding from a fiery furnace. When within a few paces of Redyan, one of the men halted.

"This is awful—I can't go nearer!" he gasped.

The others continued to advance. They put out their hands to grasp the upright lifeless form. Then a wild shriek burst from their parched throats, and turning, they fled as if pursued by a thousand demons. The figure was

A LIVID, RED-HOT STONE.

August Gebauer is a well-known saloonist on West Main Street, his place being located below Jackson Street. He returned from Lima to-day, and while there, with a colored man, was a horrified witness to the awful form of stone. He was seen by a *Globe-Republic* reporter last night and told what he knew of the awful affair, with marked agitation.

"Yes, I saw the Lima horror, Friday afternoon," said Mr. Gebauer, last night. "The reports published in the newspapers

BY NO MEANS DO THE SUBJECT JUSTICE.

"This man here," indicating a negro a few paces distant, "was also there, and saw as much as I did. Sit down, and I will tell you all about it."

Mr. Gebauer, as his name would indicate, is of German extraction, a steady-going, solid-looking gentleman, and whose words are uttered with a readiness and a frankness that at once impresses one with their truthfulness.

"I went to Lima on business," he resumed, "and I took Mr. Black there with me. When we had finished our affairs we concluded to

GO SEE THE STONE MAN.

"There were so many conflicting reports rife in Lima that we more than half suspected we were going on a fool's errand, but we were not.

"The Redyan farm lies a mile and half east of Lima, in a level stretch of cleared country, and is quite easy of access. The neighborhood is but thinly settled, and this fact accounts for the slowness with which the report of the awful occurrence spread.

"It happened in the south-east corner of a large corn field, lying some distance from Redyan's house. It is needless to go into details as to how it occurred—you have heard that. Suffice that it did occur, and the sight I saw is such a one as I

NEVER WANT TO SEE AGAIN.

"The field was thickly dotted with black stumps, and the corn had been trampled flat by the constantly coming and going crowds. When we reached the field it was pretty well filled with people. Off in the southeast corner of the field, around a large heap of sandstone rock, the people were grouped in a dense mass, all excited, some talking, others mute, apparently with horror.

"We pushed forward and soon found ourselves in the front ranks of the throng and facing the narrow entrance to a cave in the rocks.

"My God! What a sight it was we saw! I shuddered yet, and almost wish I had stayed away, for

IT HAS BEEN CONSTANTLY BEFORE ME
since that hour."

Even as he spoke a shudder went through Mr. Gebauer's sturdy form, and his voice was one of plaintive earnestness.

"Yes, the corpse of the stricken blasphemer was there, standing in the cave. A number of men were at work, striving to remove it. They worked with long iron crowbars, and kept their faces shaded or turned away, for the heat radiating from the body was frightful.

"But the efforts to dislodge or remove the corpse were of no avail, or as fast as they thrust the crowbars against it

THE SOLID IRON MELTED
"And fell in trickling drops to the stony floor, while long, forked tongues of blue flame issued from the body, driving back the desperately battling men. While untouched the corpse emitted a faint, bluish glow, such as comes from stone nearly red hot.

"The horrible thing still retains the form and features Redyan bore in life. The face is distinctly visible, set and rigid, while the eyes seem starting from their sockets. It is diabolical!

"Many days have passed since the miraculous death of Redyan, and yet the heat is as fierce and blighting as when first noticed. Think of it! Solid iron melting and running down like water when applied to the body. Why, the heat is

FIERCER AND MORE INTENSE
Than that of the hottest furnace in existence.

"Of course, Mrs. Redyan and her five children are prostrated with grief, sorrow and despair. Both Allen and Mercer counties are shaken from center to circumference, and the throngs surging about the accursed spot are hourly increasing. My only regret is that I went to the place."

It may be added in conclusion that the C.C.& I. and I.B. & W. roads here have both been

LITERALLY BESIEGED WITH REQUESTS
to run an excursion to the scene of this visitation of divine wrath.
Xenia [OH] Daily Gazette 4 August 1886: p. 1 MERCER/ALLEN COUNTY

NOTE: August Gebauer was a real man from Springfield, now buried in beautiful Ferncliff Cemetery in Springfield. As you will see by the following article, he was not happy with the notoriety. I don't think there are any caves in the Lima area, just to cover all bases. The railroads mentioned were also real. Redyan spelled backwards is "Nayder" or "nadir," meaning the lowest possible point, either of a person's character, spirits, or what have you. I suppose this story was supposed to represent the lowest possible point of a humorous hoax story, although to me, it is the very pinnacle!

A WHOPPING BIG LIE.
THE LIMA STONE MAN SENSATION
A LITTLE STORY WHICH SHOWS WHAT A XENIA BOY
CAN DO WHEN HE HUMPS HIMSELF

The Indianapolis *Sentinel*, about two weeks ago, published the yarn of a Pan Handle railroad engineer, regarding an alleged startling occurrence near, or at, Lima, in Allen County, this state, where a man was said to have been turned to a block of stone, instantly, by a bolt of some sort from heaven, after emitting a volume of blasphemy of the most horrible description against God Almighty. The story, in one shape and degree of elaboration or another, was in several papers and appeared in the Sunday issue of a Springfield journal worked up into a two column article with a half column display head, going into minutest and most astounding details. It was alleged that one, Gebauer, a west end saloonist, with a colored man named Black had been in Lima and seen the wonder, his alleged statement in an interview with a reporter being given.

The readiness with which the people catch at anything of this sort was shown by the fact that, during the day, the story was on all tongues, and a copy of the paper containing it could not be had for love or money, a large extra edition being speedily exhausted. The number of those who swallowed the big gag, solidly, of those who took no stock in it and "pooh-poohed" the whole thing, and of those who suspended judgment regarding the "what-is-it," until something further was received, was about equal, but everybody had something to say and an opinion to express, the discussion even threatened to detract from interest in the day's lesson in some Sunday school classes. Poor Gebauer found himself suddenly and apparently, not altogether unpleasantly, thrust into notoriety, and was overwhelmed by curious inquirers of all ages, conditions and walks in life.

Gebauer is represented as denying that he has been outside Springfield at all, received any letter or been interviewed by any reporter, and as saying in addition that it wouldn't be particularly healthy for one of the fraternity to attempt it now.

Local agents of railroads have received numerous inquiries as to running of excursion trains to Lima to afford people an opportunity to witness the horrible spectacle, and yesterday sales of a considerable number of tickets to that place by regular trains, are reported.

It's an ill wind indeed that blows no good. There is the very best authority for the statement that one of the foremen in a factory here, who has always been a very profane man, frequently blaspheming God, became so much alarmed and conscience stricken on reading the account that he hasn't been heard to utter a profane oath since. One or two other cases of the kind are reported.

The article which created such a stir is credited among knowing ones, to Mr. John W. Osborn, formerly of Xenia, a well-known printer and newspaper writer, as well as author of several cheap novels of the ten cent description, he receiving the magnificent sum of three dollars for two and a half hours work. He should have contracted to get up the article on a per cent. Of sales. It would have been money in his pocket....

Xenia [OH] Daily Gazette 10 September 1886: p. 1 MERCER ALLEN CLARK GREENE COUNTY

NOTE: "Humps" here means "works hard." "Cheap novels of the ten cent description" refer to the so-called "dime novels," the 19th century equivalent of pulp fiction or popular paperbacks. They featured lurid plots and sensationally purple prose. Author John W. Osborne obviously understood the genre.

8.

A Cat Named Death

Cemetery Spirits, Omens of Death, and Curious Cadavers

Take a walk through any cemetery and you will see how the fool passes away. Here rests the man who blew in an empty gun, there the woman who lit a fire with kerosene; a grassy mound covers the man who took a mule by the tail. Here is the man who jumped from a train to save a thirty foot walk, side by side with a woman who laced her corset to the last hole, and the idiot who rode a bicycle nine miles in ten minutes. Beneath this clay is the man who sucked death from a cigarette; there, beneath the weeping willow, gathered in a tin pail, are the remains of an aeronaut. Here reposes the physician who took his own medicine. Over by the gate rests the woman who kept strychnine in the same cupboard with the baking powder. There, in potters field, is the editor. The broken bones of the man who refused to pay for his newspaper are piled in a corner by the fence.

Press, [Bryant, OH] November 1896, quoted in *Stories of the Fountain City 1840-1900*, Paul Van Gundy, (Bryan, OH: The Bryan Area Foundation) 1975: pp. 109-110

Death was a constant companion to the people of the past who were not shielded from its realities as we are. Yet even in that time when death was more familiar, when families washed and coffined their own dead, cemeteries were feared as places where the worlds of the living and the dead touched. There were iron fences around old cemeteries to keep the dead in and the body-snatcher out. Lights seen after dark in the cemetery might be corpse candles—lanterns held by the dead to lure you to your doom. The spirit of the last person buried guarded the graveyard.

Today we tell ourselves that iron is not a magic metal to hold back the dead and that corpse candles are just methane from rotting bodies. We rely on funeral directors to care for our dead. Nevertheless, when passing a cemetery some of us still hold our breath so ghosts can't steal our souls. Driving past the graveyard we put our feet up or we do not walk on graves for fear of spirits dragging us down. We touch red—the color of blood and of life—to remind ourselves that we are alive. And we still shiver when we hear of a ghost haunting a graveyard.

CEMETERY SPIRITS

A horrifyingly grotesque apparition of a murdered man is seen in a North Liberty graveyard. Was this the guilty conscience of a community with blood on its hands made manifest?

TERRIFIED BY AN AWFUL APPARITION
RESIDENTS OF AN OHIO TOWN TELL OF HAVING
SEEN A HEADLESS BODY

West Union, Ohio, August 14. The citizens of the quiet little hamlet of North Liberty, a few miles west of here, are greatly worked up over ghostly manifestations in their midst. For several months past strange stories have come from there, about unearthly noises coming from the little grave yard at the edge of town. A number have claimed to have seen, while passing the place, what seemed to be a huge ball of fire flitting about from grave to grave. Very few people can now be prevailed upon to pass the place after dark.

The most intelligent account of what is to be seen there comes from Maurice Hudson, a farmer living near there. Hudson relates that when on his way home late Wednesday night, and while passing the cemetery, his attention was attracted by a peculiar noise, and on glancing in the direction of the grave yard he was almost paralyzed by the sight which
MET HIS GAZE.
Standing over one of the graves was the burly form of a negro with outstretched arms and open hands.

The body was headless—that is, so far as the head being connected with the body is concerned. Hudson states that from the neck there spurted upward a conical stream of blood to the height of five or six feet, where it was probably two feet in circumference. Dancing on the top of this stream of blood and bouncing about in every conceivable position was the head of the apparition.

After spending its force on the head the blood descended over and around the form in a spray. Hudson claims he was rooted to the spot for fully five minutes, and that when he did finally make a step the wonderful picture began to gradually fade from view, and the soft, pale light, which had surrounded the scene for a radius of probably 50 feet grew dimmer and dimmer.
A HEADLESS BODY.
An investigation the following morning revealed the fact that the grave over which the apparition had appeared was that of Roscoe Parker, the young colored fiend, who so cruelly murdered the aged Rhine couple

near Winchester, and who, in January, 1894, was taken from the County Jail in this city by a mob and hanged near North Liberty. Not long after this Parker's grave one morning gave evidences of having been opened the previous night.

Upon investigation it was discovered that the coffin had been opened and the head of the negro's body cut off and carried away. At the time it was generally concluded that the work had been done in the interest of some museum, but to this day the perpetrators of the deed and the whereabouts of the head have remained a mystery.
Cincinnati [OH] Enquirer 15 August 1896: p. 10 ADAMS COUNTY

NOTE: Roscoe Parker worked for an elderly man, Pitt Rhine, who, along with his invalid wife, had his throat cut December 20, 1893. Parker was taken from the County Jail by a mob of masked men, lynched and shot on the night of January 12, 1894. A *Portsmouth Daily Times* article of 19 June, 1885 reported that the entire body—not just the head—had been stolen "by body-snatchers" a few nights previously. It was said that the head was taken by a local physician. The place where Parker was hung quickly was shunned by the locals.

"The place where Roscoe Parker was hanged is almost directly opposite the old Patton homestead at a point where a path from the colored settlement northeast of North Liberty leads down to the pike to Winchester. Before daylight on the morning of the lynching of Parker, old Leonard Johnson...who does chores for the villagers of North Liberty, came from his home...along this path and passed directly under the body of Roscoe Parker hanging from a limb above. A grain sack that had been placed over Parker's head by the mob lay in the path beneath his lifeless body, and Johnson picked this up and carried it to North Liberty before he learned of the lynching of Parker and the purpose for which the sack had been used. Then he feared the dreaded 'hoodoo,' and never since has he traveled that portion of the path to his home. And the other persons of 'the settlement' no longer climb the fence at the bridge and take the path through Patton's woods, but very prudently avoid the 'hoodoo' by traveling the public highway, and in the daytime."
A History of Adams County, Ohio, Nelson W. Evans and Emmons B. Stivers (West Union, Ohio: E.B. Stivers, 1900) p. 394 ADAMS COUNTY

These are two strange accounts of a walking skeleton who defies bullets at a Cleveland cemetery. I have not been able to trace any earlier reports of the apparition. The second story was found in a syndicated article and was almost certainly not written by a local journalist. I cannot locate or even verify the existence of a Grudnow cemetery. Grudnow is a town in Poland and, with Cleveland's many East European immigrant neighborhoods, it is possible that this was a nickname or pseudonym for a Polish cemetery. If this was a hoax, it was a dangerous one for the prankster.

CLEVELAND CLAIMS "GHOST" WALKING
STORY OF WINTER

Cleveland, O. Feb. 10 Reports that an "apparition" is presenting nightly spectacles in Grudnow cemetery gained wider circulation today as gradually increasing crowds vouched for the authenticity of the reports.

At first noticed only by a few south side residents the "apparition" is drawing several hundred spectators nightly who gather across a small valley two hundred yards away, the nearest accessible spot to the place where the "ghost walks."

The purported ghost is described as the outline of a skeleton on a small narrow tombstone. Only the torso being visible, and it only when viewed from certain angles. Spectators describe the sight as a figure which draws its arms behind its back and always in a general walking motion, twisting and turning from left to right positions.

Increased size of the crowds which visit the burial ground at all hours of the night caused police to investigate and place a sack over the tombstone. Despite this action, however, the figure is illuminated through the covering as plainly as before, witnesses maintain.

Zanesville [OH] Signal 10 February 1931: p. 4 CUYAHOGA COUNTY

In Cleveland, Ohio, an American city in which the quota of intelligence is high, lies Grudnow cemetery.

One night a few weeks ago, a man was walking past it. He peered, quite by chance, toward the rows of tombstones. His blood went cold. He stopped in his tracks, uttered a screech.

The next moment he rubbed his eyes, looked once more, and saw nothing. A wintry wind howled about his head and he hastened toward his home.

Friends scoffed, but the next night a crowd journeyed and stood there not too close. At the same hour as before, the phenomenon occurred.

A spectral skeleton, without a head, seemed to dance about a stone, taller than the rest. Murmurs ran through the onlookers. Women screamed. Others fled. Few stayed more than five minutes.

It was the talk of the city. The next night a police officer, armed with a revolver and with plenty of courage, joined the curious.

On the dot, as promptly as the night before, the spectre appeared. And as the crowd watched with mingled dismay and admiration, the intrepid officer strode over the dark graves toward the tomb on which the apparition was visible.

At the approach of the officer, according to eye-witnesses, the spectre danced with more gusto than before. Arm bones locked behind ribs, it jumped and cavorted with abandon.

The intrepid patrolman fired three shots and the apparition disappeared. But those who held watches on the graveyard edge, two hundred yards away declared that the "ghost" had finished his allotted stay anyway.

A little sceptical, yet not without heart-quakings, the officer threw a bag over the tombstone and went away.

The following night, and at nearly regular intervals since then, the spectre appeared, as if coming through and not over the bag. Persons learned in psychical research are still at a loss to explain the phenomenon satisfactorily.

It is not easy to believe in ghosts yet...in Grudnow Cemetery, few can explain the apparitions away. May we know the secret some day?

Portsmouth [OH] Times 15 March 1931: p. 31 CUYAHOGA COUNTY

This next story of a Woman in White comes from Greene County and was submitted as part of a "true ghost story" contest held by the *Dayton Daily News* in 1914. I've edited the author's rather casual style.

THE SPECTRAL LURE

When I was a boy fourteen years old, I attended a social gathering one night. I had quite a distance to go to my home. On my road I had to pass a country graveyard in a very lonesome spot on the road. The graveyard was about five hundred yards from the highway and stood slightly higher than the road and was fenced with a high stone wall. I was driving a very gentle old family horse that had a reputation of never being frightened at anything.

As I drew near the graveyard, my horse stopped and began to back in the road till the buggy was fast on the fence at the side of the road. She showed signs of great fear. I looked to see what had frightened her and about one hundred yards ahead in the road I saw the form of a woman with long golden hair hanging over her shoulders and clad in a white robe. As she advanced toward me I could see her face, which was beautiful, but I could also see the road and fences through her, she seemed to be transparent. It came straight at me; as my horse would not go, I could do nothing but look.

It came within ten feet of me, then uttered in a most musical and strange voice these words, "Oh come on! Oh, come on!" It then arose with no apparent effort, about three or four feet from the ground, and floated gracefully over the graveyard wall, on which it seemed to rest for a moment, then beckoned to me with its hands for me to follow, then faded from sight.

You may bet I did not obey the call. The horse was nervous for several days. I was, too. Now you skeptics explain this if you can. Others have seen queer things at this same place before and after my experience. This happened in the winter of 1892 about twenty-two miles east of Dayton in Greene County, O.

Dayton [OH] Daily News 9 February 1914 GREENE COUNTY

NOTE: I wonder if this has anything to do with the apparition of a ghostly bride on Trebein Road near the cemetery at Byron, which I wrote about in *Haunted Ohio IV*? Local legend says that the phantom bride died urging her father to drive faster to the church—"Oh, come on!"?

Even in 1885, ghost hunters were investigating cemeteries after dark. One brave soul paid the ultimate price.

FRIGHTENED TO DEATH.
THE HORRORS OF A HAUNTED GRAVEYARD IN MIDDLETOWN
MISS ELLA TAYLOR BRAVELY INVESTIGATES AND DROPS DEAD

A sad death, made more deplorable by the attending circumstances, occurred at Middletown about ten o'clock Friday night. Miss Ella Taylor, an employee of the P.J. Sorg Tobacco Company, together with a number of companions, left the factory about half-past nine o'clock. A proposition to investigate shadows cast upon a monument in the Middletown Cemetery by the electric light, which were said to assume supernatural appearances, met with general favour.

The rumors that the grave-yard was haunted by the spirits of the departed dead were exploded by the investigation of the young ladies, in which Miss Taylor seemed to exhibit more courage than any of her companions. A challenge was made by one of the party that none dared to advance to the monument and touch it. Although the reflection on the object from the electric light produced a figure which in the night appeared to be that of a human being, Miss Taylor boldly advanced and touched the monument. Finding nothing more, the girls were about to depart, when they suddenly realized that they were in a graveyard at dead of night. They quickened their footsteps as they came to each succeeding tombstone. Among those who appeared most excited was Miss Taylor herself.

Shortly after the exit from the cemetery Miss Taylor surprised her companions by suddenly dropping to the ground overcome, as they supposed, by excitement. They went to her assistance and found her in an apparently helpless condition. She was taken to the residence of Mrs. Lallee, nearby, and medical aid quickly summoned. Dr. D. B. Bundy was the first to arrive and upon examination pronounced the young lady dead and stated that death was caused by heart disease, occasioned by overexercise and excitement. The remains were then placed in charge of A.T. Wilson and later on were removed to the home of her mother, Mrs. Bridget Taylor, on Clinton Street. The body still retaining warmth at three o'clock yesterday morning the theory of suspended animation was advanced, and again medical aid was summoned, not only one but several physicians being called. The decision first given was reiterated and confirmed.

The deceased was a very estimable young lady, twenty years of age, and was the idol of a widowed mother and two brothers and was highly respected by all, who now extend their sympathy to the bereaved family.

Cincinnati [OH] Enquirer 26 April 1885: p. 12 BUTLER COUNTY

NOTE: *The Brooklyn Eagle* 31 January 1886: p. 15 added the detail that someone "had cried out, 'There's a ghost!' All started to run, and Minnie Taylor fell down and expired."

When a man shoots himself on a grave, it is usually news. However, I have not been able to find the original incident on which this short account of a ghost in the German Protestant Cemetery in Cincinnati is based.

GEISE'S GHOST
MANY PEOPLE WATCH THE CEMETERY TO SEE IT.

There has been a good deal of inquiry at the German Protestant Cemetery regarding Geise, the man who shot himself on a grave Decoration Day two years ago. Some people declare that as they go by the cemetery they see Geise's ghost hovering over the grave where he committed suicide. The sexton's wife, Mrs. Dahman, says that she has watched particularly and never saw any ghost, though the grave is within a stone's throw of the house.

Cincinnati [OH] Enquirer 31 January 1892: p. 9 HAMILTON COUNTY

CURIOUS CADAVERS

The Victorian press was fascinated by petrified corpses. I don't know if such things still happen today with modern embalming and better cemetery drainage. Exhumations were perhaps more common in the old days and there was more of a chance that you'd come across an anomaly like the following bodies.

PETRIFIED WOMAN 900 POUNDS.

Bellefontaine, O. One of the most remarkable cases of petrification ever on record was discovered here when the body of Mrs. J.W. Overly, who died 18 years ago, was exhumed at the Roundhead cemetery. The body and coffin had petrified and were hard to move owing to the weight reaching nearly 900 pounds. Mrs. Overly was a small woman. At burial both she and the coffin did not weigh as much as 200 pounds. The petrification is said to be perfect.

Sheboygan [WI] Daily Press 3 April 1911: p. 6 HARDIN COUNTY

A PETRIFIED WOMAN

Down at Quincy, Shelby County...a petrified woman has been discovered. She is no Cardiff giant, but a Mrs. Kellison who used to live in Illinois. [She died while on a visit to her son and was buried on his farm. He sold the farm and it was then that the petrification was discovered.] The body had turned to solid stone, and it took a dozen men with ropes and pulleys to drag the remains from the grave. The old lady was 70 years of age, in good flesh, and weighed 130 pounds when she died. When exhumed the petrification was perfect, and the only part of her body lacking is a small portion of the left [part] of the nose. The weight of the body is now estimated by good judges to be at least 1,000 [lbs.]. The remains have been laid away in Prospect Graveyard, Quincy, Ohio, where they now are, but Mr. Kellison promised them to a scientific gentleman, who intends to present them to one of the medical museums of the State.

The Indiana [PA] Progress 18 November 1880: p. 1 SHELBY COUNTY

NOTE: The Cardiff Giant was a notorious hoax—a 10-foot man carved of stone—"discovered" on a farm in Cardiff, New York, October 16, 1869. When P. T. Barnum couldn't buy the original, he made a *fake* fake giant out of plaster and exhibited it as the genuine Cardiff Giant.

While most grieving relatives were happy to let their petrified loved ones rest in peace in a grave or museum, some had more lucrative ideas. The Elyria papers had quite a field day over an Amherst man who travelled to Iowa to retrieve the petrified body of his sister so he could exhibit the body as a show freak.

AMHERST MAN GOES WEST TO GET BODY BURIED IN 1856 AND REMOVED IN 1860 HAS TURNED TO STONE, REQUIRING SIX MEN TO LIFT.

Believing that a fortune can be made by exhibiting the petrified body of his deceased sister, A.A. Pember, Sr., of Amherst, leaves on Monday for Glasgow, Ia., where the deceased will be exhumed with a view to discovering her condition...It was in 1860 that the body of Miss Pember, who had died four years before at the age of twenty two, was removed from its place in the Glasgow, Ia. cemetery. Those who had charge of the removal bear witness to the assertion that the body had completely changed to stone in the four years of burial and that it was all that six strong men could do to handle the casket.... For years [Pember] has entertained the hope of being able to turn the phenomenon to practical account. Persons with whom he has conferred have told him that there was money in the exhibition of such a freak as this and he claims to have received offers for the privilege of exhibition. These he has rejected, however, preferring for family reasons to have charge of the exploit himself.

The reason for the lengthy delay in claiming this prize was lack of funds. But plucky Mr. Pember scrimped and saved and was able to make the trip in August of 1907. Tragically, as the Elyria papers headlined, he was baffled by the simple fact that he

COULD NOT LOCATE PETRIFIED WOMAN A.A. PEMBER LACKS LOT NUMBER AND IS FORCED TO GIVE UP QUEST.

Amherst, August 12. A.A. Pember, who went to Glasgow, Iowa, to look up the dead sister which was believed to have been petrified has returned to his home and for the present at least reports failure.

The body was buried in a cemetery a few miles out of Glasgow, but Pember was unable to ascertain the lot number and so had to give the quest up temporarily. The matter was left in the hands of a cousin in Glasgow and if anything is done Mr. Pember will be notified.

Elyria [OH] Evening Telegram 3 August 1907 and *Elyria [OH] Evening Telegram* 13 August 1907: p. 8 LORAIN COUNTY

It wasn't only showmen who were eager to get their hands on a quality petrified corpse. The scientific community often wanted a crack at it, as in this story from North Amherst.

KREUGER FAMILY ARE OPPOSED TO EXHUMING
THE SEXTON REFUSES TO OPEN THE COFFIN
CONTAINING THE PETRIFIED REMAINS
GREAT EXCITEMENT OVER THE FINDING OF THE BODY
FEATURES REMAIN THE SAME.

While medical and scientific men of the county are anxious to exhume the petrified body of Miss Louise Kreuger, which was discovered while removing the remains from one part of the North Amherst cemetery to another Saturday, the family of Kreugers, consisting of the father and brother of the deceased, refuse to listen to the numerous pleas that have been made since the discovery. The sexton also refuses to again open the grave and has given out the statement that in case it is again opened some other person must do the work.

The sensation experienced by Sexton Bemis was a most horrifying one, especially when it is taken into consideration that he slipped from the side of the grave and stepped into the box and in so doing removed the rotted wood of the two boxes, exposing the ghastly form....After being given a rigid examination [the Sexton] finally confessed that the body was petrified without a doubt and so heavy that the six men had to exert their strength to move it to the new location. He also stated that the body had been buried in hard clay and that water had been in that part of the cemetery for years. The spot is so wet that it has been laid out as a park and no graves are placed there anymore. The body was buried nine years ago last December, the deceased having been ill with typhoid fever.

When told of the remarkable interest which the case has excited and the rumors afloat that medical men would make an attempt to get the body even though the relatives failed to consent, [Albert Kreuger, brother of the dead girl] was thoroughly alarmed and said: "If we decide that they shall not have the body, we will take it up and bury it again in a stone vault where those who rob graves will find it hard to get to it. "

The Elyria [OH] Reporter 31 January 1906 LORAIN COUNTY

Other families actually relished the idea of keeping a beloved member in an excellent state of preservation close at hand, like this Cincinnati family.

A HUMAN BODY TURNED TO CHALK

At the office of Leitch Brothers steam printing works, in the city of Cincinnati, O., are the remains of the mother-in-law of Mr. A.L. Leitch, one of the members of the firm, in a thoroughly petrified condition. The woman has been dead about twenty-five years. The body, according to the statement of a prominent physician, is in a state of adipocere. Mr. Leitch has been keeping it in his office since its arrival in Cincinnati, undetermined what to do with it, but his brother informed a reporter that they were contemplating placing it on public exhibition for the benefit of science. Several physicians, he said, who have examined the body, consider it a rare specimen of adipocere, and they have broken off little pieces, a toe or a finger and put them in their cabinets of snails and crawfish and other interesting articles.

The lady died of apoplexy, and she was buried in the graveyard of Dupont, Ind. She was seventy-two years of age at the time of her death. The ground in which she had lain for the last two dozen years is mainly of limestone formation and small streams of water trickled through the limestone and came in contact with the body. A scientist stated that it is unknown just what is in the water that petrifies flesh, but it is some kind of mineral.

Last November relatives of the deceased decided to take up her bones and rebury them at Cincinnati. When the grave was opened their surprise was great to find instead of only decayed and crumbling bones, a well preserved box, an apparently new coffin, and above all a corpse which requires no less than six men to lift. It is literally a chalk woman.

The limbs and body are preserved almost perfectly. The limbs are there, but have shrunken and changed so much as to be barely recognizable. The flesh, or rather what was once the flesh, is discoloured, is dark, and has an unnatural look. Taking a knife and cutting and scraping this dark substance away the substance is found to be almost exactly like white chalk. The back of the head is slightly decayed, but this is the only part where decay is indicated. Some parts of the body are not brittle like the rest of it, but are waxy and tough.

Marion [OH] Daily Star 27 March 1883: p. 2 HAMILTON COUNTY

NOTE: Adipocere or "grave wax," is the result of saponification, a chemical reaction of body fat to bacteria in a cold and wet environment, such as is described in this article. The preservation can be quite perfect and detailed or it can be quite horrifying, as in the "Soap Lady" preserved at the Mutter Museum in Philadelphia.

And, finally, we have an actual "living corpse" from Alliance.

HIS BED WAS A COFFIN

People who are of unsound mind do many queer things. The other day Barney Frickers, an aged and wealthy resident of Alliance, O., received death's summons while reposing in a coffin. A severe illness and the loss of his wife many years ago deranged him. For two decades it had been his custom to sleep every night in a coffin of his own manufacture, believing that he was about to die. He always robed himself in a shroud before retiring. The coffin is of oak, very strong and covered with allegorical subjects. *Springfield [OH] Republic Times* 5 January 1891: p. 7 STARK COUNTY

OMENS AND PREMONITIONS OF DEATH

The 19th-century seemed very interested in death omens. It may be that the religious sentiment of the era, which emphasized being prepared to meet thy God, made knowing the day or the hour of one's demise desirable. Or perhaps they just liked a good yarn about a premonition. Even President Abraham Lincoln reported having dreams that seemed to predict his death.

All manner of things could foreshadow death: pictures falling off the wall, a clock stopping, birds tapping at the window, or a dog howling in the back yard. I heard these tales as a child and I still shudder when owls hoot in the woods behind my house at night.

The Irish shuddered at the creature they called the Banshee—a lethal messenger who screamed of death. She had two guises: as a young woman with blood-red hair or an elderly crone washing the gore-stained shirts of the doomed. Seductive or vile, her shrieks were the same: a high-pitched keening cry. When the Banshee wailed, someone would die....

THE HOWL
OF THE FAMILY BANSHEE
WARNS A MAN OF HIS COMING DEATH.
GERALD GAILOR SAYS HE WILL DIE IN TEN DAYS
HE IS PREPARING TO FIGHT AGAINST THE OMEN,
AND HAS BEEN MAKING INQUIRIES LOOKING TO A
FATAL SICKNESS WITHIN A FEW DAYS.

"I am nearly certain that I am going to die inside of ten days, and I want to arrange to be well taken care of while sick."

This fragment of a conversation with a man who called at the City

Hospital yesterday, as well as the man's queer actions, startled some of the attaches of the institution.

The stranger was seen during the morning passing by the hospital, both on the Twelfth Street and Central Avenue sides. He was noticed particularly because he stopped several times as if in doubt, and gazed up at the buildings.

In the afternoon he returned again and finally approached one of the physicians.

"How long does a person have to be in the city to be admitted into the Hospital?"

ASKED THE STRANGER.

"Any time, but if you are able to pay you must be a resident of the city a year," was the answer.

"Have you got the most scientific doctors in the city?" was next asked. "And do you think you might save a man's life if he was doomed to die?"

"Why so?" asked the doctor, becoming curious. "Are you sick?"

"No, I am in perfect health just now, but am going to be sick inside of ten days," and the stranger heaved a sign.

After considerable more guarded questions and answers, the doctor said: "Well, see here, I can't fool with you all day. Tell me what you want. Give me your name or something or I will have to leave you."

"My name is Gerald Gailor and I'm stopping in Covington," said the strange man. "It may appear strange to you, but I will tell you my story straight. Last night I

HEARD OUR BANSHEE.

"And I am afraid I will be a dead man inside of ten days."

"I didn't sleep all night. I kept hearing noises. The door of my room suddenly sprang open several times and then the windows rattled. I just got into a doze once when I heard a moaning and a wailing that made my tongue freeze stiff. It finally changed to laughter, and then I heard all sorts of noises. I got up and lit a match.

"As I glanced toward the window the sight that met my eyes caused me to fall back in the bed.

PEERING IN THE WINDOW

There I saw the face of the most hideous and inhuman woman you ever saw. She had a white cap on her head and had her nose pressed against the window-pane.

"I nearly fainted for a moment, but came to my senses and the thought flashed through my brain that it was someone trying to scare me. But it was real, because my room is on the second floor."

The man then stopped his tale and turned to go.

"But what was it?" asked the doctor.

"Why, don't you know?" asked the man in surprise. "That was the family banshee as sure as I am a man.

MY MOTHER DIED

"The same way and my grandmother. Just before their deaths they heard horrible moanings and the cry of the banshee, and then died within ten days.

"I've heard grandmother say that her relatives for generations back have been warned of death by the family banshee.

"If I am taken sick within the next ten days I want the best of care. I don't hardly believe in this business, and I'm going to fight it, but I want to take all the precautions. If you are sure I'll be treated right, I'll come here." And the strange man left and wandered down Central Avenue toward the river.

Cincinnati [OH] Enquirer 13 May 1892: p. 4 HAMILTON COUNTY

NOTE: In a regrettable anti-climax, I have not found any follow-up to this story to see if the man really did die. Both first and last names can be spelled a variety of ways, which made the search more difficult. He mentions a "family banshee"—these deadly entities seem to be attached to different Irish clans.

The same City Hospital in Cincinnati was home to a different sort of howling Messenger of Death, a mysterious black cat. Like the notorious Oscar, a modern cat who roams Steere House Nursing and Rehabilitation Centre in Providence, Rhode Island, the animal told of death coming silently on little cat feet.

"DEATH"
THE BLACK CAT AGAIN AT THE CITY HOSPITAL
AND GIVES WARNING OF THE DEATH
OF ALECK HUTT, WHO WAS HIT ON THE HEAD,
AND A WOMAN NINETY YEARS OLD.

Some months ago a black cat appeared in the front office of the City Hospital.

Whence it came and to whom it belonged no one knew, but tabby soon made herself at home. She wandered all over the building and appeared regularly in the kitchen for her meals. At nights she confined her wanderings to the corridor below the front office.

A few nights after tabby's first appearance Night Clerk Hudson was startled by a mournful miauling emanating from the depths of the cellar. Almost immediately the telegraph instrument clicked off the death of one of the patients. The next night the corridor was again filled with the miaulings of the black cat, and again a patient died. This miauling warning of death continued night after night, until finally the hospital attaches nick-named the black cat "Death."

For over a month "Death" gave warning of an approaching visit of the grim monster and then it suddenly disappeared. Nothing was seen of it until early yesterday morning. The clock in a neighboring steeple had just tolled the hour of 3, when Night Clerk Hudson was startled to hear a long drawn, mournful miaul in the cellar. The miauling continued, and when Hudson's hair had again resumed its natural position, he secured a lantern and descended into the cellar. Guided by the miauling, he made his way to a corner where he found the long lost "Death." Satisfied, he returned to the office in time to hear the telegraph instrument clicking. It announced the death of Aleck Hutt, a colored barber living at 25 Broadway. He was struck on the head during a fight on a steamboat May 16. He came to the Hospital and a few days ago developed delirium tremens. The Coroner was notified and has ordered a post-mortem to discover if the blow caused death.

Another death announced by the black cat was that of Nida Elder, a colored woman 90 years old. Her relatives reside at No. 305 John Street.
Cincinnati [OH] Enquirer 27 May 1892: p. 4 HAMILTON COUNTY

NOTE: Patients at City Hospital were each given a number. The hospital wards were connected to the front office by a telegraph. To notify the office of a death, the nurse would click the patient's number with a special "death signal."

Millionaire businessman Thomas J. Gladwell of Toledo seemed to have a time machine, so accurate was his vision of the exact manner of his death and burial.

WEEK BEFORE HE WAS KILLED
GLADWELL TOLD JUST HOW IT WOULD OCCUR
HAD A VISION AND SAW MARE KICK HIM
RELATED HOW HE WOULD BE TAKEN TO HOSPITAL
AND BE BURIED UNDER AN ELM TREE
DREAM WAS TRUE IN EVERY PARTICULAR

Toledo, Ohio, June 29. It appears that the gift of looking into the future was bestowed upon Thomas J. Gladwell, the millionaire broker and horseman, who was killed last night by the kick of a favorite pet horse.

Mr. Gladwell, who has been the owner of large strings of fast trotters and pacers for the past 30 years, was at the matinee of the Toledo Driving Club at the Fair Grounds last Saturday afternoon. He had always taken part in the races, and last Saturday, when he failed to put in an appearance on the track with his flyers, several horse owners gathered round him and asked him the reason, and inquired if his health was poor. Mr. Gladwell is reported to have replied in substance as follows:

"There is nothing the matter with my health. I never felt better in all my life. I am not superstitious, and do not believe in ghosts, spirits, and all that sort of thing, but I assure you gentleman that I saw a peculiar vision last night while lying in bed.

WAS WIDE AWAKE.

"I was wide awake and realized all that was going on just as fully as I do now. While lying on the bed thinking about one thing and another, a bright vision appeared before my eyes. The dark room was all lighted up. I saw myself as plain as I see you bandaging the leg of that sorrel mare, the pacer. I led her into the stable and struck her on the haunches with my open hand, when she let fly with her heels, struck me in the forehead, crushed in my skull and allowed my brains to drop out.

"I saw myself lying bleeding and helpless on the stable floor, my colored stable boy running to my assistance, myself trying to get up and then falling back again helpless. I saw myself carried to the ambulance and taken to the hospital. There I saw myself die, and lastly I attended my own funeral and saw the coffin containing my body lowered into a grave in Forest Cemetery under a spreading elm tree. The vision told me this was all to happen on Friday evening, June 28, but I concluded to heed the warning to-day, and that is why I am not driving. The vision made me nervous, and I can't force my mind away from it."

IT CAME TRUE.

The vision as related by Mr. Gladwell to his friends came to a full and complete realization last night. He apparently forgot all about his vision or he was in the hands of fate and could not avoid what death had in store.

He was bandaging the leg of his sorrel mare and led her into the stable, and as she stepped into the box stall he placed his hands on her hips and being of a nervous temperament this startled the mare and she let go with her heels, catching her owner squarely on the forehead and crushing in his skull.

There were the pools of blood, brains dashed out, attempts to get up, colored stable boy calling for help, ambulance, trip to the hospital and death there, all enacting in perfect sequence with what Mr. Gladwell described as seeing in his vision. Even the part of the vision relating to the grave under the spreading elm tree will be fulfilled, as Mr. Gladwell purchased a burying site around this tree years ago and left a sketch of how and where he wanted to be buried in case he was called away suddenly. The location brings the grave directly under the elm tree where the grave was dug to-day to receive his remains to-morrow.

A WONDERFUL CASE.

This is a most wonderful case of a person foretelling every little detail in connection with his death and seems to be without a parallel. The vision as outlined by Mr. Gladwell had been mentioned several times during the past few days by those who had heard him relate the story of what he saw and when they learned of his death last night and how it occurred the most of them were not surprised, but said they rather expected it....

Cincinnati [OH] Enquirer 30 June 1901: p. 1 LUCAS COUNTY

Some premonition-of-death stories are ironic.

Theodore H. Becker, a saloon-keeper of Hamilton, has frequently remarked of late that he did not think he would live very long, although he seemed in good health. The other morning he told his wife that he believed he would lie down and die. A moment later he went into his bedroom, remarking to her as he crossed the threshold, "I will be dead in half an hour." She thought he was joking, and paid no attention to him. In about fifteen minutes Mrs. Becker had occasion to go into the bedroom and was horrified to find her husband lying stretched upon the bed stone dead.

Van Wert [OH] Republican 26 September 1889: p. 2 BUTLER COUNTY

Others are meant to tug at the heartstrings:

"I'M GOING TO DIE,"
LISPED THE FOUR-YEAR-OLD TO HIS FATHER
A PREMONITION.

Wilmington, O., Nov. 3

An interesting and singular incident of a premonition of death has just been brought about through the death of little Jimmie Wickersham, of Greenfield, near here. He died Monday, and was not yet four years of age.

Five days previous to his death, when apparently in the best of health, he came to his papa, and in his childish prattle said: "Papa, I'm going to be sick, awful sick, and I'm going to die." Within three days afterward he contracted a severe cold, but it was not considered serious. Nothing further was thought of his remarks of the previous day until Sabbath evening, when he was taken suddenly worse, and he again repeated what he had told his papa to his grandma, and at an early hour yesterday morning he died.

His childish words of but a few days previous were proved to be only too true. It is the talk of the community as being a most remarkable case of premonition in one so youthful.

Daily Gazette [Xenia, OH] 4 November 1896: p. 3 HIGHLAND COUNTY

Visions of headless creatures were another recognized death omen. These next two stories came from the 1914 *Dayton Daily News* "true ghost story" contest.

IN GREENE COUNTY

During the war of 1861 I was at a neighbor's house. I looked out of a window and saw a man with no head and brass buttons on his coat. As I went home, a bear with no head run me for three or four hundred yards. In about three weeks I heard of my brother being starved to death in the Andersonville Prison.

This all happened near New Jasper, in Greene County, Ohio.

C.H.G.

Dayton [OH] Daily News 3 February 1914 GREENE COUNTY

NOTE: This story is eerily like "The Headless Soldier," from Fairfield, Ohio, in *Spooky Ohio: 13 Traditional Tales.*

Mysterious White Ladies also were seen as messengers of death.

THE TOKEN OF MY AUNT'S TRAGIC DEATH

Some forty years or more ago in early autumn, the evening being cool and the work having been attended to out of doors my mother closed the doors before sitting down to finish her evening's work. After lighting the lamp and arranging her sewing she proceeded to sew on the machine and I was set to my task of sewing on buttons.

I was then seven years of age.

The younger children proceeded to have their accustomed romp with father before settling down for the evening. After becoming tired they quieted down and some of them had already gone to sleep and everything was quiet and still when we heard the outside kitchen door open and someone come in and upon looking through the sitting room door into the kitchen, we were amazed to see a lighted candle, as we had brought the lamp into the living room.

As the light grew brighter and drew nearer to the living room door, mother grew pale and father and I became so frightened that we appeared unable to speak as the form of a woman robed in white holding the light in her right hand came into full view. She passed the door, turned around and passed through the kitchen door and disappeared, the door not being in view from where we were. The ghost, as we supposed, passed through as it opened and closed and everything was dark and quiet. After recovering from their surprise and scare, father proceeded to investigate, looking through the kitchen he passed out into the yard but could find no trace of anyone having been about the premises.

We could never discover the identity of the strange and weird visitor and could not account for the visit unless it could be explained by the accidental death of a dear aunt of my mother that same evening by the accidental discharge of a gun with which she was going to shoot a squirrel about sundown, my mother always claiming it being a token of her death.

Dayton [OH] Daily News 29 January 1914 MONTGOMERY COUNTY

MORE CEMETERY SPIRITS

I began the chapter with graveyard ghosts; I will close it with more cemetery spirits, starting with a 10-foot spook in Hamilton.

A TEN-FOOT GHOST SEEN IN THE OLD BOUDINOT CEMETERY AT HAMILTON A BOLD YOUNG MAN WHO FAILED TO LAY THE SPIRIT

What is claimed to be a genuine ghost has made its appearance in Hamilton, Ohio.

The apparition has been seen in the old Boudinot burying ground, in the First Ward, by a number of parties.

About a year ago the grounds were put into the hands of the City Council, and an effort made to convert them into a park. The grand old trees that had stood for a century and shaded the tombs were cut down, and the grave-mounds were levelled to the earth, the stones being carried away. The grave was robbed of its once solemn beauty and the hallowed associations of years disregarded. Day after day the graves were torn open by the plow and the

ROTTING BONES

Thrown promiscuously upon the ground. A few days ago the plow-share turned up a tomb-stone bearing the inscription:

"Charley, aged 12, son of Herman and Anna Carter."

Soon after this rumors that were calculated to keep the immediate residents in the house after night were circulated, and some superstitious ones declared that in the old cemetery there were ghosts. A few evenings since, Joseph Myers, who resides on Boudinot Street, had a strange experience. While he was sitting in his doorway shortly before retiring, he looked in the direction of the park and saw a queer looking object appear. From the deserted Carter tomb arose a shrouded figure.

It was about ten feet in height and carried a torch in its outstretched hand, making at times quite a brilliant light.

In a short space of time the figure seemed to rise and glide toward the street. Myers was somewhat nervous for a short time. He arose, however, and walked across the street and pursued it for the purpose of investigation, but before he could approach the mysterious figure, it suddenly disappeared.

It is claimed that the

SPIRITS OF THE BODIES

That belong to these graves which have been disturbed nightly promenade the grounds.

A young man residing on Park Street boldly asserted that he had no fear of any such thing as a ghost, and that he would fathom the mystery of the apparition.

Last Friday night he took a seat in the extreme eastern portion of the cemetery to carry out his design. About midnight

THE GHOST AROSE

Before him, and he became so badly frightened that he started at a break-neck speed in an easterly direction, and on the following day was discovered hidden in a blackberry patch near Reily, some twelve miles distant from the corporate limits of Hamilton. Since this adventure he cannot be persuaded to go outdoors after sunset.

Cincinnati [OH] Enquirer 27 July 1890: p. 9 BUTLER COUNTY

There is a horrific tale called "The Croglin Grange Vampire" told by Augustus Hare in *The Story of My Life* (1896/1900). The hideous Thing in this story from Van Wert is strongly reminiscent of Hare's unearthly creature found in a churchyard vault.

HORRIFYING EXPERIENCE OF A MINISTER WITH A VAN WERT GHOST

We clip the following from Sunday's [Cincinnati] *Enquirer* and as it relates the experience of the narrator in Van Wert, it will doubtless be interesting reading. The gentleman alluded to is quite well known to us but we are not at liberty to use his name:

Washington C.H., July 9. A Methodist minister, lately a resident of Hamilton County, Ohio, who has been visiting friends in our city, relates the following thrilling episode in his life, which occurred while he was stopping at Van Wert, Ohio.

'It was on a beautiful moonlight evening in June, and the atmosphere was just about as sultry as it has been at any time during the present summer. I was enjoying myself in the company of some relatives who lived about three miles from Van Wert, on the old Willshire road. At a late hour I arose to go, but my friends insisted that I should remain for the night, as my way would be very lonesome. It was suggested that some ghost might appear to me at the cemetery or some individual might rob me. This was a beautiful burying ground, and was situated about midway on my route. I was quite amused at their artful method of persuasion and laughed vociferously. It was very ridiculous to me, indeed, that there should be a rattling of dry bones, or the apparition of a spirit in a modern cemetery. The people of to-day had made too much advancement, as I thought, for such idle fancies as that.

Thus I proceeded on my way with no thought of danger—indifferent to the warnings that had just been given me. As I drew near to the cemetery, however, and began to see the tall, white shafts of marble looming up among the evergreens my imagination was tensioned to its utmost capacity, and, I confess, I was a fit subject for terror. It seemed as if all the spook stories to which I had listened in my childhood chased each other in quick, succession through my brain, and the very chirrup of the crickets or the incessant song of the whippoorwill intensified the loneliness of this little nook of earth. The long line of dark trees that threw such strange shadows across the field and mellow light that fell from the moon upon every grotesque stump or stately monument, only served to intensify my loneliness.

I arrived at last at the corner of the cemetery, and, oh horrors! right in the very center of this field of dead men's bones, and from the shadow of a broad new tombstone, I saw a tall black creature rise and stand erect. The apparition seemed in the distance like a huge cadaver clothed in a robe of sack-cloth. The dreary eyes were sunken deep in their sockets, and the few irregular snags that served for teeth were pressed like fangs against the thin and wrinkled lips. The monster gazed a moment in all directions, then with a steady measured movement it made directly for me. I stopped and gazed upon the creature, and started back bewildered, but, at once regaining my senses, I concluded to proceed, and, if possible, to put on the appearance of unconcern. As I proceeded the spectre proceeded also, and, as certainly as I live in the present moment, it seemed as if we would both meet at the same point in the road. After going a short distance I slackened my pace, in order to let the mysterious something have all the room in front of me it might desire, and in a few moments I congratulated myself on being about twenty feet in the rear.

Contrary to my anticipations, there was no conversation opened between us but in a strange, ghost-like manner, the long withered form moved ahead of me until it reached a little, old, abandoned burying ground at the right of the road. This spot was far more desolate than the new cemetery, for it had become entirely neglected, and at that late hour of the night appeared as an interminable thicket, so completely were the weeds, bushes, briers and trees tangled and matted together. Into this uncanny place my ghostly terrifier passed and disappeared. I have never understood the nature of this apparition up to the present time, and I am perfectly willing to give my name to anyone who would be inclined to doubt the occurrence.'

The Van Wert [OH] Republican 14 July 1887: p. 5 VAN WERT COUNTY

NOTE: The road called Willshire Road is now Shannon Street or State Route 118. The "new cemetery" is Woodland Cemetery of Van Wert. The older cemetery was on West Main Street. Its inhabitants were moved to Woodland. You can find the Croglin Grange story at http://augustus-hare.tripod.com/croglin.html

9.

A Family Bewitched
The Hoffman Poltergeist of Wooster

The demon, now acknowledged to be around the place, adopted a new method of annoyance. A sharp, clipping noise, as if from a pair of invisible shears, was heard all through and around the house and, worse yet, all the clothes of the family, their table cloths and bed coverings were cut and gashed, the slits being all in the shape of a crescent. Of course, the news of these unearthly doings soon spread, and people from all directions crowded to see and hear what was going on. There are still preserved in some families pocket-handkerchiefs that were folded in the pockets of their owners when they visited the place, but, yet, were cut and marked in his peculiar way by the demon of the scissors that kept up his "clip-clip."

–"Wizard Clip" from *The Strange Story of Harper's Ferry: with Legends of the Surrounding Country*, Joseph Barry, (Martinsburg, WV: Thompson Brothers, 1903): p. 212 –

The year 1871 was a significant one in the annals of paranormal events: The mysterious Sandusky/Milan faces-in-the-windows first appeared in 1871. There was a heavy rain of snails in Tiffin. Perry Township in Carroll County, was terrorized by a 15-foot snake. And one of the strangest, least-known poltergeist cases erupted in the town of Wooster, in Wayne County. I have collected other stories about poltergeist slashers, but the case is unique in its impressively disruptive scale. This is the story of a family bewitched, of poltergeist attacks that ripped apart the fabric of family life like shattered silk.

The first notices in the *Wooster Republican* were dramatic and lurid:

SPIRITS ON THE RAMPAGE!
A FAMILY BEWITCHED!
STRANGE DOINGS IN WOOSTER

If the Rev. Cotton Mather, of witchcraft memory, were living in these degenerate days, he would have his hands full of business in this city, at the house of Mr. David Hoffman, near the corner of Pittsburgh

Avenue and J. Stibbs' Lane; the family is said to be haunted by malignant spirits, who are uncomfortably rampant in their evil doings, diabolical in their transactions, and mysterious in their ways.

According to the 1870 census, the family was a small one for the era: David Hoffman age 52, his wife Mary (45), daughters Kesiah (25) and Etta [Henrietta] (17) and son Jacob (13). David, Mary and Kesiah had been born in Pennsylvania. They lived in Killbuck Twp., Holmes County, where David worked as a miller at Sharp's Mill, two miles south of Millersburg, "where the family were regarded as respectable, intelligent and Christian people."

Life seemed to be good in Holmes County. David said he was "doing well at the mill, had a good salary and a good home and in every way in comfortable circumstances, until disorder in a mysterious way visited his family."

Like many poltergeist infestations, it began with something very simple.

> It first commenced, he said, a year ago last June, by his missing two dollars from his pocket book, after which he privately hid his money, but that too, disappeared in the most unaccountable manner. Articles of food and clothing, in daily increasing quantities, went the same way. Crockery ware fell from shelves and broke to pieces, stones, gravel, eggs and other things were thrown about the house, apparently without human agency, the badness seeming to have headquarters in the cellar. The family, from being annoyed, at length became frightened, and imagined that a change of abode might bring relief from the spirits, removed to Wooster last summer, Mr. Hoffman remaining at the mill where he was unmolested by any evil visitation. But his family, who lived in Mr. Snook's house, West Liberty St., was not so fortunate.

As we have seen in some other poltergeist cases, the Wooster poltergeist seemed obsessed with clothing.

> The clothing of the mother and eldest daughter was taken, some returned, from whence no one could tell, all cut to pieces as if with shears, and some secreted in out-of-the way places, for instance, all their underclothing was found stuffed into the mouth of the cellar drain, a silk dress hid under a wood pile in the cellar, and skirts, &c., buried in sand.

Rather than rapping out its messages, the Wooster poltergeist wrote notes that seemed to precipitate out of the ceiling or the cellar. In a more traditional vein, the entity taunted Mrs. Hoffman about a treasure hidden in the basement.

Many written notes were thrown, apparently from the cellar, bearing all kinds of messages. One was that if Mrs Hoffman would come down to the foot of the cellar stairs on her knees, on a certain specified day and hour, she would there find a box containing two thousand dollars. Prior to this the family had become afraid to enter the cellar; and as she could only go down the steps backwards on her knees, Mrs. Hoffman afraid of bodily injury, was dissuaded by neighbors from making the attempt. But she went to Holmes County and brought her husband to Wooster, hoping that he could get the lucre, and abate the spirits, or IT, as she calls the evil agents of her fireside. Another note was received, stating no one could get the money but herself. It has not been secured up to the present time.

Some of the prominent spiritualists of Wooster, learning of these transactions, held a circle meeting, but received no signs from that other bourne.

The troubles raged on. Mr. Hoffman, at a sacrifice was compelled to give up his situation at the mill and join his family in Wooster. A few weeks ago, they moved to where they now reside, followed by IT.

By request of the family, a clergyman from Wooster visited them, and offered prayer. Shortly after he left, a scrap of paper dropped strangely to the floor upon which was written, that, as they (the family) had "prayed to Got," the spirits wouldn't bother them for a while. All was quiet for a few days. Then more clothes were taken, which after an absence of one or two days, would be found in the house or yard, cut to pieces. About ten days ago, while another reverend gentleman was there, a piece of new calico, sufficient for three dresses disappeared. A neighbour lady next day found it, uncut, under a pile of wood, and also a blanket shawl, under a box of potatoes, in the cellar.

Frequently at nights there are poundings on the walls, stones, from pebbles to those as large as a man's fist, thrown in the rooms, and a general rumpus created, as if imps were holding high revelry. On one occasion Mr. Hoffman called upon IT to cease, without avail; whereon he indulged in a little tall swearing, when all became serene. A young man called there last Friday evening; said if the spirits could cut up his hat and handkerchief they were welcome. A small stone dropped on his head, which when picked up he found red hot; and upon taking out his handkerchief discovered it cut to shreds. As another instance very peculiar, a young gentleman and confirmed skeptic in Spiritualism, with other persons visited the house on last Sabbath afternoon, and on his return to this brother's residence, to the amazement of all, at least twenty holes were found in his handkerchief, which had not been out of his pocket at the haunted house. Mr. Hoffman answered one of the spirit notes, placing his reply quietly in the cellar, but just as he got into the room, his own note dropped at his feet on the floor—all his family present.

Until last Friday, nothing of Mr. Hoffman's clothes had been touched. That night his two pair boots—all he had—were taken, and also the table knives, but the boots were mysteriously returned next day, accompanied by an exceedingly vulgar note. On last Saturday all his clothing, excepting an old working suit, was taken, and words written on the side of the house to the effect that they would not be returned.

Mr. and Mrs. Hoffman and the eldest daughter have no clothing but that on their backs; while in the house are piles of cut up garments of all descriptions, of good quality—a dozen dresses, silk, delaine, calico, &c., cloth sacques, four shawls, underclothing, and any quantity of lesser articles. It is a shame—this wanton destruction of property. From a man comfortable in life, Mr. Hoffman is getting into reduced circumstances. He said he lost about a thousand dollars during the last year.

The whole matter is confounding. There are, however, several plausible theories for the cause of seemingly marvellous transactions. Careful watch has been kept, yet no clue of the perpetrators of the outrages has been discovered. Hundreds of men and women have visited the premises. It is said that the Spiritualists propose holding meetings at the house, and get up a circle to see if anything can be developed. We will keep our readers posted on the subject. *Wooster Republican*
Massillon [OH] Independent 3 May 1871: p. 1 WAYNE COUNTY

NOTE: "That other bourne" is a reference to *Hamlet*: "The undiscovere'd country, from whose bourn/ No traveller returns." It was a catchphrase used by Spiritualists for "death" or "the afterlife."

This next article suggests several origins for IT, drawing on a more traditional view of ghosts and haunted houses. In keeping with the arc of many of these poltergeist cases, there is an attempt to find a deceased spirit to blame and the Spiritualists are called in.

MORE ABOUT THE HAUNTED HOUSE!
THE SPIRITS STILL ON THE RAMPAGE!
FURTHER STRANGE DEVELOPMENTS

The evil spirit or IT, haunting the house of Mr. David Hoffman, continues in its turbulent ways, and still remains a mystery. It is the theme of conversation and speculation among all classes of the city, and creates the sensation of curiosity, amusement, or fear, according to individual temperament. Practical people charge that the so-called spiritual manifestations are the legerdemain tricks of a living female member of the family, but thus far have no facts to sustain the theory, although considerable detective ability has been exercised.

The family indignantly deny, and with plausible argument assert their innocence, and invite investigation by the hundreds who visit their house. They state that they are as much confounded at what takes place as other persons, and are very anxious to be relieved of their unknown malignant enemy, who is ruining them financially, and in every manner giving them the greatest discomfort. They are afraid to sleep in separate chambers, and therefore bed in one room, frequently disturbed and frightened by unearthly noises. Nothing they possess appears to be safe. Clothing, furniture and provisions alike disappear. Crockeryware flies to pieces, five dollars' worth of lard, a quantity of eggs, butter, and several other things pertaining to the larder; unceremoniously disappeared lately. To that, without food or raiment, and worried, as Mr. Hoffman expresses himself, until 'almost crazy,' it seems proper that IT had better cease from troubling and let the weary be at rest.

So many people are so constantly calling at the house that the family admit but few, on account of pressure. About three hundred were refused last Sabbath. On one occasion, several were declined admission because some spiritualists were at the moment, deep in the mystic rites of holding a circle, to which faith, it is said, Mrs. Hoffman is almost persuaded, having no other particular religion.

The evil genius of her house, she sometimes is constrained to believe, is the spirit of a deceased sister, who died in Holmes County, Ohio, a few months before IT began operations. They used to quarrel a good deal about clothes before the sister put on immortality; and it may be that the force of habit was so strong as to lure the departed one when in a wayward mood, from the bright side of the New Jerusalem to renew old times with her sister, and to cut up her clothes. Such, at least is Mrs. Hoffman's idea, when she reflects upon the past, and those who have gone before. Again, she imagines that it might be the ghost of her father; yet thinks he wouldn't have the heart to bewitch her family. And so on, until many dead are under suspicion of not being as good as they might be.

In fact, for "ways that are dark," the operations of the house are peculiar. Mr. Hoffman, who is a commonplace man, and well known for many years in Wayne County, as an upright citizen cannot see through the millstone, although himself a miller. ["See through the millstone" is a colloquial expression meaning to be able to see through some difficult matter.]

He wants to go away for it never molests him only when he is with his family, when the spirit business is about pat, cutting up his clothes, purloining his money, which he worked hard for, and taking away the provisions he furnished for the family. All his good clothes are gone. His old working suit he protects from the destroyer by placing it under his pillow at nights. His money—what little he has—he saves by wrapping his pocket book in a handkerchief which he ties around his body under his shirt. He remains with the family because of their beseeching tears to stay as protector. They become almost frantic with grief if the old man offers to go. He is a kind father and a good husband; and if the outrages upon him are committed by members of his family it would be ungrateful, if not worse.

David Hoffman's position is one of the most poignant features of the whole affair: "He wants to go away for it never molests him only when he is with his family." Yet he "is a kind father and a good husband." And he was repaid by what seemed like the Devil quoting scripture for his own purpose:

When his boots were returned, all cut to pieces, a copy of the New Testament lay over them, opened at XVIII chapter of Acts. [These Biblical verses refer to unclean spirits being cast out, the sorcery of Simon Magnus, and various miracles.]

At two subsequent times the Testament mysteriously opened at III chapter of Acts [Peter and John heal a lame man and a warning to people who do not heed God's prophets.] and XIV of St. John [The consoling verses about "Let not your heart be troubled" and "I will not leave you comfortless."] The leaf was turned down in each instance, but no verse marked.

Many seemingly strange things are done. For example, a trunk was packed and locked, preparatory to moving. When no one was near the lid was raised by an unseen hand and the clothing thrown out upon the floor. The trunk was repacked and locked; again the lid was lifted, and a muff at the bottom thrown out, without in the least disturbing the apparel on top. This manifestations ended by IT sawing the lock out of the trunk.

Night appears to be the season of greatest annoyance, full of noises, rappings and general disturbance. One night the two daughters were awakened from sleep by the sensation of being punctured with pins, and sprang from the bed and ran into their parent's room, where they remained the rest of the night, afraid to return to their own chamber.

The clothes of the family having been nearly all destroyed, the spirits turned their attention to that of visitors, and play havoc. Several persons' clothes have been cut while in the house, one lady having her dress ruined, and another rent, and this, too, done in daylight in the presence of individuals who were on the lookout for such depredations.

One afternoon lately, at the request of C.M. Kenton, editor of the Shreve *Mirror*, our reporter accompanied him and two other gentlemen to Mr. Hoffman's house, where they were shown every courtesy, by way of exhibiting piles of cut up garments, etc., and relating the various annoyances to which the family are almost daily and nightly subjected. When about to take their departure, it was found that the reporter's hat was slashed, so to speak, into ribbons. The hat was upon a small stand in the room, where all were, and could not have been moved from its place or the action would have been observed. The cuts were clear, as if done with some lancet-kind of instrument—performed expertly, and upon the principle "What thou doest do quickly." It was afterwards learned that IT mistook him for an orthodox minister of the Gospel; hence his loss is some preacher's gain.

Typically poltergeists dislike authority figures, particularly members of the clergy.

There are many other strange incidents "too numerous to mention." However, it is confidently believed by every sanguine person that the mystery of the Bewitched will soon be solved, from the fact that Mr. S. B. Cooper, a well-known and respected citizen of Wooster, has written for the celebrated clairvoyant, Madame Thomson, of Cleveland, to come to this city and lift the veil that shadows the house of Hoffman. The Madame gave him valuable information on two occasions; the first a triumph; but the second, digging for treasure at 2 o'clock, A.M., in the hill-side near the railroad depot, was unfortunately, not a success, on account of the interference of the police. *Wooster Republican*.

The Massillon [OH] Independent 17 May 1871 WAYNE COUNTY

NOTE: I have not been able to trace a Madame Thomson, although she may be E. or E.F. Thompson, a clairvoyant who advertised that she could produce a picture of the person the client was to marry. Poltergeists sending people on wild goose chases for treasure is a popular motif of the period, as we've seen from the note telling Mrs. Hoffman about the $2,000 in the basement and several other stories in this collection.

THE HOFFMAN GHOSTS

Several investigations have taken place into the curious ghostly phenomena going on in the town of Wooster, Ohio—but according to the
local Press, without the slightest light having been thrown on the mystery.
Our readers will remember, from an account printed in these columns a
short time since, that the manifestations occur in the family of a miller
named Hoffman, and are much of the same type as those recorded in the
last century as the work of the famous Cock-lane Ghost. There are almost
continual noises, furniture is thrown down, clothes are cut to pieces or
hidden away, crockery flies briskly about the house, food disappears from
the larder and is found buried or stuck up the chimney, and other mischie-
vous pranks of the same sort are continually played, to the annoyance of
the family, and the amazement and awe of their neighbors.

The matter has now become, we are assured, the theme of animat-
ed discussion through the whole surrounding country. It was alleged by
many at the outset that the whole affair was a clever piece of legerdemain,
carried on by the women of the Hoffman family. This charge they denied
with indignation, and invited the most thorough investigation. All classes
have been asked to come and see for themselves, and people have accepted
the offer in great numbers, and with much closeness of scrutiny. In fact,
the pressure of visitors has been so heavy, that at last some discrimination has been rendered unavoidable, and the Wooster *Republican* says that
three hundred persons were refused admittance on one day. Committees
of examination have been at work for weeks, but strangely enough, not
even a clue to the affair has been attained. All who go, see, hear, and attest to the same things. Some visitors—doubtless the most inquisitive and
incredulous ones—have been subjected to the same persecutions as the
Hoffmans themselves. For example, ladies have had their dresses cut and
rent, to quote the words of the *Republican*, "in daylight and in the presence of individuals who were on the watch for such depredations." Again,
a reporter's hat was slashed into ribbons—the hat having been during the
whole time of the owner's visit "upon a small stand in the room where all
were, and could not have been moved from its place, or the action would
have been observed."

Mr. Hoffman, the head of the family, who took up his abode elsewhere for a time—the ghosts never troubling him individually under such
circumstances—has returned home. He has taken this step because of the
entreaties of his wife and daughters to come and protect them. We have
already explained that a change of residence on the part of the ladies is
followed by no relief.

Mr. Hoffman's contumacy in returning to the domestic hearth, against the apparent wish of the unseen demons, is sharply punished by them in the old way. They cut his clothes, and steal his money, and pull his hair, and play him all manner of disagreeable tricks. Lately, too, they have devised a fresh and poignant torture for his daughters. On managing to get to sleep, after the excitement and worry of the day, these persecuted females are suddenly aroused by the sensation of being punctured with pins. This, it will be observed, is a leaf from the book of many of the old-fashioned spectres, and, before the Hoffman ghosts are found out, the whole ancient catalogue of thaumaturgical exploits will probably be gone through.

Meanwhile it must be recorded, to the credit of the mystic operators, that their reputation for professional skill is considerably raised by their protracted escape from detection. The number of investigators has been greatly multiplied, and the chances for catching the ghosts tripling are of course multiplied also. But neither the Presbyterian divines nor the table-tippers, neither the pedagogues of the region nor the physicians, can boast, so far, that they have thrown the least light on the mystery, or have gained any advantage the one over the other.

Several Ohio newspapers have been represented at the house of the Hoffmans, sometimes by their editors and sometimes by reporters; and all their accounts seem to be exactly confirmatory of each other and of what we have described. The whole business is an amusing repetition of past history and we doubt not the final exposure will bear out the parallel. Pending that event, we must own that the longer it is deferred the more surprising the matter is, and the more valid is the claim to precedence set up for the Wooster ghosts over their ancient friend of Cock-Lane.

The New York Times 24 May 1871

NOTE: The Cock-Lane Ghost was the talk of 1762 London. Although the manifestations were of a poltergeist type, they were attributed to the ghost of the restless spirit of "Scratching Fanny," a former resident of the house. She rapped out that she had been murdered by her husband. He denied it and claimed that someone was trying to extort money from him. The case was investigated by Dr. Samuel Johnson himself. Spoiler Alert: A 12-year-old girl was responsible. You can read more about the story in Dr. Johnson's account in *The Gentleman's Magazine* for 1763, or in *Cock Lane and Common Sense*, Andrew Lang, 1894.

And then the Spiritualists arrived.

SPIRITUALISM INSTALLED!

The report of facts, published in the *Republican* at different times during the last six weeks, relative to the marvellous transactions of the ministering spirits haunting David Hoffman's house in Wooster, has ceased to be a local matter. Through the press it is known all over the country, until our city has rather a spiritual than truly orthodox religious reputation....

People from distant parts of the country—from New York to Kansas, Canada, &c.—have written to us for information as to the truth or falsity of the so called Wooster spirit manifestations. Many citizens also have verbally asked the same question. To all we have to say that we simply recite the strange occurrences as they take place; at the same time rejecting every solution of the manifestations that are based upon the hypothesis of supernatural agency. But yet, as an exchange remarks upon the subject: "most people turn a willing ear to every revelation of the marvellous. Superstition and credulity can scarcely be regarded as salient features of our nineteenth century civilization, and yet few of us would like to confess how, after all we have given our faith to the supernatural Ghost stories, which have not lost their secret charm for the wisest as well as the simplest. Of course in the light of science and of reason, all these things are nonsense; but after all, it is nonsense for which we cannot help keeping a soft spot in our hearts.

There is no abatement of the strange proceedings at our haunted house. The spirits still live, and seem to be more irresistible than ever.

The newspaper unwittingly hits on a key to the whole poltergeist phenomena— at first the Spiritualists "did not know whether it was spirits or the family."

But after profound research and labored investigation, success perched upon their banners. The discovery was made by a sure test—"music in the soul"—and in this melodious manner: A common tin pan, second hand, and a little wooden stick were placed under a table; the table covered with a cloth of sufficient size so as to completely envelope it; around, at a distance from a table, the circle of men and women arranged. The lights were put out, deep darkness supervened, and silence reigned so intense that one couldn't hear anybody pick up a pin. Then the stick commenced hammering the pan with a rub a-dub dub. Eureka! A lost pleiad found, and

Mrs. Hoffman and eldest daughter crowned and anointed as first class mediums! It was glory enough for one night!

This occurred some two weeks ago. Since then there has been better music; such as the spirits touching the light guitar and playing second fiddle to the circle, performed in the same manner as the stick and pan. Madame Thompson, of Cleveland, the great clairvoyant and illuminator of the 'ways that are dark,' 'hidden hands,' etc., came to Wooster on the express last Saturday. A good sized stone flew across the room of the haunted house several times to attract attention, on which was written that on that evening the circle would have the biggest meeting they ever had. The information proved correct. The faithful marched out, the observed of many observers on the street. The spirits were obedient—made music, &tc., according to programme. The Madame proclaimed that it was spirits, but being so many strong mediums in the Hoffman family, confusion was created and that if she would take one of them away harmony could be restored. That was all that she could do at present, but more anon.

As novelties, taking place at the house, a young man of the mercantile persuasion, whose veracity is not to be doubted, reports that he saw stones flying around the room with written notes attached to them, tied on with strings; and saw a table dance a shoo fly over the floor, and nobody near it—all this in the broadest kind of daylight.

An elderly gentleman visited the family one afternoon. He was forcible in telling the mediums that they were the bully ghosts themselves. He got his sure reward and just deserts. A hot stone dropped at his feet, and the next instant a handful of gravel and sand was thrown in his face; at the same time a note dropped on the bare footed part of his scalp, upon which was written, as the bad boys said to the prophet Elijah, 'Go up, thou bald head!' but no reference was made to the two she bears.

The other day a white apron ready made was thrown up from the cellar, and had been made out of one of the medium's confiscated undergarments by the spiritual sewing machine that keeps dark in the cellar.

A lady, who, with others, paid a curiosity visit there last Sabbath lost a cuff. It mysteriously 'went where the woodbine twineth.'

Old Mr. Hoffman is now in his shirt sleeves, the last coat of a half a dozen was cut to pieces Friday morning. Saturday morning the family found their garden ruined. Peas, that had been two foot high were pulled up and cut off; onions, salad, &c. in the same way—all the spirits' work, they say.

One of the strangest occurrences is, that one of the daughters purchased a pair of shoes, and for safety, left them at a neighbors, who hung them upon the wall. Next morning the shoes were missing and no trace of them could be discovered. The next day, Mrs. Hoffman put some meat in a vessel on the stove for dinner. When about ready to be served, the lid was taken off, when it was found that with the meat, boiling away, was one of the shoes cut into fine pieces, and thus the spirit cook spoiled their broth.

And so IT goes on rampant. *Wooster Republican*.

The Independent [Massillon, OH] 31 May 1871: p. 1 WAYNE COUNTY

NOTE: The shoes cut to pieces is one of the creepiest images in this story. The reference to Elijah and she-bears comes from the Bible, 2 Kings 2: 23-4: where the prophet Elijah is mocked by children and curses them so that they are eaten by two she-bears. "Went where the woodbine twineth" means "disappeared." The "lost pleiad found" refers to the Pleiades star cluster, where only six out of the seven stars are readily seen.

The Hoffman case was discussed far beyond Wooster, even as far as England and New York.

If the evil one himself has not taken up his residence in Wooster, it certainly looks as if he had disciples there. And it is very probable that it will eventually be discovered who these disciples are. *New York Sun*

The Atlanta [GA] Constitution 5 June 1871: p. 4

But then, abruptly, the news coverage of the bewitched family ends. The last article I have been able to locate was a sarcastic squib in the *Holmes Co. Republican*, from the Hoffman family's former home town, Millersburg.

"The Hoffman family of 'spirit rappers' have removed from Wooster to Akron."

Holmes Co. Republican, [Millersburg, OH] 21 September 1871: p. 3

Poltergeists usually wear themselves out after about 6 months. Since I don't have a precise date for when the manifestations started, I can't say that this was the case here. The family may have fled to Akron, only to find that IT had come along, as it did when they moved to Wooster from Holmes County.

Was Mrs. Hoffman, at a hormonally difficult time of life, the focus of the spook? And did the attacks end when she was declared a "first-class medium," conferring on her some special status, some role she could claim for her own beyond household drudge? The female mediums of the early Spiritualist movement often assumed masculine roles such as preaching or lecturing while in trance—a liberating experience.

I do not know the end of the Hoffmans' story. I would like to dig deeper in future. What follows is mostly conjecture, trying to tease out a record of relationships based on dry records like city directories. I examined Akron city directories from 1879 through 1908. Mrs. Hoffman and her son Jacob, who is listed as following various occupations like "laborer" and "dyeing and scouring" (a part of the textile industry involving hand-washing with soap or urine) seemed rooted at the rear of 123 S. Main, also known as 123 Maiden Lane. David is listed as a teamster, a laborer, a worker at a livery business, also at the Akron Water Works.

I have to think that for a man who had had a good, respectable job as a miller, working as a teamster, outside in all weathers, associated with a group with a reputation for being tough men, was a step down the financial and social ladder. He was, after all, in his 60s. He must have looked back longingly at those golden years in Holmes County when he was a happy and respected miller.

In 1879, David is listed as boarding at 602 S. Broadway in Akron. Mrs. Mary Hoffman and Jacob M. Hoffman, dyer, live "Alley, rear 123 S. Main.," a little over a mile from David's boarding house. Did he board out because he was on call for his job? Or was the couple separated by something more than a few city blocks? Only once, in the 1888-89 directory, is David listed at the same address as his wife, although he has another address as well. The couple did not divorce, but they never lived together again.

David seems to have died in 1894. Mrs. Hoffman is first listed as "Wid. David" in 1895. She ceases to appear in the City Directory in 1904, although Jacob is still there for a few years longer. The daughters vanished into marriage or death.

Did the son, Jacob, working at a hard, dirty job, ever dream about what might have been if IT hadn't appeared? He might have gone to school, gotten a job where he could have kept his hands clean, married and had a family of his own instead of living with his mother. Perhaps he was a mama's boy, happy to have her cook his meals and mend his clothes, taking his mother's side against a father who had failed to protect his family.

I wonder about those separate addresses for the Hoffmans. If Mrs. Hoffman, rather than the teenaged children, was the focus of the attacks, did Mr. Hoffman blame her for the family's woes?

Hoffman himself was untouched by IT until his wife, eager for the money she was convinced was hidden in the cellar, convinced him to come to

Wooster. He gave up a good job to live in a madhouse where food disappeared and crockery was smashed, clothing was purloined or shredded; where he had to sleep with his one remaining suit under his pillow. No matter how fond of his family, he must have regretted returning.

As I have remarked before, certain poltergeists take a great interest in the human wardrobe, either constructing strange tableaux out of clothes or maliciously destroying them. So much of what poltergeists do can be understood in symbolic terms: they sometimes target religious objects or clergymen, certain persons in the house are tormented more than others, and clothing, which could be seen as a surrogate for a living person, a symbolic "skin" of that person, is shredded in a rage.

Someone was furious. Someone was full of anger that could not be expressed except by wielding a pair of phantom scissors on the clothing of spouse, child, or sibling, symbolically murdering the family.

With our modern emphasis on communication and self-esteem, we find it hard to understand. Many families turn to their church or community; they weather crises and stresses without becoming infested with entities like IT.

But the Hoffmans' last refuge: prayer and the Bible had been turned against them. The strummed guitar of the Spiritualists was no match for the powers of Darkness. There was nothing left to take when they moved—a family torn to pieces, like their garments.

10.

Death in Black Silk
Ohio's Women in Black

She is...the mother of lunacies, and the suggestress of suicides...
And her name is *Mater Tenebrarum*—Our Lady of Darkness.

– Thomas de Quincey –

*She is darkness made visible; murder in twilight satin. Corseted to a skeleton,
she drifts like black smoke, silently, behind you. You turn. She lifts her veil....*

For several decades between 1870 and 1910, ghostly female figures in
mourning clothes and veils caused panic wherever they appeared. Like
the contagious UFO flaps of the 1960s, as soon as one town had a ghost
scare, others reported similar apparitions.

What were these veiled mysteries doing, walking the streets, gowned entirely in black? The Victorians would have instantly recognized such a woman as being in mourning for a loved one, perhaps a husband. The mourning customs of the Victorian era were well-codified. Prince Albert died 14
December 1861, plunging Queen Victoria into the deep mourning that she
wore for the rest of her life. The Queen's prolonged mourning solidified and
intensified the fashion. This led to such oddities as a widower's new bride
putting on mourning after the wedding in sympathy for the loss of his previous wife and baby clothes being threaded with black ribbons. A widow was
expected to wear dull black clothes and a mourning veil for at least a year.
Gradually she could add shiny fabrics and jet jewelry to her wardrobe, and
eventually go into "half-mourning" in purple, grey, and white fabrics. Every
gradation of mourning was described and generally the rules were strictly
followed. It was only during the First World War that the authorities, afraid
that morale would be undermined by seas of people in black, asked that full
mourning be no longer worn. Oddly, considering the consternation the image aroused, insurance companies and undertakers used the phrase "The
Woman in Black" as a euphemism for "widow" in the early 20th century.

Wearing black marked you as one touched by Death and entitled to
special consideration. Yet the same veiled figures could touch off terror in
an entire town.

Women in Black panics occurred all over the country. During a cluster of Pennsylvania incidents, the Women in Black were regarded as omens of death, either by disease or mine disaster—just at a time when there was a movement for safer working conditions in the mines. It's tempting to look for some social pressure that would conjure up these bogey-women. Women in full mourning were scarcely an unusual sight in the 1860s-1910s. Why were they so frightening to witnesses?

Certainly casting them as death omens, as in the Pennsylvania panics might explain some of the fear they aroused. Or we might speculate that something about fluttering veils and dull black cloth triggered a Grim Reaper response in viewers. There is also a long folklore tradition that widows are ill-omened creatures, as if they were infected by their husbands' deaths and could spread the contagion.

There are common motifs in the Women in Black panics: the creatures almost always appear out of doors. They move noiselessly and disappear quickly. They are often described as tall and skeletal. They are usually heavily veiled.

This is a classic Woman in Black story—she moves silently and she disappears "with a suddenness that is unpleasantly startling."

CLIFTON'S GHOST.
A WOMAN IN BLACK, WITH MUFFLED FACE
UNCANNY EXPERIENCES OF TWO BROTHERS WHILE WALKING HOME
ONE IS FOUND, SENSELESS, LYING ON THE SPIRIT'S FAVORITE WALK
WITH STARTLING SUDDENNESS SHE APPEARS WITH OUTSTRETCHED ARMS AND WAVES THEM BACK
A MYSTERY THAT PUZZLES

Clifton has a ghost.

It is not an ordinary, every-day ghost, with white robes that flutter without a breeze and the other common-place perquisites.

It does not drag chains clanking after it, nor does it make the unfortunate beholder's hair stand on end and his blood take on an Alaskan temperature with groans as if torn with all the tortures of the nether regions. Nor is midnight its chosen hour.

It is a quiet, well-behaved ghost, chainless, groanless. It assumes no tragic postures, nor does it float away and melt in the distance in an irritating manner. It simply disappears

IN THE TWINKLING OF AN EYE.

She—for it is feminine in this instance—wears a dress of the most pitchy black, a hat of the same hue, which waves a white plume, and she muffles her face beyond recognition in a black material, light yet opaque. In her wanderings not a sound does she make, but appears and disappears with a suddenness that is unpleasantly startling.

So far, her visitations have been confined to two brothers, boys of about 15 years of age, who are boarding with a gardener, or truck farmer, by the name of Tony Fisher, who lives and has his garden on the northern boundary of Clifton, between Central and Resor Avenues. After night the neighbourhood of Fisher place is about as gloomy a place as can well be found.

Adjoining Fisher's grounds are those of Gardner Tice, and between the two places and Resor Avenue is a piece of land used as a pasture. It is owned by Captain Hosea. Part of it is heavily shaded, and on three sides it is surrounded by high and thick bushes. Through it diagonally runs a path from Resor Avenue to Fisher's grounds. This is

THE GHOST'S FAVORITE WALK.

Though the first time it was seen was on Resor Avenue, some distance toward Clifton Avenue. For some reason, the ghostly visitations have been kept as quiet as possible, but their reality is attested by the two boys.

They claim that they first saw the woman in black in May last. The brothers, who work in the city and return home after dark, were, they claim, walking out Resor Avenue to take the short cut through the pasture. They were nearing the latter when, through some invisible yet powerful presence, they were compelled to stop. Startled, they looked ahead and suddenly the figure of a woman, dressed as described, appeared distinctly, every line being clearly defined. As they looked the being stretched out her arms on either side, as if to bar their way, and with an undulating movement.

SEEMED TO WARN THEM

From going further and to force them back. Her face was covered "not by a veil, but by something thicker," and her features could not be seen. The boys were startled so that they could not move at first: then they went nor stood they on the order of their going. They reached home by a roundabout way, told their story there, but did not repeat it outside.

The boys avoided using the path across the pasture for some time, but finally grew bold enough to try it again. The path runs by an old stump that stands in the center of the field. The stump is rotten, forming "foxwood" that emits a phosphorescent light. Not many days ago the boys chose different times for going home. The first reached there in safety.

After waiting for several hours for his brother to come and growing fearful that an accident had happened, he, with a son of Fisher, started to look for him. In almost the center of the lot they found

THE BOY LYING SENSELESS.

He was as one dead, and after they had carried him home they spent a long time working over him before he regained consciousness. He was unable to give much of an explanation. He had not seen the ghost, but while walking had been thrown down by a gentle but irresistible force and became unconscious. He bore no marks of violence

Shortly after the brothers had climbed the fence to the pasture on their way home and had taken a few steps, the old stump assumed an unwonted brightness and the woman suddenly appeared advancing toward them. They skedaddled.

The boys have told their story to the Marshal of Clifton, and he has determined to make a thorough investigation and catch and examine the ghost if possible. He will place some officers in ambush and then use the boys as decoys.

Cincinnati[OH] Enquirer 28 September 1889: p. 4 HAMILTON COUNTY

The next story's ghost—"Grim Death in Female Form"—has taken the shape of one of the avenging Greek furies—hair loose and streaming, wearing a long, dark robe.

JULIA, PERHAPS.
GRIM DEATH IN FEMALE FORM STRIDES ALONG BRUSH CREEK AT DEAD OF NIGHT.
IT IS ATTIRED IN SOMBER BLACK, AND HAS OFTEN BEEN SEEN OF LATE.

Peebles, Ohio, November 11. The people of Dunkinsville, a small place six miles south of here, are greatly excited over the actions of a mysterious object in the form of a woman which haunts the vicinity of the iron bridge crossing Brush Creek, and by its sudden appearance strikes terror to the hearts of the belated pedestrians who are chancing that way. The first time the apparition was seen was last Sunday night, when two young ladies and their escorts, while returning from church, were passing over the bridge, saw coming toward them a medium-sized woman robed in black.

As the mysterious being neared them the first thing that attracted the attention of the ladies was the appearance of the woman's feet, which were encased in what they though was a pair of white slippers. There was nothing especially startling in this other than the slippers were rather out of season in such cool weather. As the ghostly object glided by them, to their astonishment they saw that the woman was barefooted. As she passed they looked more closely at the slight form

IN SOMBER BLACK

With no wrap to shield her from the cool night air, her long, dark hair in disorder streaming far below her waist, and a face which bore the stamp of death and shielded by a hand which for whiteness rivaled her countenance. They were transfixed with horror as the being glided by them without a sound and passed across the bridge, and out of sight. Not one of the party had the nerve to follow and investigate, but hurriedly quit the scene. Wednesday night the mysterious object was seen by Abbott Wesley, who was returning home at a late hour, but his courage failed him and he, too, left the vicinity in haste. Other residents claim that they have seen the same thing, and the believers in the supernatural connect its appearance with the remarkable mystery which puzzled the neighborhood years ago. Old residents will remember the excitement created over the mysterious disappearance

OF JULIA EICHEL.

A young girl who was employed as a domestic in the family of Leslie Mangus, a former merchant at Dunkinsville. One wintry night, when the snow was several inches deep the young girl bade the family good-night and retired to her room. The next morning her shoes and hat were found in her room, but the girl had disappeared as mysteriously as if the earth had swallowed her up. Diligent search failed to find any trace of her, and not a single track could be found in the snow about the house. From that day to this no trace has ever been found, and the superstitious believe that it is the spirit of this girl which wanders about the spot unable to rest until her body is found. Others say the old graveyard in the vicinity has given up one of its dead, which wanders about frightening travelers. The

SAME THING WAS SEEN

A number of times by reliable persons about six years ago and excited much talk at the times, but Sunday night was the first time it has been seen lately. The story goes without comment and those who laugh at superstition may discredit, but those who saw the mysterious object are firm in their convictions that it was a supernatural being, and not the vision of an imaginative mind.

Cincinnati [OH] Enquirer 12 November 1893: p. 9 ADAMS COUNTY

Although understated, this next story is one of the most chilling of all the Ohio Women in Black tales I've found. It makes me think of Pauline Moran, the terrifying Woman in Black in the original 1989 movie of that name.

ROBED IN BLACK AND VOICELESS, APPARITION OF A WOMAN GLIDES ABOUT NOISELESSLY
IN SCHOOL BUILDING AND JANITOR LIES IN WAIT TO FELL WHAT THE SUPERSTITIOUS PEOPLE OF BRADFORD JUNCTION BELIEVE TO BE A GHOST

Special Dispatch to *The Enquirer.*

Bradford Junction, Ohio, January 4. The superstitious people of this community claim to have seen a mysterious apparition of a woman in the third room of the public school building here and they say they believe that the schoolhouse is haunted. They say that the apparition first made its appearance in the building several weeks ago. One evening while the pupils of the third room were drilling for a school entertainment a strange, pale woman, dressed in black, suddenly manifested herself in the doorway, and after remaining there a moment, disappeared without uttering a word. Nothing was thought of the matter at the time, as it was supposed that the woman was going to some other part of the building and had opened the door of the third room by mistake.

FIGURE STOOD MOTIONLESS.

A few days later Janitor W.J. Addington entered the room at dusk, to close the windows for the night and was surprised to see the black-robed figure of a woman standing motionless at the other side of the room. Supposing that she was one of the lady teachers Addington exclaimed, "Hello! You are remaining late."

At the sound of his voice the black-robed figure glided noiselessly to a door on the other side of the room and disappeared without replying. Her actions impressed the janitor as being rather strange, and he hurried across the room and into the hall, but the woman had disappeared. He next went to a window overlooking the walks leading to the street, but saw no one leave the building in that direction. The janitor searched the other rooms and the basement, but found no trace of the woman. Next day he inquired if the third-room teacher had remained after school hours, as the teachers often do, but she said she had left the building when school was dismissed for the evening.

Not long after Misses Bertha Addington and Minnie Stiles, two young women who assist the janitor to sweep the building, were badly frightened by the appearance of the woman in black in the third room while they were at work there, and they rushed into the hallway calling for the janitor. Addington searched the room and the building, but could find no trace of the woman.

AFRAID TO GO BACK.

Since then nothing can induce the two young women to enter that room after school is dismissed. A girl pupil named Gillespie was badly frightened by the apparition and others remember to have seen a black-gowned woman near the window of the room as they passed along the street.

Janitor Addington is a veteran soldier who does not believe in ghosts and will endeavor to solve the mystery by "laying" this one with a club at the first opportunity. Local Spiritualists have become interested in the case and talk of sending to Indiana for a famous medium to interview the alleged spook.

Cincinnati[OH] Enquirer 5 January 1902: p. 9 MIAMI & DARKE COUNTY

NOTE: The ghost's silent gliding movement reminds me of a famous English Woman in Black, at Cheltenham, where the ghost was seen by multiple witnesses at once, haunted the same house for an extended time period, and was even touched. An account appears in *The Cheltenham Ghost* by Bernard Abdy Collins.

Did the unfortunate Mrs. Aleshire see a vision of Death in her black-clad visitant?

SHE SAW A GHOST.
A SERIOUS ACCIDENT CAUSED BY SIGHT OF A SUPERNATURAL VISITOR

Washington C.H., O., Oct. 19 Mrs. Aleshire, a woman about 40 years old living on Washington Avenue met with an accident caused by the sight of a ghost, which almost cost her her life. The house in which the family resides has been thought to be haunted for years, and many mysterious sights have been witnessed there by persons who chanced to live in the house, a young lady having died there under strange circumstances. Mrs. Aleshire was in the act of starting downstairs into the cellar, when, just as she left the top step, a mysterious something resembling a woman dressed in black arose apparently through the cellar floor and faced the horrified woman. Mrs. Aleshire carried in her hand a kettle of boiling hot apple butter, and when she beheld the ghost she fell down the long, steep flight of stairs to the bottom, lying in this state on the floor until neighbors called in by her little daughter arrived. A physician was summoned and an investigation revealed the fact that the woman's arm was burned by the apple butter almost to the bone, some of the flesh being ready to drop off. Her leg was also broken and she is in a sorry plight. She declares that she saw a genuine ghost, and the family moved out of the haunted house.

Waterloo [IA] Daily Courier 19 October 1891: p. 2 FAYETTE COUNTY

A thread of dark, dull crepe runs through newspaper ghost stories from the 1870s through the 1910s. Let us follow where it leads: through ghost scares and Women in Black panics.

Toledo's suburb of Ironville has a ghost. It has been seen by passengers on the street car line running to Ironville. It takes the shape of a woman in black who signals the car to stop. When the conductor tries to help her aboard he grasps at her arm, and she vanishes. Ironville citizens are aroused and strict investigation will be made.

The Stark County Democrat [Canton, OH] 2 March 1893: p. 1

THE FIFTH STREET GHOST

The curiosity of the people on West Fifth Street has been aroused to a painful state by the queer actions of a woman. Those who have seen the mystery say that she is dressed entirely in black and that she wears a heavy black veil. She is said to appear every night at the corner of Clay and Fifth Street, where she will stand to a late hour, as though looking for someone. Many of the ladies in that neighborhood are afraid to leave the house after dark. There are theories out concerning her. Some think it a crazy person who is waiting on some imaginary person, others that it is someone trying to raise an excitement, while there are those who think it some wandering spirit.

Delphos [OH] Daily Herald 26 June1902: p. 8 ALLEN COUNTY

Spring Hill is reveling in the mystery of a ghost, or at least some mysterious person, who has been perambulating around at night and scaring timid persons who had heard the story. The "mystery" is said to be a woman in black and there are various vague stories afloat as to who and what it is. Last night a number of persons were out endeavoring to solve the mystery, but so far have not met with much success.

Daily Gazette [Xenia, OH] 16 September 1896: p. 3 GREENE COUNTY

The Grim Reaper comparison, which is rarely explicitly stated in these stories, is evoked in this description from Lakeview.

A STRANGE APPARITION

Bellefontaine, O., Sept. 18. A strange apparition has been terrorizing the citizens of Lakeview, and from the frequency of its appearance has become known as "The Woman in Black." She paces the street at midnight, encircled in a heavy black robe, and so folded over her head as to conceal the features.

Hamilton [OH] Daily Republican News 18 September 1899: p. 8 LOGAN COUNTY

Cumminsville was a particularly active place for the Woman in Black.

A STALKING GHOST
CUMMINSVILLIANS DISTURBED BY A MIDNIGHT APPARITION

Quite a sensation was caused on the Marietta and Cincinnati Railroad, between the Clifton crossing and the depot, last Tuesday evening, by the appearance of a mysterious figure, said, by those who have seen it, to be a woman who walks the track between the above-named points, between the hours of 12 and 1 a.m. This figure appears only at certain intervals, sometimes a year or six months elapsing between the visit, and when followed, as has often been the case, the figure leads whoever pursues along down the track until nearly to the depot, when it fades away, disappearing in the direction of Millcreek. Sometimes the alleged apparition is clothed in white, but more frequently in black.

One evening, recently, Mr. Michael Costello, night watchman at Dodsworth's distillery, who had heard of the thing being seen, but disbelieved "any such nonsense," as he called it, was at the crossing shortly after twelve o'clock, and was conversing with a friend concerning the supposed ghost, and vehemently asserted that if he ever saw it he would not hesitate to follow up the figure, and if possible, unravel the mystery.

He had hardly done speaking when his friend grasped his arm, and pointing excitedly up the track said: "There she comes now. See if you will keep your word." Costello immediately walked to the center of the track down which the figure was advancing, intending to intercept it, but was considerably surprised to find nothing but the empty air, the mysterious being having dissolved into thin air.

Whether this is an optical illusion or an unquiet ghost revisiting the glimpses of the moon is a subject that will bear investigation. The appearance of the figure on several occasions is vouched for by several citizens who would not knowingly make a false statement.

Cincinnati [OH] Enquirer 22 December 1882: p. 4 HAMILTON COUNTY

CUMMINSVILLE

Hardly a night passes but that a pilgrimage is made by some party or another to attempt to get a glimpse of the black-robed woman who walks the C.W. and B. Railroad track between the hours of twelve and one o'clock, but their efforts have thus far been unsuccessful.

Cincinnati [OH] Enquirer 27 May 1883: p. 15 HAMILTON COUNTY

NOTE: That is the Cincinnati, Washington & Baltimore Railroad.

CUMMINSVILLE GOSSIP

The mysterious woman in black has not been seen in the Presbyterian Flats for a week. It is the general belief that it is something superhuman.

Cincinnati [OH] Enquirer 2 January 1887: p. 1 HAMILTON COUNTY

NOTE: Presbyterian Flats was the area east of Hamilton Avenue and north of the railroad tracks. Just look at the dates on the last two Cumminsville WIB stories—this is a long time for people to be deluded about a real person or a hoax. Cumminsville was also the site of a haunted house. (see the appendix, "Shavings from the Coffin of News.") Periodically the newspapers would proclaim the Cumminsville mystery "solved," but for something as ephemeral as a ghost-scare, it had unusual longevity.

A lavishly described Woman in Black from Portsmouth:

A GHOST AS IS A GHOST

Chillicothe has had its gum shoe man, Scotland has had its witches, Saul started back at the miraculous wonders of spiritualism performed by the witch of Endor; Hamlet met the spectre-like vision of his dead father; Cincinnatians have flocked around their haunted maple tree; and the devil has been discovered in Eastern Tennessee, but Fourth Street, in the city of Portsmouth, Scioto County, Ohio, stands unapproachable as the ghost-haunted, spirit-possessed, wonder-stricken place of the world.

It has only been a few months ago when the window-panes of a house on West Fourth Street displayed to an awed congregation of citizens, who flocked far and near to view the wonderful phenomenon or ghostnomenom, the exact picture of a dead Magdalen. Far and near in the press was the wonderful wonder portrayed by the ready pens of the readier writers, and even in pictorial papers on this side of the Atlantic, and in the Old World, was the startling picture of the ghost of Mollie Sullivan seen looking through the laced curtains and trellised bars of a Fourth Street mansion window.

But we wander. Soon imagery would have peopled every window with spectre-like images of dead courtesans, if we were not recalled again to earth and spirits by the consideration of the thrilling story that comes to our ears from two affrighted females, one who resides in the Third and the other in the Fifth ward of the city.

Tuesday evening, when the dusky shades of night gathered around the city, and the thunder clouds darkened the darkness more darkly, two unprotected females were journeying down the north side of East Fourth Street, when a ghastly, ghostly woman, neither flesh nor fish, but of seriform substance, clad in black silk, with a long flowing train, barefooted and bareheaded, swept past them with the velocity of lightning coming from no where and returning to the same place in an incredible short space of time. Her breath was as cold as the breath of the frigid icebergs that guard the lonely stalactites of the north pole. Her eyes were like the meteors just escaped from some furnace heated as only furnaces are heated in the dominions of Satan. The rustle of her dark dress, that sent back the lightning from it, was like the whispered breathings of spirits in the novels we shrink from and yet read. Take it all in all it was the sudden apparition of death in black silk, doomed to travel on Fourth Street, barefooted and head uncovered, to make her exit from nothing and to disappear as spirits leave, and suffer nothing to linger behind it, to tell why such things are thus.

Portsmouth [OH] Times 26 April 1873: p. 2 SCIOTO COUNTY

NOTE: The really intriguing thing about this jokey, literary article is the opening list of past and contemporary spook sensations. The Gum Shoe Man haunted Chillicothe streets in October of 1872 and again in March of 1873, as in this squib from 1872:

"The gum shoe man is frightening the Chillicothe ladies. He do wear gum shoees, and when night comes on he slips noiselessly up to the lady promenaders and clutches their arms. This has been repeated so often that the Mayor has called out the militia, and if they catch 'old gum shoes,' they will make it red hot for him."

Portsmouth [OH] Times 12 October 1872: p. 3 ROSS COUNTY

Gum shoes are rubber- or crepe-soled shoes, like our sneakers. A gum-shoe man was either a detective (who needed to creep about quietly to spy on his subjects) or, originally, a thief or burglar.

Possibly the devil in Eastern Tennessee could be the Bell Witch poltergeist that supposedly terrorized the Bell family of Adams, Tennessee from 1817 through 1821. It wasn't written about until 1894, though, so there may be another case I've missed. I could not find the haunted maple tree of Cincinnati, although there was a haunted tree in Kentucky. The "dead Magdalen" was, as you read in the chapter "The Face in the Window," Mollie Sullivan/Stuart, a lady free with her favors to the paying public. "Seriform" means "shaped of silk." The Witch of Endor called up the ghost of the dead prophet Samuel for King Saul in the Old Testament. (First Samuel: 28: 3-25). The "unprotected females" on Fourth Street were prostitutes.

FEMALE GHOST CAUSES SCARE
WOMAN IN BLACK, WHO HIDES IN BARN, RUNS NIGHT RACE WITH HORSE

Springfield, O., Jan. 8 A ghost has caused terror among the negroes living on Ohio and Illinois Avenues, this city, and a number of families have sought other quarters since the scare began. It is said that one day about two weeks ago a bird resembling a bald eagle alighted on John Alexander's barn. It attracted much attention, for it sat there some time. That night near midnight a woman in black emerged from the barn and made her way down the road toward the country. In terror Alexander watched the ghostly visitor, and at last he mustered up courage to pursue her, after he had seen her for several nights. He rode his horse nearly to death for a long distance into the country, the apparition keeping just in front of him and finally disappearing. Alexander's neighbors were told and they all have kept watch. They say that each night when the woman in black is about to come out of the barn a huge arrow is silhouetted against the sky directly overhead and pointing down toward the roof.

The Evening Telegram [Elyria, OH] 8 January 1910: p. 4 CLARK COUNTY

NOTE: Ohio Avenue is very close to the current site of Clark State College— Leffel Campus. The Signs and Portents in this story are a bit quirky: A huge arrow pointing at the roof of the barn before the woman in black arrives? It's like an image from a Roadrunner cartoon, although it also reminds me of a giant pointing hand seen in the skies over Findlay in 1888. Was the big bird really an eagle (and if so, why "resembled") or a vulture, dark symbol of doom?

This is a most unusual story of the yin and yang of apparitions: The Woman in Black accompanied by a Girl in White. But were they real or phantoms? It should have been easy enough to follow them and find out where they were staying. And why would living strangers instantly be classed as "ghosts?"

IN BLACK AND WHITE
TWO MYSTERIOUS FIGURES SEEN ON THE STREETS
AT KENTON
GHOSTS EXCITING THE TOWN

Kenton, April 22. For several days past various rumors have been afloat regarding some nightly apparitions seen in the principal streets of our little city, just before the bewitching hour of midnight. The "ghosts," as they are called, have been seen by many, and described as being two women—a young girl dressed in white and an aged woman in black. They seem to have a preference for the middle of the street, walk rather slowly, with arms linked and heads bowed down.

Recently a crowd of boys tried to capture them, but when very close to the figures they disappeared with a suddenness that almost left them breathless, and they took precipitate flight in an opposite direction, losing their hats in their haste to get away. Others declare that when spoken to one of the "ghosts" replies with a strange, weird voice, unearthly in its sound, which strikes terror to the listeners, who invariably flee without ceremony. Small children are afraid to be out after dark, and larger ones, who are slightly inclined to believe that the supernatural sometimes manifests itself in such ways, are not known to delight in prolonged nocturnal rambles. However, it has created all kinds of rumors and has so far eluded detection or capture. Searching parties have been organized several nights, with a determination to capture and solve the mystery but so far their efforts have been fruitless.

Cincinnati [OH] Enquirer 23 April 1888: p. 1 HARDIN COUNTY

I finish this chapter with one of my favorite Women in Black stories, one that illustrates why she was so feared.

THE WOMAN IN BLACK

The readers of the *Journal* will remember that about six years ago, several items appeared in these columns in relation to a mysterious personage that was frequently seen at night on Chestnut Street, and known to the habitués of that neighborhood as "the Woman in Black." It was related that this mysterious female was seen flitting in and out of yards along Chestnut Street at all hours of the night, and that her ingoings and outgoings were made without reference to gates or doors, as she passed directly through fences with a facility that was both surprising and astounding. But this was not the most fearful thing incident to the situation. It was marked by divers persons that wherever the Woman in Black made her frequent ingress and egress, a death was sure to occur in the family residing there. Statements to the above effect were repeatedly made to the reporter for the *Journal* at the time, by persons whose statements on any subject would be received with credence by this community. Unbelievers in this mystery were made to acknowledge that they certainly saw—if not the Woman in Black, certainly a spirit robed in very dark clothing, and she moved through fencing with the greatest facility, as though it were a mere shadow and not substance of posts and plank.

Of course, the usual surveillance was kept up on this "apparition," with the usual results, in such cases. Parties followed the Woman in Black for a certain distance, when she suddenly vanished from sight and—well, this programme was repeated indefinitely until, at length, the Woman in Black disappeared altogether. Whether death ceased to visit that pleasant neighborhood, we have never been specially advised, but as the "grim monster" neither respects persons nor neighborhood, it is fair to infer that Chestnut Street has presented its usual bill of mortality, which—we are pleased to add—has always been very small. But, this is preliminary to an incident we were intending to relate.

About three weeks ago, a gentleman who is well known to this community, was passing along Chestnut Street near Jefferson, and, passing the house of an acquaintance, he recognized the mistress of the mansion standing at the gate, and he exchanged with her the compliments of the evening. At the same moment he observed a female, in black costume, standing immediately in the rear of his lady acquaintance, and he thought [it] strange that an introduction was not extended. While ruminating on the incident, the Woman in Black flashed across his mind. And he instinctively turned about to again look at the dark, silent figure inside the gate. To his surprise—we may say consternation—the Woman in Black was gliding along noiselessly a few paces in the rear. He halted, and the black figure came to a stand-still. Our informant repeated this proceeding several times, with the same results. Then he suddenly turned and rapidly advanced towards the Woman in Black. The apparition instantly vanished. Growing a little nervous at this demonstration, our informant determined to test the matter still further, and shortly afterwards he repeated his walk along Chestnut Street, and he was again confronted with the Woman in Black, who was standing in the same place he first saw her, half an hour before, but she was alone, the lady of the house having retired indoors. As our informant passed the gate, the Woman in Black glided through the fence and proceeded after him. He halted half a dozen times and the apparition did likewise. He at first tried to account for the incident supposing that it was caused by the shadow of the gaslight at the corner. But there was no person in range to make the shadow, and it could not have been produced so distinctly under any circumstances. Full of conflicting emotions, our informant made his way home, and it was several days before he could shake off the bad effects of the incident. The denouement is the saddest feature of the incident. A few days after the appearance of the Woman in Black on Chestnut Street, death visited the premises where she was seen, and bore away one of its most lovely inmates.

If our informant was not a gentleman of excellent character, and entirely trustworthy, we would not trifle with the feelings of our readers by the recital of this most singular incident.

Dayton [OH] Daily Journal 11 October 1870: p. 3 MONTGOMERY COUNTY

A drift of smoke, a shiver of silk, a veil of cold crepe drawn across your face. The Woman in Black will be gone by the time you turn.

11.

The Horrors

Vampires, Madness, and a Haunted Morgue

There are horrors beyond life's edge that we do not suspect, and
once in a while man's evil prying calls them just within our range.

– H.P. Lovecraft –

When I started this book, I had a cozy vision of a Victorian Papa
reading the newspaper aloud to the family around a parlor table in a
pool of lamp light. That vision has been dispelled by articles like the bone-
chilling ones found in this chapter.

The following is a true story collected by Rich Wallace of the Shelby
County Historical Society. "It happened in Cynthian Township near the
Miami-Erie Canal in the fall of 1880. This eyewitness account appeared in
the *Sidney Journal* in December of 1897:"

"Winter set in very early that year, and it was extraordinarily cold.
By late fall, they were cutting ice two feet thick on the canal, and storing
it in the great ice houses which then lined the banks. A certain man had
died, when the weather was at its coldest, and I was one of the three men
chosen to keep the night watch.

The body was laid out in the parlor of the home on an old-fashioned
bier, which was too short, as he was a very tall man, and was covered
with a black pall, which hung down over the feet. There was no fire in
the room, and the window was opened about two inches, with the result
that the corpse was frozen as hard as marble. Notwithstanding this, the
undertaker left a jar of some embalming fluid, with which the body was
to be covered every two or three hours. We three sat in another room,
and punctually at the proper hours performed this gruesome function,
whiling away the rest of the time as best we might.

Just as the clock struck midnight we heard one of the women come
downstairs to prepare some coffee and food for us, and I suggested that
before we partook of it we should attend to the body again. We crossed
the wide hall, the wind moaning in gusts around the house, and the
freezing atmosphere already chilling our blood, and entered the parlor.

I went in first, the candle in my hand. I had taken two or three steps when I stopped, simply appalled. One leg of the frozen corpse was rising and falling beneath the pall, silently, but unmistakably, as though kicking in convulsive agony. Peterman, a powerful young German, who was next to me, caught sight of it the next moment, and, throwing his hands, with a cry of *"My God!"* fell fainting to the floor.

How long I stood gazing at the ghastly movement I do not know. The hot tallow fell unheeded from my hand, until it formed a little mound. At length I was aroused by Peterman coming to his senses, and commencing to vomit terribly. This changed the current of my thoughts, and I ran out for a basin. Before I could return he saw the leg move again, and fell in another swoon. Finding him thus, my fear suddenly left me, and I was determined to solve the mystery. I walked to the bier and pulled back the pall.

I found there a lean and savage black cat, gnawing at one of the frozen legs, and the arching of whose back, in the effort to tear the flesh, had caused the horrible appearance. Though I knocked it away and kicked it, the brute, with eyes glowing like coals, sprang back each time to its awful meal and I dared not touch it with my hands for fear a bite or scratch from those tainted fangs and claws should cause blood poisoning. It was literally mad with hunger. At length I fetched a long, heavy bootjack, and beat it over the head with that until it lay still, when I threw it out of doors. The only way it could have gotten in was through the window, but how it squeezed through such a narrow aperture is a mystery. Peterman was sick in bed for months after the shock, while as for our third companion, he ran at Peterman's first scream and did not appear at all."

Sidney [OH] Journal December 1897 [Thanks to Rich Wallace of the Shelby County Historical Society for this chilling account. www.shelbycountyhistory.org/schs/archives/events/horroreventa.htm] SHELBY COUNTY

NOTE: Traditionally, corpses were not left alone; someone always sat up with the body. There were some folklore traditions that said if a cat jumped over a corpse the dead person would become a vampire.

Vampires were also believed to be behind the dreaded lung disease consumption, now known as tuberculosis. There was no cure until the advent of antibiotics, but families often tried a dreadful, desperate remedy as seen in this story.

A STRANGE SUPERSTITION

The family of Philip Salladay came from Switzerland, bought and settled on a lot in the French Grant soon after the opening of the country for settlement. Hereditary consumption developed itself in the family sometime after their location in Scioto County. The head of the family and the oldest son [Samuel] had died of it, and others began to manifest symptoms, when an attempt was made to arrest the progress of the disease by a process which has been practiced in numerous instances, but without success.

Then the surviving members of the family resolved to resort to the strange "cure," to disinter one of the victims, disembowel him and burn his entrails in a fire prepared for the purpose, in the presence of the survivors. This was accordingly done in the winter of 1816-17, in the presence not only of the living members of the Salladay family but of many spectators who lived in the neighborhood. Maj. Amos Wheeler, of Wheelersburg, was employed to disembowel the sacrificial victim (Samuel Salladay) and commit his entrails to the flames. [Another account says that Major Wheeler cut Samuel open and took out his heart, liver and lungs.]

But like other superstitious notions with regard to curing diseases, it proved of no avail. The other members of the family continued to die off until the last one was gone, except George.

SOURCES: *Historical Collections of Ohio In Two Volumes*, Vol. II, Henry Howe, (Cincinnati, OH: C.J. Krehbiel, 1902) p. 568 SCIOTO COUNTY
A Standard History of the Hanging Rock Iron Region of Ohio: an Authentic Narrative of the Past, with an Extended Survey of the Industrial and Commercial Development, Volume 1, edited by Eugene B. Willard, Daniel Webster Williams, George Ott Newman, Charles Boardman Taylor (The Lewis Publishing Company, 1916) pp. 44 & 71-72 SCIOTO COUNTY

This is the first time I have seen this practice mentioned in Ohio, although it was well-known in New England, particularly in Rhode Island. In New England, consumption, which was then almost invariably a killer, was called the "White Death" and victims were believed to come back as vampires to feed on the remaining family members. The only "remedy" was to dig up the dead person, take out his or her heart and burn it, and feed the ashes to the sick. In the Salladay's case, the remaining relatives did not ingest the ashes. It seems to pile horror on horror to first disinter the decaying body of a loved one, go through the entire vile ritual, only to see more loved ones sicken, wither, and die.

You can find more information about this practice in *Food for the Dead: On the Trail of New England's Vampires*, Michael E. Bell. I report several stories about New England's vampires in *The Ghost Wore Black: Ghastly Tales from the Past*.

The Victorians were obsessed with a fear of being buried alive. Many devices were invented to prevent this such as bells attached to the hands of the dead and electronic devices that, if the body stirred, would open speaking and breathing tubes into the grave. Some people left instructions for the undertaker to cut their throats to make sure they were dead because they would rather die on the embalming slab than be buried alive. When the Civil War made embalming, which required draining the blood, universal, the Victorians breathed easier that they could rest in peace.

BURIED ALIVE.

The Cleveland "Plaindealer" tells the following strange incidents as having occurred in southern Ohio: "An old gentleman, named Delos Winans, became frantically angry with his son because he had lost a large sum of his father's money on a bet. His frenzied feelings soon got the better of him, and he immediately thereafter fell down in a senseless condition. Great excitement in the family ensued. The mother ran screaming for assistance, which was soon forthcoming in the persons of several neighbors.

Mr Winans was found in an apparently lifeless condition, with blood flowing from his nose and mouth. A subsequent examination by a physician led to the announcement by him that Mr Winan had died from the bursting of a blood vessel. So evidently had the vital spark fled that no effort at resuscitation was made, and the remains were prepared for burial as promptly as possible.

The funeral of the deceased took place the following Wednesday. Mr Winan's body had only been coffined the previous day, up to which time it had lain draped in a shroud in the parlor. Notwithstanding the wonderful life-like look of the skin, and the color of the face, it occurred to no one to suggest a postponement until death was absolutely certain. The funeral was largely attended, and everybody remarked the life-like appearance of the deceased. The 'remains' were temporarily placed in one of the vaults of the cemetery, owing to the fact that a brick tomb commenced for their reception had not been completed.

At ten o'clock on Thursday night the village was thrown into great excitement by the report that a ghost had been seen in the cemetery a short time before, and that the old lady who first saw it was frightened into a fit, from which it was doubtful she would recover. Thinking that probably the ghost was personated by some scoundrel, who had played the trick several times before, a number of persons armed themselves with shot guns, proceeded to the cemetery and commenced a cautious inspection—their hearts thumping in their bosoms in spite of their assumed bravado.

They had not long to wait, for there, flitting among the tombs, was a white object plainly to be seen. With trembling hands they raised their guns and fired, when—strange fact for a ghost—they saw the white creature fall between a couple of graves. Picking up courage, they cautiously approached the object and turned a lantern upon it. Their feelings can be better imagined than described when they found that the ghost was the lately deceased Mr Winan. While a portion of the party picked up the bleeding and senseless body of the old gentleman, and started homeward with it, the remainder hastened to the vault.

There they found Mr Winan's coffin broken open, and lying upon the floor, and the coffin of a deceased lady, that had been placed upon it, likewise thrown down from the shelf, and standing on end, also partly broken open, displaying its ghostly inmate. The vault door which was rather a weak affair, had been forced open by the resurrected man. The party then went to Mr Winan's house, and here they found that his wounds were not serious and that he had recovered his senses. He had been carried to the cemetery in a trance. Early on Thursday evening consciousness flashed upon his mind that he was coffined alive. This lent additional strength to his struggle to get free, and he finally succeeded in bursting open the coffin.

North Otago [NZ] Times 27 March 1868: p. 4 UNKNOWN, Possibly GREENE COUNTY

NOTE: See Jan Bondeson's 2002 book, *Buried Alive: The Terrifying History of Our Most Primal Fear* and *The Lazarus Syndrome*, by Rodney Davies.

FROM THE GRAVE CAME A VOICE, AND NOW IT IS BELIEVED THAT SOWERS WAS BURIED ALIVE.

Circleville, Ohio, June 29. The little village of Tarlton is agitated because of the strong presumption that Sebastian Sowers, one of its oldest citizens, was buried alive. Sowers was a veteran soldier and a subject of catalepsy. About 9 o'clock one Saturday evening two month ago he dropped dead, apparently, in the street, and his body was interred in a shallow grave in the village graveyard the following day. The same evening a belated villager returning to his home through the graveyard was startled by cries of distress proceeding from the new made grave. Without stopping to investigate he rushed into the village and gave the alarm, but everyone treated his story with incredulity and laughed at his so-called cowardice. Later developments have confirmed the villager's gruesome story, and if the consent of the relatives of the deceased can be obtained the body will be exhumed and the facts brought to light. It is not improbable that Sowers was in a cataleptic sleep—a supposition to which the lifelike appearance of the corpse before burial gives color.

Cincinnati [OH] Enquirer 30 June 1896: p. 4 PICKAWAY COUNTY

Stories involving dynamite fatalities are startlingly common. The explosive seems to have been treated rather casually, as just another handy household product for use around the farm. One man memorably stored several sticks in his stove and, forgetting about it, lit the stove....

IN THE BUCKEYE STATE
FARMER'S SUICIDE
HE TOOK A QUANTITY OF DYNAMITE TO A FIELD
AND BLEW HIMSELF TO ATOMS.

Payne, O., March 23 Samuel Haggerty, a prosperous and wealthy farmer living three miles south of town, committed suicide in a most shocking manner Friday. He took a quantity of dynamite and went to the field, announcing his intention to blast stumps. Later a violent explosion alarmed the neighbors and on investigation they found a few scattered remnants of the despondent man. Esquire Rubin was called and held an inquest which established the fact that the deceased had placed several pounds of the explosive in a large stump, sat thereon and deliberately lighted the fuse. Despondency over the loss of his wife is thought to be the cause.

Spirit of Democracy [Woodsfield, OH] 28 March 1901 PAULDING COUNTY

BLOWN TO PIECES ABOVE THE EARTH
AERONAUT WHOSE "ACT" CONSISTED IN PART OF
EXPLODING BOMBS IN MIDAIR
THE VICTIM OF FATAL ACCIDENT
BLOOD AND PIECES OF BODY RAINED UPON
SPECTATORS.

Greenville, Ohio, Sept. 1 Thirty thousand people yesterday saw Professor John L. Baldwin, aeronaut, blown to pieces by dynamite in a balloon 6,000 feet above the earth. Blood, particles of bone and pieces of flesh rained down upon the faces of the spectators bearing the first gruesome news of the aeronaut's fate. This man's wife and three children were among the spectators.

Less than ten minutes before he met his terrible fate Baldwin had taken his wife and little ones into his arms and kissed them good bye. As the balloon was liberated and he shot gracefully up into the air he tossed kisses to the multitude. No one realized that it might be a farewell, but thought it was only a part of the show.

In addition to making his ascension and parachute jump Baldwin's act included the liberating of a number of small parachutes and the explosion of dynamite bombs while suspended in mid air. He had reached a height where the big balloon as large as a barn on the ground seemed hardly larger than a barrel. He started the parachutes on their flight to the ground and then made preparation for the explosion of the dynamite bombs, nine in number.

Only something went horribly wrong:

It is supposed that he was rattled, having exhibited a nervousness, prior to his ascension, and failed to drop the bomb in time. A loud explosion was heard in midair and the balloon was lost to sight in a cloud of smoke. When it cleared away the balloon and a portion of the parachute were visible, but the balloonist was missing.

A thrill of horror spread through the crowd, and then came a sight that turned men faint and caused women to collapse.

As if a blood rain were falling, particles of bone and flesh came raining down upon the thousands of upturned faces. Like a flash the truth was known throughout the vast crowd and there was a hurried stampede for the place where the balloon was slowly falling to the earth. Not a sign of the hapless aeronaut was found, but a portion of the parachute was torn away. Small fragments of the body were gathered over an area of several acres and taken in charge by Undertaker Turpen, and will be sent to his home in Logansville, Ind., for burial.

The wife and children watched the ascension and saw the husband and father blown to atoms. It was his 1201st ascension.

Sandusky [OH] Star Journal 1 September 1905: p. 1

Harrisonburg [VA] Daily News 2 September 1905: p. 1 DARKE COUNTY

A truly gruesome little note comes from Ironton:

A cask containing mutilated remains of a human, was found floating in the Ohio river at Ironton, and some of the Irontonian wine-guzzlers, seeing the reddened water oozing from the bung-hole, thinking it was wine, drank it. How their stomachs felt after opening the barrel can be better imagine than described.

Portsmouth [OH] Times 27 December 1873: p. 2 LAWRENCE COUNTY

NOTE: To be fair, there was a bitter rivalry between Ironton and Portsmouth. This squib may reflect the communities' sniping. I fervently hope this is an apocryphal tale.

Words fail me...

LIKE FALLING ON A SWORD.
ONLY IN PLACE OF THE SWORD WAS
A RED-HOT POKER
SUICIDE OF A CRAZY GERMAN

Columbus, O., Feb. 26 Means of suicide are without number but it was left to Conrad Zapp, a demented German, living at No. 595 Krouse Avenue, this city, to contrive one of the most extraordinary methods of self-destruction ever heard of.

He left the city Friday afternoon and in his aimless wanderings reached Groveport, a village about nine miles southwest of Columbus. There he was taken into custody by Marshall Thompson and placed in the lock-up.

He had access to the hot stove and during the night he heated the poker red-hot, placed the hand end against the wall and threw himself against the point. The terrible instrument of death ploughed its way into the abdomen, searing the parts entered.

Trenton [NJ] Times 26 February 1893: p. 8 FRANKLIN COUNTY

Big snake stories were part of the standard sensational repertoire of the papers. Fields, barns, and grain bins were teeming with vermin and habitats had not been overrun by humans so the reptiles were able to grow to some epic lengths.

SNAKES!
A STRANGE REPTILE CAPTURED BY JOHN FISHER
HIS FIGHT WITH THE MONSTER.

Saturday afternoon, as John Fisher and Frank Lamont, who drive a huckster wagon from this city, were returning from Gomer, the team which they were driving came to a sudden stop about a mile this side of Gomer and all persuasion on the part of the driver to start the team was in vain. Finally Fisher got out, thinking that something was wrong about the bridles...when he stepped on a large snake which was laying in the middle of the road directly in front of the horses. Lamont, seeing the danger in which his partner was in, sprang from the seat and picked up a fence rail for the purpose of dispatching the monster. Fisher was not much excited, and, as the reptile did not seem in any haste to make away, procured a long willow stick with a V shaped prong on the end for the purpose of capturing the strange intruder. It was Fisher's intention to catch the reptile just behind the head with the prong, load it into one of the egg cases and bring it to this city alive, as it was different from any of the snakes which live in this part of the country.

The reptile in the meantime was lying quietly in the dust, and was evidently stupefied from some cause, and Fisher did not have any difficulty in catching it as he desired. After he had the prong fastened securely about the head he proceeded to raise its body up at the same time catching hold of its tail with his other hand to make a less strain on the forks. He succeeded in raising it up about a foot from the ground when one of the prongs broke.

The reptile sprang at Fisher and caught him on the fore finger of the left hand at the middle joint, making a small wound, and struck out immediately for the deep grass by the roadside. When Fisher was bit it angered him and when he saw the snake making its escape he gave chase and catching the snake with both hands carried it to the wagon, a short distance away, and dumped his freight into an egg box. After he had picked the reptile up it bit him on the right hand and tore the lining of his coat in several places. After fastening the snake in the box it was brought it to this city without any difficulty.

The snake when measured was found to be seven feet and five inches in length and not less than a foot in circumference. It is of a dark, nearly black color, and when seen in the box was covered with small light gray spots. In its head is a hooked shaped tooth in the upper jaw. This tooth or tusk is about an inch long and is hid from view, except when its mouth is opened. Fisher says that when it is lying stretched out these spots appear in the shape of diamonds about an inch and a half long and half an inch wide in a row on each side of the body.

Fisher has the snake at his home on the south east corner of Market and Tanner Street where it can be seen.

Although he was bit in two places by the reptile the wounds have not swollen and he experiences no pain. Fisher will send the snake to the Zoological Gardens at Cincinnati in a few days.

Lima [OH] Daily Democratic Times 31 August 1885 ALLEN COUNTY

Seven feet was a mere babe compared to the following creature:

> In this swail, about the year 1841, was captured the monster snake
> of the county. A hunter wading in grass almost to his head, just high
> enough above the wavy surface to fire deadly shot at ducks chased from
> their secluded retreats, heard a surging noises at some distance in his
> path. His eyes met those of a mortal enemy. The snake's forked tongue
> vibrated angrily in a frightful mouth raised above the grass. The barrel
> of the hunter's faithful gun soon contained a heavy charge of buck shot.
> Having taken careful aim he fired, dispatching two balls to the centre
> of the monster's head, and a third knocking out one eye. The writhing
> squirm and roll of death followed.
>
> The snake measured eighteen feet eleven and one half inches long and
> three feet nine inches and a quarter at the "belt." Careful examination
> showed him to be thirty-three years old. The neighborhood was of course
> somewhat aroused, and a congregation of men around the dead body
> determined upon a dissection. It was a happy thought, for within that
> serpent's skin was contained a part of a human skeleton and a small packet
> containing needles, buttons, and other notions. It will be seen by reference
> to the chapter on Woodville that a peddler was once mysteriously missing
> from the hotel at that village... this story cleared the atmosphere of scandal
> by making known the last chapter of the life of the Woodville peddler.
> The snake also contained half a bushel of bogus coins and a machine for
> making them. It further contained the pocketbook of a man from the
> East who had come to the township to buy land, and whose boots the next
> morning were found hanging on a tree.
>
> *History of Sandusky County, Ohio: With Portraits and Biographies of Prominent
> Citizens and Pioneers*, Homer Everett, (Cleveland, OH: H.Z. Williams and
> Bro., 1882) p. 808 SANDUSKY COUNTY

NOTE: For more information on big snakes see *Boss Snakes*, Chad Arment.

This next story is just one of several strange tales I've found that blend what is
framed as a true encounter with a ghost or malevolent entity with Theosophy
or some other occult philosophy. It is an unsettling combination.

DOOM OF A HUMAN VAMPIRE

There are questions which all our philosophy is not able to solve,
and mysteries in our every-day life which human reason cannot fathom.
Whoever reads the following story will be convinced of the truth of this

assertion. Between Xenia and Yellow Springs, Ohio, there is, or was, at least some twenty years ago, a small collection of rude cottages and dilapidated tenements, which has, from time immemorial, received the designation of Old Town. This is the exact place where Daniel Boone, on the occasion of his famous traverse of the Northern States, was imprisoned by the Indians. Just before dusk of an autumn day, some twenty years ago, William Wilson, lately Postmaster of Yellow Springs, was passing through this little settlement on his return from Xenia. He had just reached a lonely place in the northern outskirts of the village, when his horse suddenly paused in the center of the road, with extended nostrils, leering ears, and otherwise exhibiting notable signs of terror. Mr. Wilson, who had been carelessly jogging along, leaving the animal to itself, raised his eyes. He saw in the path before him a fearful-looking object, with a form like that of a man. Its arms and feet were marked, and the nails upon them were very long and uncouth, and appeared to be stained with blood. His beard reached far down upon his breast, and was, in places, extremely white, but in others it appeared clotted with blood.

The first impression of Mr. Wilson was that this repulsive-looking object was a hunter of the vicinity, who had decked himself out in this fantastic fashion for the purpose of giving him a fright. Accordingly, he motioned the intruder sternly out of his path. The figure did not move. A convulsive uplifting of the hands, a slight rolling of the eyes, was all the evidence given to life.

The rider then attempted to incite his horse to ride over the figure. This failing, he endeavored to rein his horse out of the road, and pass one side of the strange being, but in this he also failed. The animal only snorted and reared, while its fright was evidently increasing from moment to moment.

Mr. Wilson was one of those stern and implacable sort of men who waste no words when their anger is aroused. Without uttering a single remark therefore, he quietly slid from the back of the horse, threw the bridle over his arm, drew his "bowie" from his pocket, advanced to the side of the figure, and aimed a furious blow at its breast. The blow was evaded, not convulsively, as if by a man, but by the gradual withdrawing of the body, as if by some invisible power, and with an unfailing ease.

Again and again did Mr. Wilson endeavor to bury the weapon in the form before him, but in vain. The sweat came out on his forehead as he saw with what ease the figure withdrew itself, waving here and there, as if keeping time to his blows, rather than seeming desirous of escaping a deadly thrust aimed at its life. At last, however, he arrived at a position abreast of it, and the horse suddenly leaped past it, endeavoring to break away. Mr. Wilson restrained the animal's impatience long enough to spring upon his back and dashed furiously away in the direction of his dwelling. The figure made no effort to precede him, but kept exactly abreast of his horse's shoulders. It did not appear to make any effort. Mr. Wilson...has no recollection of seeing its feet or arms in motion, and is inclined to think that it moved without giving any of the motions which would be exhibited by a man running.

The horse did not slacken his furious gait, nor did the rider attempt to check him until the three intervening miles were passed. Arriving at the door of his stable, just back of his house, in the southern outskirts of Yellow Springs, the animal came to a halt while his rider slid to the ground. The mysterious object at the same time, placed itself in the stable door.

Furious with rage, Mr. Wilson again drew his knife and struck at the figure. The same evasive movement was made, and the horse, at the same instant, sprang past it into the stable. Mr. Wilson then replaced his knife, half resolving to leave the mysterious object to itself, and began to occupy himself with unsaddling and feeding the terrified beast. A few moments were consumed in this labor, during which time the figure remained standing in the doorway, and then Mr. Wilson darted out of the stable, employing all of his agility to close the entrance ere the figure could follow.

Circumstance, still stranger than any of those which had preceded! The frightful form appeared on the outside of the door, he knew not how, gradually taking the same horrible semblance it had before possessed! Again drawing his knife, Mr. Wilson advanced toward the figure, manifesting in his glaring eyes and rigid features the fiercest anger. The strange object quietly retreated before him, keeping its face toward his own, its hollow and sepulchral eyes steadily fixed upon him, and managing without any visible exertion, to evade his furious blows.

In this way Mr. Wilson pursued the figure to the house, through the woodshed, around the barn, around the well, and, finally, time after time, around the house. Tired with his repeated and long continued exertions, Mr. Wilson paused, holding his weapon guardedly before him, and scrutinizing the figure from head to foot. It seemed to grow more and more horrible to his sight. The clotted gore upon its beard appeared to become a bright red, and its long nails seemed dripping blood! More than all, an awful expression of agony was now visible upon its ghastly features.

"Man, spirit, or devil!" cried Mr. Wilson, for the first time finding his voice; "who and what are you? Why are you here, and what do you want with me?" The very moment Mr. Wilson's voice rang out upon the air, the figure appeared convulsed with joy, uplifting its hands in prayerful attitude, and raising its eyes toward heaven.

A spell appeared to be removed from its faculties by those intonations of the human voice, for it instantly spoke: "My friend," it said, "have pity upon me, and listen! I am a spirit who was once mortal like thee...I lived upon this earth about four thousand years ago." Here a groan interrupted the voice of the mysterious being, and it wrung its hands in evident agony of thought. Mr. Wilson was too much surprised to utter a word. Thoroughly beside himself with astonishment and dread, he waited for the continuation of the revelation, which soon came, in these words: "I was passionate and obstinate, from my earliest youth, neither fearing God nor regarding man. At the early age of fourteen I was guilty of an enormity, forbidden by all the patriarchs and prophets: I commenced eating blood!"

The clotted gore upon his head appeared to glow with a redder hue as the words were uttered: "I at first killed animals, solely for their blood, sucking the vital tide from their veins! Erelong, I acquired such a perverted taste that I relished nothing but blood-warm, reeking blood! Still another long interval of self-degradation, and I found that the blood of animals was no longer sufficient for my taste. I wrestled, for a season, with this terrible craving, but it finally conquered. My own child was the first victim—then my wife—then my friends—then anyone I could murder unawares. For years lasted this awful course of iniquity, but I was finally detected, summarily tried, and as summarily put to death.

"I awoke to another state of being—but that terrible craving still remained! I became conscious of the fact, and then I knew what it was to be in hell! O, the agony I suffered! Think not that it was beyond my power to do any further evil—that I was debarred from sin. I tell you that I had the same power of slaughtering my fellows, of being the same vampire at their mangled throats! O, how my demoniacal capabilities were increased! How rapidly I progressed in the downward change from man to beast! I could see, by the reflection of my features, that they were becoming the features of a beast of prey!

"At last, in an hour whose misery and infamy can never be revealed, there came an angel to me, and said: 'You once had a soul. It was a temple up to which nature itself had struggled, and in which reason was placed as the keeper. But, instead of advancing, you began, since you could not remain stationary, to go back to the nothingness from which the spirit of man had slowly and painfully struggled. The beast had become man. With you it seemed fatality that man should become beast. Listen, therefore, to your doom. A soul once consciously existent, can be annihilated by a repeated and continual violation of its inborn sense of right.

Insanity, imbecility, idiocy, bestiality, and then an unconscious being during thousands of years, the whole dark chapter to be eventually closed by the total destruction of all your faculties and powers. The world has only to look at the features of a collection of hardened criminals in a prison to see that they have gone back one or several degrees toward the brute. The same destroying influences have only to be continued a sufficient time—you understand. O most unfortunate spirit, and behold what is your fate!'

"Such were the words of the angel. They were, in Divine mercy, sufficient to break the spell which had so long and terribly bound me. I formed a resolution to arise to my original estate, and I have never faltered a moment in this resolve, whatever the trials and temptations I have undergone. I received permission to travel to distant planets; I visited many millions of worlds. An hour is all I can remain on any one planet, and I can never visit it but once. Already I experience such a fact and such a sensation as you would experience in entering the water—I am lifted up, borne aloft, taken from my feet! I go, but know, O mortal, that from the point where we are placed in existence, as mortals, we can advance to the condition of gods or return to the level of the brutes."

The next moment Mr. Wilson was alone. He has never pretended to give any explanation of the facts here recorded, nor does the writer. I can only repeat what I said before, that there are facts, actual facts, in our every-day life which are beyond our wisdom and superior to our science.
Cincinnati [OH] Enquirer 22 March 1879: p. 10 GREENE COUNTY

NOTE: A man named William Wilson lived in Greene County in the 1870s, but was not the Postmaster of Yellow Springs. Although *Dracula*, by Bram Stoker, was not published until 1897, people of the time would have been familiar with the concept of vampires. Articles on Eastern European vampires were seen in the papers. See, for example, "A Flesh-Creeping Narrative of Vampirism in Hungary" in an 1870 *Cincinnati Enquirer*. There seems to be a Theosophical underpinning to this article: eating animal blood/flesh maddens; astral travel; a striving for enlightenment and to rise above our base animal nature. A tall tale, but with some ripping yarn moments.

Religious insanity was a popular theme. Newspapers particularly liked to report on Spiritualists who went mad.

SACRIFICE OF A MEDIUM

A man whose name is Samuel Cole, residing in Washington County, Ohio, who was made insane by the workings of the spirit-rapping delusion, became possessed of the idea that he must offer, like Abraham of old, a sacrifice to the Supreme Ruler of the Universe. He accordingly proceeded to carry his object into execution, by taking off one of his feet, which he succeeded in doing some days since, in a very scientific manner, and with a heroic determination that would compare with the self-sacrificing deeds done in earlier ages. His family fearing that some other of his limbs might be demanded in a like cause, had him conveyed to the Lunatic Asylum at Columbus, where he is now in the enjoyment of as much liberty as the nature of his disease will warrant the superintendent of that institution in granting him.

Adams Sentinel, [Gettysburg, PA] 14 March, 1853: p. 5 WASHINGTON COUNTY

NOTE: Abraham was told to sacrifice his beloved son Isaac in Genesis 22: 1-19.

The phrase "met an unnatural death" was commonplace in the papers. The advances in medical technology and health we take for granted did not exist. There were no x-ray machines, no antibiotics. If an elderly person fell and broke a hip, he or she would usually die of pneumonia within a relatively short time. The county death records are full of causes of death easily preventable today, but death sentences then: diphtheria, cholera, smallpox, typhoid, measles. The list of deaths was long and appalling: eaten by hogs, fell into a tub of boiling lye, bit by a mad dog, burned by an exploding lamp (an ever-present danger with coal-oil lamps), took Rough on Rats (an arsenic-based rat poison).

In the nineteenth century, suicide was often regarded both morally and legally as a crime. Newspapers were often brutally frank about suicides :

MADE TORCH OF HIS BODY.
HORRIBLE DEED OF AN INSANE MAN WHO ATTEMPTED SUICIDE BY BURNING HIMSELF OVER LOSS OF MONEY IN POKER GAME

Brooding over the loss of his savings in a poker game, Frank Frei, aged fifty-one, a tailor who has a little shop on the first floor to the tenement house at 1414 Clay Street, Cincinnati, O., went mad and in his insane frenzy attempted to end his life in a horrifying manner.

After stabbing himself furiously with a pair of tailor's shears until the upper part of his body was a mass of bleeding wounds the demented man poured gasoline over his naked body and over the furniture in his two rooms and set himself and the house on fire. With his body a human torch,

Frei defied the neighbors and the firemen who were called to extinguish the fire, barricaded himself in his room, and, with the flames circling about him, danced and howled like a demon. He was finally conquered by streams of water thrown on him and beaten into submission with an ax handle.

Frei was taken to the City hospital, where it was stated his death was expected. The firemen succeeded in putting out the fire, which threatened the tenement house and had caused a panic among the tenants.

The Mansfield [OH] News 8 August 1908: p. 11 HAMILTON COUNTY

NOTE: This is actually a subtle and restrained account of this horrific event. The *Cincinnati Enquirer* article on Frei was one of the most gruesome pieces I've read in a period newspaper.

Let us finish this catalog of Victorian horrors with a story from a county morgue.

RESTLESS CORPSES
GHOSTLY STORIES ABOUT THE COUNTY MORGUE
THE CLAMMY HAND THAT STRUCK A POLICEMAN
WEIRD ADVENTURE WITH THE DEAD ROOM DOOR
HOW A WATCHMAN LOCKED IN THE STIFFS
THREE UNCANNY TALES

The ghostly stories that originate in the County Morgue would fill a monstrous volume. A place so full of the spectacle of death, so impregnated with the peculiar smell and "feel" that arises from the constant proximity of deceased humanity could not fail to produce many weird and startling tales.

Superintendent Shaw had an experience not long ago that hastened the approach of gray in his hair. He was sitting alone in his office at a late hour. Three corpses lay in the crates in the inner room, and the constant "drip, drip"

OF BLOODY WATER

As it fell from the slabs into the buckets below, was the only sound to be heard. The door was slightly ajar.

The Superintendent was dozing when the door leading to the death room closed with a sharp click. Mr. Shaw was somewhat startled, but he opened the door a few inches and sat down again. After a few minutes the door again shut with a bang. The Superintendent, who is afraid of neither ghosts nor human beings, took up a lamp and entered the inner room.

There was nothing wrong apparently. The three lifeless forms lay in their boxes dimly outlined under the sheets that covered them. No sign of life was about. But while Mr. Shaw stood gazing about, the door again swung slowly around and closed with the familiar click, leaving the Superintendent imprisoned with the dead. The thing was inexplicable. Mr. Shaw

EXAMINED THE LOCK

And the hinges of the door, without arriving at a solution of the mystery, and then retired to his office, closing the door after him. The incident has never been repeated.

A few evenings since a patrol dashed into the alley in the rear of the Morgue, and soon two stalwart policemen walked into the dead room, carrying a corpse on a stretcher between them.

The man had died in agony, and his arms were bent convulsively at the elbows, so that the hands almost touched the shoulders. Superintendent Shaw straightened out the arms with much difficulty and then went to another part of the room.

At this juncture one of the policemen bent over the body to see whether he could recognize the man. Suddenly he gave a yell as one clumsy hand of the corpse raised and brushed against his own fingers. A moment later he jumped back thoroughly terrified as the other hand of the "stiff" flapped up and

DEALT HIM A BLOW

On the face with its icy fingers.

The Superintendent laughed loud and long at the agitated copper. The explanation was simple. The arms of the corpse had stiffened in a bent condition and when Mr. Shaw straightened them out they resumed their original position with such force as to deal the blue-coated officer a smart slap in the face.

There are always unexplainable noises about an old or unused house, and it is so with the Morgue. One watchman had an uncanny experience recently, and now he is no longer an attendant at the house of death.

It was long after midnight and the watchman was sleeping on a cot in the office with the light turned down. A dull sound as of some object falling in the inner room awoke him thoroughly. Taking a light he walked

INTO THE DEAD ROOM.

And examined the bodies lying there, one of which was that of a suicide.

He had hardly returned to the office when the sound of steps, so the watchman afterward declared, came from within, followed by a peculiar wailing sound, such as is sometimes produced by a hard, wintry wind. Yet the air outside was still, as the watchman observed when he opened the outer door (in order to have a way to escape), and there were no cats or rats in the solid brick building to explain the peculiar sounds within.

Slipping over to the inner door, as if the ghosts would hear him, the watchman turned the lock, and then sitting down on the stone step of the entrance, he waited until morning before entering the dead room. There all was quiet and nothing had been disturbed.

Cincinnati [OH] Enquirer 29 March 1891: p. 17 HAMILTON COUNTY

12.

The Babe in the River
The Ghosts of Murder

There's the scarlet thread of murder
running through the colourless skein of life.

– Sir Arthur Conan Doyle –

To judge by the newspapers, it was the Golden Age of Murder. Wives poisoned husbands; husbands cut wives' throats; unfilial sons slaughtered aged parents with axes for their property. Peddlers were popular targets, as were men on their way home from market with wallets full of cash. Trusting young ladies seduced by plausible rogues had lives cut tragically short; so did their babes, who were apt to be tossed off a bridge. In a century so liberally strewn with the mangled corpses of murder victims, it was inevitable that some restless spirits would rise to plead for justice or frighten the innocent.

MURDER WILL OUT

"When a boy of twelve years of age I was an ardent fisherman with no more superstition in my nature than may have been inherited from the Highland Scotch blood of my father...," wrote the author of this entry in the 1914 *Dayton Daily News* ghost story contest. He described how the family had moved to a remote village and was careful to preface his story by saying that he hadn't met any of the neighbors or heard any local gossip. He wanted, he said, to "prove that I was entirely uninfluenced by any local gossip or traditions—an unprejudiced witness."

After helping with the move, he eagerly went out to fish.

> While daylight lasted I enjoyed pulling out rock bass, sunfish, and an occasional pike. Before the long northern twilight could darken into night the full moon rose and lighted the scene most gloriously.
>
> I lingered on the bank until perhaps ten o'clock, then gathered up my big string of fish and started for home, happy and unafraid. Climbing into the road I started for the road, whistling in my joy as I thought of the splendid fishing I was to have in the future.

It was then I came in sight of what, in my eagerness to reach the creek, I had failed to notice—a lonely house that stood about ten feet back from the road. It had a fence in front of it and a little porch facing the "pike."

Upon this porch, in the full blaze of the moonlight, stood the figure of a woman, wrapped in what appeared to be an old and soiled counterpane.

Long, disordered black hair hung around her face and fell in dark masses over the breast. Nothing but the hair and face were visible—but never shall I forget that face! More than three score years have passed since then, yet I can close my eyes and see it as I saw it that night in the moonlight. In those many years I have looked upon hundreds of dead faces but never upon one on which death and decay were marked in such terrible characters as they were upon that face in the moonlight.

Blotches of decomposition showed on the livid white gray of the skin, the jaw was fallen, the eyes wide open, their glare a dead horror which the moonlight revealed but did not brighten.

There I stood in the moonlight unmoving, with those awful eyes staring, as it seemed, at me: and there, for perhaps a minute, stood I, also staring, my gaze fascinated by the dead horror. I say "horror," for it was more a paralyzing horror than a fear that I experienced at that never-to-be-forgotten moment.

I was neither an exceptionally cowardly nor an extraordinarily brave boy. Perhaps I was, in a manner, drunk with fear—perhaps there was a subconscious idea that someone was trying to frighten me—I could never tell the real motive: but, dropping my fish and rod, I walked straight towards the horror, my staring eyes fast fixed upon the baleful object. As I reached the little gate and tried to pull it open, it fell forward against me. To clear myself of the wreckage it made I looked away from the "object" for just a moment. When I looked up and passed through the gate I discovered the figure was gone—had in a fleeting second, "made itself into air into which it vanished."

Knowing that I would not only be ridiculed but accused of cowardice, I told no one of the incident. Several days afterward, when I had made the acquaintance of some of the neighbour boys, we all went fishing together, and again I stayed out with them until after nightfall. As we started for home I noticed that my new friends took a roundabout path in order to strike the road halfway up the hill. I asked them why they didn't take the road at the bridge (as I had done that moonlit night). Said they:

"We ain't goin' to go by that ha'nted house at night." Keeping silence as to my own experience I asked for information concerning the haunted house and was given these gruesome facts. About eighteen months before the time I heard this story, a man and a woman had occupied the house.

The woman disappeared. The man explained that she had gone on a visit to relatives. Shortly after that he also left. For some reason suspicion of crime was awakened, and a search of the premises made.

The body of the woman, wrapped in an old counterpane, was found buried under the hearth. My recollection of the affair is that the "haunting" began before the discovery of the body, and that it was this that created a suspicion of foul play.

We moved away from the neighborhood shortly after that, but before we left I had occasion several times to pass the house without again seeing the ghost (?) of the murdered woman.

C.E.C.

Dayton [OH] Daily News 5 February 1914 Probably MONTGOMERY COUNTY

NOTE: "made itself into air into which it vanished" is from Shakespeare's *Macbeth*, describing how the three witches disappeared.

THE GHOST OF MARY SENEFF

In 1880 pretty, young Mary Seneff had lived for a few days as a servant with Ellen and Henry Athey near New Philadelphia. According to Mrs. Athey's confession, she got into an argument with Mary, accusing her of trying to seduce her husband. She ordered Mary out of the house; Mary refused to go and in a fit of rage Mrs. Athey hit Mary with an ax repeatedly, killing her. Then she dug a grave in the ash pit by the house and hid the body. Eventually she confessed to her two brothers and her husband and they dug the body up and threw it into Sugar Creek. Mrs. Athey was tried and sentenced to life in the Ohio Penitentiary. A *New York Times* article of 4 July, 1880 about the murder of "Mary Leneff" repeats some titillating local gossip about Mrs. Athey's temper and her attack on another woman. It is also suggested that the motive for the crime was that Mrs. Athey feared that Mary would expose her incest with her brother.

Horrific murders almost invariably give rise to local ghost stories. But it is unique to find the murder victim appearing in three separate incidents, once in front of two witnesses.

GHOSTLY MERMAID
A MURDERED WOMAN RISES FROM HER WATERY GRAVE AND CONFRONTS A FARMER

A farmer living in Jefferson Township, Ohio, relates the following ghost story: He states that on last Tuesday night, while returning home from town, and when approaching Sugar Creek Bridge, his attention was attracted by a loud splashing in the creek below. Immediately a white form arose slowly out of the water and glided noiselessly toward the shore, beckoning to him with its hand. A ball of bluish light surrounded the head, and the farmer declared that he plainly distinguished the features of Mary Seneff, the girl who was murdered and this was at the very spot where her body had been thrown into the water.

The farmer states that he was terribly frightened, and no amount of urging could induce his horse to move a step. We give the balance of the story in his own words:

"I watched the form a minute, and to my horror it came slowly out of the water and walked quietly up the bank toward me. From the light of the furnace I could now plainly see the identical Mary Seneff standing within ten feet of me. She was dressed in white, and in one hand held some strange looking garment above her head. With the other hand she pointed to a deep scar on her neck and an ugly ax mark across her forehead. The form then quietly moved backward toward the creek and slowly disappeared down the bank and into the water."

"I have always been a firm believer in ghosts," said the farmer, "but I am as positive as I live that I saw the murdered Mary Seneff on that night. I am unable to account for the strange apparition, and it makes my blood chill to talk about it."

The integrity of the farmer has never been questioned, and we give the story as related by himself. It is stated that he has frightened some of the old ladies of the neighborhood by the yarn.

[*Cincinnati Enquirer*]

Printed in *Brooklyn [NY] Eagle* 20 March 1881: p. 2 TUSCARAWAS COUNTY

THAT GHOSTLY MERMAID: SEEN AGAIN NEAR SUGAR-CREEK BRIDGE

Black Band, April 3. And now comes a workman named Joshua Engler, who claims positively to have seen the ghost of Mary Seneff: also Mr. Engler furnishes the reporter the following card for publication.

"Canal Dover, Ohio, March 1881.

"I was at the Salt Works on Saturday evening, and returning home about two o'clock in the morning, got within about twenty yards of Sugar-Creek Bridge, where Mary Seneff was thrown into the water, when I saw the shape of a woman about ten feet from the shore, come out of the water and walk up and down the creek. I watched it for five minutes. It started down the Stone Creek road and turned the bend at Hosea Fisher's, then it disappeared. Joshua Engler."

Mr. Engler says he could not see any features, but plainly recognized a female form clad in a white robe. It moved noiselessly up and down the bank after coming out of the water, and then went off down the road. Several other citizens claim to have seen the apparition, and the excitement over the matter is on the increase.

Cincinnati [OH] Enquirer 4 April 1881: p. 2 TUSCARAWAS COUNTY

Two weeks later, Mary's ghost was again spotted.

A TROUBLESOME GHOST: MARY SENEFF'S GHOST SEEN AGAIN BY A COUPLE OF STALWART GRANGERS

Black Band, Ohio, March 27. Poor Mary Seneff has been dead and buried for nearly ten months, but, according to the stories we hear, her ghost seems to be giving some of the people hereabouts a vast amount of trouble. Two weeks ago a belated farmer saw her shadowy form emerge from Sugar Creek at the very spot where she had been thrown into the water. Now come two men, named Spare and Mowzer, living about three miles west of here, who on last Monday night also claim positively to have seen the murdered girl's ghost. We give the story in Mr. Spare's own words as told in the presence of an *Enquirer* man to-day.

"Mr. Mowzer and I," he said, "had attended a sale during the day, and did not start home until probably half-past nine o'clock at night. To shorten the distance we cut across the fields, which took us past the Athey house, where Mary Seneff was murdered. When we were approaching the house we were both astonished to find it brilliantly lighted up. It was then nearly ten o'clock, and we knew the house had not been occupied since the murder. We stopped a minute at the gate, and while discussing the matter a shadowy form made its appearance at the window facing us. The head and face were plainly visible, and Mowzer involuntarily threw up his hands, exclaiming, 'My God! That's Mary Seneff.' I'll admit that we were both frightened, but more so when we saw the figure raise the window and noiselessly glide out. Our first impulse was to run: but Mowzer whispered to wait a little. The form was clad in what seemed to be a loosely fitting gown made of white material. It moved up to within a few feet of us and then halted. The figure now had the appearance of a thick shadow, but seemed to gain in substance the longer we looked at it. Presently it began receding and motioning to us to follow. Unconsciously we moved up the road a little further, and saw the form move around the corner of the house and walk slowly toward the ash-pile at the out-house, where Mrs. Athey had buried the body of Mary. With one hand she pointed at the partly filled grave and with the other frantically beckoned us to approach, but we had seen enough, and with one accord both of us took to our heels and ran. People will laugh," said Spare, "when they hear the story, and say we were full; but I knew we were both perfectly sober, and are as positive as we live that it was Mary Seneff's ghost, although I never believed in such things."

The story has frightened the lads of the neighbourhood badly, and they now go around by the road to spellings instead of cutting across the fields.

Cincinnati [OH] Enquirer 2 March 1881: p. 1 TUSCARAWAS COUNTY

NOTE: Grangers were members of The Grange (The National Grange of the Order of Patrons of Husbandry) an organization that educated and improved practices for farmers. Spellings were spelling bees.

Here is a link with more information on the murder of Mary Seneff, as well as some horrific details. http://unknownmisandry.blogspot.com/2011/07/female-on-female-violence-ellen-athey.html

This next story is the basis for the haunting of what is now Hammel House in Waynesville.

OHIO GHOSTS EVEN PROVE INTRUSIVE

Correspondence of the *Cincinnati Commercial*

Waynesville, Ohio, Feb. 19. Our town is in a fervent excitement over a haunted photograph gallery. For more than a week the artist, Mr. W. F. Slater, has been unable to take a picture owing to the appearance of the figure of an old gentleman behind the sisters. Until to-day he failed to hold the shadow on the negative, but he is now able to print the ghost who looks like a fine old man of 50, dressed in olden style. The artist's bottles and negatives have been shaken, his lamp blown out, &c., and he is so scared that nothing would induce him to spend the night there. Old residents revive the story of a peddler being murdered 50 years ago in the building in which the gallery is; in fact, they say his body was thrown into a well which is immediately under the gallery. But those who have seen the ghost's picture say that he was never a peddler when in the flesh.

The New York Times, 23 February 1881 WARREN COUNTY

NOTE: W. F. Slater was a 19th- and early 20th-century photographer who worked in Franklin, Lebanon, Middletown and Waynesville.

Stories about the ghosts of murder victims were perennial favorites. Since the popular adventure and fantasy novelist H. Rider Haggard (*King Solomon's Mines, She*) is mentioned, this may just be a local legend.

A GHOST WITHOUT A HEAD

A clever business man of southern Ohio, who has an imagination second only to that of Rider Haggard, contributes this:

While stopping one winter in a small village about fifty miles from Cincinnati, near the Little Miami river we used to congregate in the corner store of evenings and talk over the exploits of the day and have a good time generally.

There was one of the number who was always on hand, who lived a mile and a half down the pike.

He would always come up early in the evening and stay till about 10 before starting for home.

The pike ran through a deep hollow about a half mile from the village. I had often heard it told that a horrible murder had been committed near that place and that people had seen strange sights and heard sounds that would make their hair stand on end. I paid no attention to such tales, as I don't believe in such things myself. Some of the villagers were most positive that they had seen and heard sufficient to satisfy them, and no money would induce them to go through that hollow after dark.

The murder that was said to have been committed was that of a woman having her head cut off. Uncle Jack, as we called him, who lived down the pike, used to say he always whistled to keep his courage up. This evening Uncle Jack was more sober than usual. We often would ask him during the evening, "What is the matter? Have you seen the headless lady?" But he would only shake his head and say nothing. About 8 o'clock it commenced to snow, and by 10 it was about four inches deep. As it drew near time for Uncle Jack to start for home he would sigh and say he wished he was at home. "Come, boys, some of you go with him across the hollow. He is afraid of the headless lady." No one would go. So I said, "Come, Uncle Jack, I'll go; I am not afraid of ghosts." As we got close to the hollow I began to whistle. Of course I wasn't afraid, you know. Uncle Jack never said a word, but I could hear him sigh every few steps.

It was still snowing as we neared the hollow, which was lined on each side with tall trees. The snow hanging to the limbs made it look rather gloomy, without any ghosts added to it. As we began to descend the hollow I began to feel like I didn't weigh quite as much as I did on the hill. When we got about the middle of the hollow Uncle Jack, with a groan sank down flat in the snow and said: "Look, there it is!" I turned, and horror of horrors! There she stood, not more than three yards from us, without a head, the blood streaming down her shoulders, her hands covered with blood. As I turned to see where Uncle Jack was, expecting every moment to feel the bloody hands on my arms, Uncle Jack raised up and said, "Where is it?" "There it is," but it was gone. "Come, Jack, let's get out of this," and we did get too. Of course, I wasn't scared nor afraid of ghosts, but I went four miles round to get home, you bet.

Logansport [IN] Pharos Tribune 2 April 1889: p. 3 WARREN or possibly MONTGOMERY COUNTY

Stories like this next one from the *Brooklyn Eagle* need to be taken with a jumbo grain of salt. *The Eagle*, although it published legitimate news, was inclined to print journalistic hoax stories, including this corker of a tale of a "heartrending and cruel crime." How do I know it's a hoax? Well, I thought that I was certain—because Mt. Nebo existed only in Athens County. But the helpful librarians of the Youngstown Library found a long-defunct village of Mount Nebo. I thought that there were no caves near Youngstown—but it turns out that there are some coal mines and some shallow sandstone caves, according to the very helpful Tom Metzgar of the Mid-Atlantic Karst Conservancy (www.karst.org). The Youngstown librarians also reported that the owner of the coal mine was the Dilworth family of Pittsburg, not Conrad Dittmar.

But I think the lurid language and the age-old story of a peddler murdered for his money, as well as the fact that this story appears in many different newspapers, tips this towards the end of the local legend spectrum. I've been wrong before—I originally thought that the tale called "The Undertaker's Revenge" from Ironton was just folklore until a librarian sent me news clippings telling the whole true, sordid tale of the disemboweled doctor. I'd be happy to be proved wrong about "Blood Stained."

BLOOD STAINED.
THE TREASURE WHICH GHOSTS ARE SAID TO GUARD
STORY OF A HEARTRENDING AND CRUEL CRIME
THE TRADITIONS WHICH PERTAIN TO A CAVE NEAR YOUNGSTOWN, OHIO

CONFIRMATION OF AN ASSASSIN'S EXPLANATION
HOW A PEDDLER DISAPPEARED
ATTEMPTS MADE TO PENETRATE THE HAUNTED
SPOT

[Youngstown, O., dispatch to *Cincinnati Enquirer*.]

In the side of a ravine near the Village of Mount Nebo, ten miles southeast of this city, is a cave which is an object of horror to the superstitious and of peculiar interest to the adventurously inclined.

One night twenty years ago, so the story goes, two men sought shelter in the cave from a blinding snowstorm. One was a simple minded old peddler, who for years had supplied the farmhouses in the vicinity with his wares, which he carried in a pack upon his back. The other was a friend whom he had long known and whom he had met an hour before, belated like himself and seeking shelter from the storm.

Once in the cave, a blazing fire was soon started, which effectually shut out the cold blasts of wind and snow, and the two men prepared to pass the night as comfortably as possible. The peddler drew from his pocket a handful of money and after counting it slipped it into a money belt which he wore about his waist. He made no effort to conceal the fact that the belt was heavy with gold, and talked as simply and unsuspectingly as a child of the time, soon coming, when he could forsake his pack forever, and, with the money he had saved, end his days in peace and comfort. After readjusting the belt about his waist he lay down and was soon fast asleep, his pack serving him for a pillow.

His companion, whom the sight of the gold had excited to desperation, feigned sleep, until the breathing of the peddler, assured him of his complete unconsciousness. Satisfied of this, the man, his eyes glittering fiercely in the firelight, drew from his pocket a large clasp knife, opened the blade and drove it, with devilish precision, into the sleeper's heart.

It was all over in a moment. The dark blood gushed from the wound in a thick stream, there was a nervous twitching of the hands, the eyelids half opened, and the eyes turned inwardly, the neck stiffened and drew the head back, and all was rigid and still again.

The murderer groped for the belt and drew it out, wet and slimy with blood. He hastily poured the gold out and looked at it, and ran it through his hands. In the fascination of the gold he forgot all else, and only remembered the crime and the victim when a stream of blood trickled down from the corpse's breast and formed a pool where the gold lay. Then a consciousness of his position dashed upon him, and he tossed the body into the darkness in the back part of the cave, and with the bloody clasp knife dug a hole and buried the gold for which he had paid so terrible a price.

He would not remain in the cave with the body of his murdered friend and he rushed out into the snow, intending to return some time and recover the fortune—for there were thousands of dollars in the peddler's hoard. The clasp knife he still retained, and with it he blazed trees along his path so that he might be able to find his way to the cave more easily on his return.

A month later he was lying in a hospital at Cleveland, haggard and helpless. He had been found in the snow miles away from the scene of his crime, so badly frozen that amputation of his hands and feet was performed in a desperate effort to save his life. Pitying Samaritans had cared for him, little suspecting that the object of their sympathy was a murderer.

He lingered in the hospital for months, and then they told him he must die. The remembrance of the crime which he was expiating so terrible became too much for him to bear. He sent for his niece, to whom he told the story, and died.

Scarcely waiting to see the maimed body of the murderer consigned to the grave, the niece and her husband hastened to Mount Nebo and made inquiries concerning the disappearance of the peddler. By means of the blazed trees which the murderer had described they found the cave, only to discover that its walls and rock had fallen in and barred up the entrance. The husband set to work, assisted by farm hands who lived in the vicinity, to remove the rocks. After they had progressed a few feet they were startled by unearthly voices and lights that sounded and gleamed through fissures in the rocks from the darkness in the interior of the cavern. The exploring party immediately abandoned the work, and a moment later the rocks again fell in, filling up anew the space which had been excavated.

Since then many unsuccessful attempts have been made to open the cave. One was by Mr. Conrad Dittmar, who owns the premises upon which the cave is situated. He declares the place is undoubtedly haunted, and testified to having heard and seen the voices and lights which frightened the first exploring party.

A party of four men living near Mount Nebo attempted to open the entrance, and had the temerity to camp out over night at the mouth of the cave. After dark, while sitting around their camp fire, they distinctly saw the ghostly figure of a man standing a few feet from them. Upon being addressed the figure faded away into nothingness. The hair of one of the party became instantly perfectly white, and a day or so later he died, so they say. The survivors declare that the figure they saw corresponded exactly to the description of the murdered peddler given by those who remember him.

One individual who ventured to the place after dark exhibited scars and bruises for weeks afterward in proof of his story that he had been picked up bodily by unseen hands and tossed into the creek that runs along the bottom of the ravine.

A spirit medium who visited the place said that the fortune would not be recovered for many years to come.

The trees standing on the hillside immediately around the cave are black and lifeless, and have the appearance of having been burned with fire.

The story of the murder is well authenticated, and the ghost stories are implicitly believed by the residents of Mount Nebo and vicinity.
Brooklyn [NY] Eagle 26 February 1882: p. 2 MAHONING COUNTY

The belief that a man could not rest until his bones were properly buried was given greater weight when the person was a murder victim. Here's a classic tale illustrating that belief.

DISCOVERY OF SKELETON LAYS OHIO "GHOST" SPOOK NEAR PAINESVILLE HAS NOT APPEARED SINCE BONES IN WELL WERE BURIED

Painesville, O., Aug. 15 A "ghost" which farmers living near Paines Hollow say has been haunting them for seven years is "at rest" today. It disappeared several days ago with the burial of the skeleton of Henry Lipenstick which was found in an abandoned well on a farm.

Lipenstick, a farm hand, disappeared seven years ago. Since then the farm is said to have had poor crops. A farm house burned down, and the "ghost" was blamed for that. Owner after owner has come and gone.

Carl Logies purchased the farm about a year ago. Whenever he went to his barn at night Logies said today he would see "a white wraith-like figure" walking about. At times he declared he followed it with his gun in hand and it always disappeared in the direction of the well.

Determined to find out what caused the apparition Logies cleaned out the old well which had been filled with stones. He came upon the body of Lipenstick. Sheriff Spink was called and he and his deputies suspected murder. The next day the sheriff ordered the body buried and now the "ghost" is gone.

Frank Lorman who owned the farm at the time Lipenstick disappeared is in the Lake County jail. He was bound over to the grand jury on charges of murder.
New Castle [PA] News 15 August 1922: p. 6 LAKE COUNTY

I've written in several of my books about Crybaby Bridges—that ubiquitous "urban legend" (although they usually take place in a rural setting) about the crying ghost of a baby whose body was never recovered from a stream or river. We like to think that these are just gruesome stories to be told around the campfire. As this selection of articles shows, they were, shockingly, not always legends.

WOMAN AND CHILD
A PHANTOM STORY OF THE SCIOTO
STRANGE SIGHTS WITNESSED BY TWO RELIABLE
FARMERS AND PORTSMOUTH
A FIGURE WHICH FLOATS ALONG LEAVING
A COLD WAVE BEHIND IT
THE APPARITION GOES TO THE BRIDGE
SPANNING THE RIVER
AND DROPS ITS LITTLE COMPANION
INTO THE WAVES

Portsmouth, Ohio, July 16. People living in the neighborhood of the great bridge that spans the Scioto River at the foot of Second Street, and especially residents of the West Side who are compelled to cross that structure in the night season, are experiencing the sensations of a strange excitement occasioned by the mysterious visitation of a still more mysterious person, who appears not in the traditional white garb of ghostly callers, but walks the streets clad in the sable garments of sorrow. Her companion on these nightly pilgrimages is a small child, which she carries closely clasped to her bosom. She is heavily veiled, the drapery falling in double folds about her head and shoulders.

THE PHANTOM FIGURE
First made its appearance several weeks ago, but the report of its existence was not believed and did not settle down to anything like a tangible resting place until last night, when there was a denouement that leaves no doubt in the minds of those who witnessed it or of those who know the parties to the scene, and in whose integrity and cool, calculating observation and discrimination they have the most thorough and unyielding confidence.

About ten o'clock last night Messrs. Nat Smith and Joe Henry, West Side farmers, who had been in the city making purchases, started home. Between Market and Jefferson Streets, on the way to the bridge, it is very dark, made so by the heavy foliage of the shade trees that line the sidewalk. It was while passing through this darkness that the gentlemen first

FELT SINGULAR SENSATIONS.

A feeling of uneasiness, undefined and perplexing, came over both men simultaneously. A moment later a woman clad in the deepest mourning, and bearing a child in her arms rushed past them. An icy chilliness enveloped the strange form, and it pierced the men as it went by. This chilly atmosphere seemed to bear the woman along, as no sound of footsteps could be distinguished.

At Jefferson Street the woman turned toward Front, crossing over and turning down Jefferson in the shadow of the buildings. The men, who were now thoroughly interested in the movements of the woman, followed her. Her progress was very slow, the form merely floating along with the evening air. This let the men ahead, and at the corner of Front they waited for the woman to pass. The same chilly experience was felt here, and the vision rushed on down the street. Smith and Henry followed. At the corner of Scioto Street the strange figure headed for the Scioto River bridge. When the men reached the bridge she was but a foot in front of them. The same

AWE-INSPIRING DREAD

Was around them, and they hesitated at a nearer approach. Slowly the form floated along over the bridge until the middle span was reached, when it approached the railing and, glancing over, peered intently at the water below. Smith and Henry stepped to the side of the bridge to await future movements. Scarcely had they done so, when they were horrified to see the woman raise the child in her arms, and, with a wild cry, dash it over the bridge. Both men turned in an instant and looked down at the water, but there was no break in its current, and nobody could be seen descending. Now thoroughly terrified, the men again looked up at the woman. For the first time her face was revealed. The heavy veil was thrown back, and features sad, but singularly beautiful were shown. A second later the apparition ascended, and gradually faded away, the men watching it in wonder until the

LAST FAINT OUTLINE DISAPPEARED.

Numerous theories of the causes that prompt this strange apparition are advanced. Does the ghostly visitor seek to reveal the mystery connected with the death of Steve Rayburn; does it strive to clear up some hidden

secret concerning the woman who came to the Weber House last winter, remained there during confinement, and then left with her child and has never been heard from, or is it connected with the falling of the bridge or the death of poor Morgan many years before? These are questions asked in regard to the strange visitor in black. There is evidently a deep meaning to it somewhere, and further manifestations will be impatiently looked for.
Cincinnati [OH] Enquirer 17 July 1888: p 5 SCIOTO COUNTY

NOTE: Steve Rayburn was found on July 2, 1888 half-submerged in the Scioto River with head injuries and bruising from his fall from the Scioto River Bridge. Murder was suggested because the railings were considered high enough to prevent an accidental fall and a fall would have caused much more damage to the body. A witness saw him with two unknown men on the bridge and it was thought he was lured under the bridge and killed. "He was a man who had enemies of the worst kind."

"Poor Morgan" was William Morgan, a man who supposedly gave away Masonic secrets and disappeared mysteriously. The Bridge fell in heavy flooding in 1844.

CHILD MURDERER
A FATHER THROWS HIS OWN CHILD IN THE OHIO RIVER

Cincinnati, March 7. On Thursday afternoon there was discovered in the Ohio River, near North Bend, the body of a white infant child from appearances a week old. The case has developed into a most shocking and heartless case of infanticide. It was brought to light by the volunteer detective work of two women—Mrs. Arnold and her daughter, Mrs. Moore. The facts are given as follows:

A couple, purporting to be James Dubois and wife, took rooms three weeks ago in a boarding house here at 134 Elm Street, kept by Mrs. Arnold. On Sunday last Mrs. Dubois gave birth to a male child in perfect health. Wednesday Dubois announced that he intended to take the child to a niece living near Hamilton, O. For this purpose he placed it in a basket, and Mrs. Arnold and Mrs. Moore assisted. Dubois left the house at 7:40 o'clock and returned at 11 o'clock. The papers of Friday morning contained an account of the finding of the dead body of a male infant in the Ohio River near Cleves.

Meantime Mrs. Moore and her mother went to Cleves, had the body exhumed, identified the clothing beyond question, and Saturday afternoon returned to the city and told the story to the police, and the man was arrested. The man at first denied everything, but broke down and said he went to the middle of the Chesapeake and Ohio Bridge and threw the babe into the Ohio. From papers found on him it appears his name is William A. Boyce and that his home is Portland, Ind. His wife is said to be the daughter of F. J. Settle, of Muncie, Ind. Dubois gave as the cause of the crime his inability to support the child.

Newark [OH] Daily Advocate 7 March 1892: p. 1 HAMILTON COUNTY

I had collected the previous story about a year ago. Quite by accident, just before going to press, I stumbled across the story that ends this chapter and could scarcely believe it—it was the ghost of the child in the story above.

IN WHITE AND WAILING PITEOUSLY
A PHANTOM BABE CONFRONTS MISS DELLA JONES
THRILLING EXPERIENCE OF A YOUNG LADY
ON ELM STREET
AN AWFUL CRIME RECALLED BY THE APPARITION
'TWAS IN THE ROOM WHERE THE GHOST WAS SEEN
THAT THE INFANT WAS BORN
WHICH W.C. BOYCE, ITS FATHER,
THREW INTO THE RIVER

The occupants of the house at 134 Elm Street are in a terrible state of agitation over the supposed presence of a ghost.

The unearthly apparition is said to have haunted the dwelling at irregular intervals for several years. It made its appearance again last night, as it is claimed. About 11 o'clock the spectre was seen by Miss Della Jones, who has a room on the second floor of the above number. Miss Jones, who is a young unmarried woman, is employed on West Fourth Street.

The house at No. 134 Elm Street is an apartment building, and is located on the east side of the street, south of Fourth. At one time it was well known to the police, the old [illegible] game having been successfully worked on several unsuspecting victims there. However, these occupants were forced to vacate, and since then the police have kept aloof. Since March, 1892, it has been claimed by a number of persons that the house is haunted, they affirming that they saw supernatural sights and heard unearthly sounds, which caused them any amount of uneasiness. In these instances, however, they never could or would repeat their experiences, and the matter was passed by. Miss Jones affirms that she saw the spirit of a baby and heard its wailing.

A HARROWING EXPERIENCE.

She says that about 11 o'clock, after she had been in her room reading for about an hour and had lowered the light preparatory to going to bed, she heard a peculiar cry. She could not distinguish at first what it was, but after a moment she thought it sounded like the mewing of a cat. As the noise continued she recognized it as that of a child. It seemed to come from near the head of the bed, and she looked in that direction in the hope of learning what caused the noise and hoping to find nothing more than a cat there.

Just as she turned she saw emerge from the gloom near the head of the bed an object in white. The object started toward the center of the room, and as it did, so its outlines became more distinct, and Miss Jones recognized the features of a baby. It was dressed in its swaddling clothes, and seemed to float near the floor. Its face was distorted, and it seemed to be crying.

As the phantom seemed to make straight for the center of the room, Miss Jones became transfixed with fright. Beads of perspiration started out on her forehead, and her limbs refused to obey, but as the apparition began to fade away her composure partly returned, and with one scream she turned, unlocked the door and fled down the stairs.

Mrs. Meyers, who is the landlady, and her daughter heard the scream and hurriedly rushed into the hall to see what was the matter. Miss Jones had just reached the bottom of the stairs and looking wildly about attracted the two women, who hastily grabbed her. At this moment Miss Jones's nerves, which had been at a high tension relaxed, and the prostration which followed caused her to faint. Restoratives were immediately applied and she soon returned to consciousness. After she had been allowed a few minutes to compose herself she told the above story. An investigation was immediately begun, but nothing could be seen or heard. The ghost story was scoffed at by the other occupants of the house, but Miss Jones would not vary one iota from her first statement, and stoutly maintained that she had not been deceived and as evidence of her conviction refused to again occupy the room last night.

A CRIME RECALLED.

This story recalls a case of infanticide that occurred in the house in question about three years ago. A mother gave birth to a child in the same room which Miss Jones occupied, and the mother and father of the helpless infant conspired to get rid of it. The father murdered it by drowning it in the Ohio River.

On Friday morning, March 4, 1892, *The Enquirer* gave an account of the finding of an infant's body in the river at North Bend. The description given led to the identification of the waif and the arrest of the parents on the charge of murder followed. Less than a year previously Sallie Settles, of Muncie, Ind., was seduced under promise of marriage by William A. Boyce of Portland, Ind. On the advice of the mother of Sallie, Boyce married the girl on February 17 following.

The first clew that led to the detection of the perpetrator of the crime was furnished by Mrs. Libbie Moores, a dressmaker, of 234 Kenyon Avenue. She had read the account in *The Enquirer* of the finding of the child's body, and she immediately recalled that a few days before she had made an outfit similar to the one worn by the dead babe. She had taken the dress to 134 Elm Street. Mrs. Moore's mother, Mrs. Arnold, lived at this number, and rented furnished rooms. About three weeks previous a man giving his name as Dubois, claiming to be a sewing-machine agent, and a woman claiming to be his wife, took up their abode there. The woman was young and pretty. On Sunday, February 31, 1892, the so-called Mrs. Dubois gave birth to a male infant. Dr. L.M. Denman was the attending physician. At the time Dubois made a remark about his wife disliking children, and that they intended placing the babe with relatives. On the following Wednesday Dubois placed the babe in a basket and started out with it, saying that he was going to take it to a nurse. It was 8 o'clock when he left the house, but did not return until three hours later.

BOYCE ARRESTED

Through Mesdames Arnold and Moores [efforts], Dubois was arrested. After being arrested and closely cross-questioned by Colonel Deitsch he broke down and confessed. He said that his right name was Boyce. He had taken the baby down to the Chesapeake and Ohio Bridge, and, seizing the child by the arm, hurled it into the river. He insisted that his wife knew nothing of the deed. He said that he wanted to place the babe in the City Hospital, but it would not be accepted. The next night, when he placed the child in a basket, he says that he wandered up and down several streets with it undetermined what to do. At one time he wanted to leave it on a doorstep. As he neared the C. and O. Bridge he claimed that he saw a man sitting on a wagon and offered him $10 to help him get rid of the child.

Boyce claimed that this man murdered it, but it was later brought out that he had committed the deed himself. He had first choked the infant into insensibility and then thrown it into the river. As he was about to let go of the child one of the little sleeves of the dress caught on his finger and the sleeve was torn out. Boyce was convicted and sentenced to the penitentiary for 20 years.

It is thought by the occupants of the house at 134 Elm Street that the apparition seen there last night is the spirit of the murdered baby, and that it is crying for its mother.

Cincinnati [OH] Enquirer 24 April 1895: p. 8. HAMILTON COUNTY

NOTE: The *Cincinnati Enquirer* 11 March 1892: p. 4 described in heart-rending detail the funeral of the Boyce baby. A plaque on the tiny coffin read "Our Darling" and people filed for hours through the morgue to view its remains. When some people objected that the baby had not been its parents' darling, others announced that the child was now the *public's* darling.

13.

Haunted by Fire

A Fire-Spook in Springfield

The story begins, as so many stories do, with an orphaned girl. She is a mystery. She was born sometime in 1873. She was 11 when one or both of her parents died, possibly in the Sixth Cholera Pandemic. Her father's name was James Markle, and despite searching all variants of the last name, I have not been able to locate her parents in any census or graveyard. They were said to live in Mendon, Mercer County, a town twice destroyed by fire in 1906 and 1907. An apt birthplace for an incendiary poltergeist.

MYSTERIOUS FIRES
A BOARDING HOUSE ON SOUTHERN AVENUE THE
SCENE OF BLAZES OF REMARKABLE ORIGIN
HOUSEHOLD GOODS BURST INTO FLAMES
WITHOUT ANY APPARENT CAUSE
ASTONISHING AND PUZZLING ALL
THE BEHOLDERS

The people at the extreme west end of Southern Avenue, in the vicinity of Reeser's green houses, are mystified over the unaccountable and mysterious origin of the number of small fires, which have broken out in the past few days in the residence occupied by Mrs. Jane McGowen 279 West Southern Avenue.

The first mysterious blaze broke out in the kitchen loft early Wednesday afternoon, a bundle of papers and clothing were discovered on fire.

The flames were extinguished by Will Reeser, Mr. Kirkwood and other boarders. About an hour afterwards, Mrs. McGowen declared she smelled fire and the bed and bed-clothes in one of the boys' room, no-where near a stove or any fire whatever were discovered ablaze. Just before supper Wednesday evening, the underwear and other clothing lying on the machine in the kitchen, fifteen feet from the stove, were found burning brightly, the machine itself even catching.

Then a short time afterwards the inmates became thoroughly mystified and frightened by discovering the window shutters in the summer kitchen on fire, followed by the papers on the gasoline stove blazing up.

Towards midnight the top shelf in Will Reeser's sleeping room was discovered on fire. During the early part of the evening Miss Minnie McGowen's [sic] dress caught fire from some unexplainable cause and was extinguished with difficulty, but the most mysterious phase of the whole matter was the fact that the young lady put on a new clean apron after supper, and she was horrified to find out immediately afterwards that the strings were on fire and that the back part of her dress had even caught from the blaze.

The inmates had become thoroughly frightened by this time, and it was determined to sit up and try to discover the origin of the strange occurrences. About 9 o'clock Thursday morning Mrs. McGowen, who was sitting up, was startled to see the table cloth blaze up at both ends of the table. Assistance was hastily called and the fire put out.

Perhaps the most mysterious part of the whole affair was the fact that the table cloths, napkins, and a few other small household goods again caught fire about 10 o'clock yesterday morning. These things were on a shelf in the pantry leading from the kitchen and were at least twenty-five feet from the coal stove in the kitchen.

The news of the strange visitation of fire has spread all over the neighborhood and many people called at the house yesterday and today.

Mrs. McGowen is a lady of intelligence and does not believe any supernatural power is persecuting her, but she is very nervous over the constant menace to her property. She says some person must be starting the fire, but she has no idea whom to suspect.

Springfield [OH] Republic Times 19 December 1890 CLARK COUNTY

There is a strange pattern of either misspelling or misstating Minnie's last name throughout these newspaper stories. It is as if, as an orphan, she had no fixed identity.

Several things strike me about this next account. The outbreak came while there were other young women in the house, including Mrs. McGowen's step-daughter, [a *Cincinnati Enquirer* article giving much the same information as this says that Miss Pearl Netts and her mother were visiting.] The clothes of a deceased daughter of Mrs. McGowen were a target, along with Mrs. McGowen's bed, which Minnie apparently shared.

Census records tell us Mrs. McGowen had lost two of four children. In this article Minnie is called Mrs. McGowen's "step-daughter." In the previous article, her name is given as "Minnie McGowen." Was there actually any relationship between them or did the reporter mistake the domestic servant for a daughter of the house? Did she mother Minnie when her "real" relatives were not around? Could Minnie pretend that she was a daughter—until people with a better claim came to call?

I wonder about the relationship between the landlady and Councilman Netts' niece. Mrs. McGowen lived in the home of her own daughter—Mattie Netts—from 1900 to her death in 1910. Did Minnie feel snubbed by Miss Netts? Did her anger blaze forth in a tangible form? Or was something else going on in Springfield? A note in the paper from 1 December 1890 mentioned that there were "fire-bugs" at Springfield. To that date they had burnt two stables and attempted to fire the First Presbyterian Church. Although Minnie was the logical suspect, knowing what we know about poltergeist outbreaks, arson was in the air in Springfield in December of 1890.

MYSTERY DEEPENS
FOUR MORE FIRES BREAK OUT IN MRS. MCGOWEN'S BOARDING HOUSE
A BOX OF CLOTHING BELONGING TO A DECEASED DAUGHTER BURSTS INTO FLAMES
TWO BEDS FOUND ABLAZE
ONE ON THE TOP OF THE HEADBOARD

The fire mystery at Mrs. McGowen's residence on Southern Avenue grows more mysterious daily. All efforts of the lady, her boarders, the police, and reporters to discover the origin of the blazes have thus far proven fruitless.

This forenoon four more fires were discovered just in time to save the house from destruction.

The first blaze was discovered about a quarter after 8 o'clock by Mr. Chris Benning, a boarder, who had just finished polishing his boots upstairs and on coming down discovered the cover on the center table in the sitting room on fire. At least three persons, Mrs. McGowen, Misses Minnie Merkle, Mrs. McGowen's step-daughter, and Pearl Netts, niece of Councilman Netts, were in the room not five minutes before the table cover caught fire. A close inspection of the covers reveals the fact that the blaze burned directly across the corner in a straight line and not in a zig zag course as is generally the case. This fact strengthens the theory that chemicals have been thrown on the garments.

The second fire blazed out in the bed in Will Reeser's room upstairs about half an hour after the first one.

Miss Netts was upstairs five minutes before this mysterious blaze occurred, accompanied by Miss Merkley.

They were in the sitting room down stairs when Miss Merkley cried out in much alarm that she smelt something burning upstairs! Both ladies then rushed upstairs and opening the door of Mr. Reeser's room were almost suffocated by a rush of smoke. The lower part of the bed was ablaze and the room dark with smoke. Assistance soon arrived and the fire was put out. While they were talking in frightened tones about the mysterious visitation, one of the parties turned around and beheld Mr. Reeser's coat, hanging behind the door, on fire, and a blanket on a chair near the head of the bed, was at the same moment discovered in flames.

The third fire came frightfully near getting such a start as to prevent its being extinguished. Mrs. McGowen passed through the sitting room where the first blaze started about 10 o'clock, with a blanket from Mr. Reeser's bed. She took the blanket into the backyard and hung it on a clothes line and returning after not more than 10 minutes absence, was horrified to see her own bed in the sitting room in flames. It was extinguished with difficulty, workmen from Reeser's greenhouse being called over. The bed had been made up about an hour before by Miss Merkley.

The fourth outburst occurred at a little after noon and was discovered by Miss Merkly, just as a *Republic-Times* reporter was leaving the house. In this instance it was a chest of clothing which belonged to a deceased daughter of Mrs. McGowen. The young woman died about four years ago and her clothing was packed away shortly after the funeral since which time it has not been touched. This is the most mysterious of all features yet developed and has done much to arouse a feeling among the superstitiously [inclined that some supernatural] agency is responsible for the phenomenon.

The insurance agents of the city have secured the services of chemist J.D. Lisle who will make a thorough examination of the premises in search of any chemical preparation which may have been used to cause combustion. If he fails the spirits will have to bear the blame until some stroke of good fortune vindicates them.

Later word comes by telephone that three more blazes have been extinguished since 1 o'clock.

Springfield [OH] Republic Times 23 December 1890

All in a day's work for an incendiary poltergeist. If you look at the history of mysterious fires of this sort, the pattern is classic: the fires start with incredible rapidity and come in quick succession with multiple fires in a day, sometimes numbering in the dozens. (A later article in the *Cincinnati Enquirer* states that 25 fires occurred in one day.) The coat on the back of the door flaring up just as the bed was extinguished is also typical. The bewildered residents can scarcely turn around without a new fire starting.

In this case, the introduction of the dead daughter motif is also typical—it is easier to blame the dead than the living who are apt to fall into "spasms" as Minnie did when accused.

I recently read an account of an outbreak of mysterious fires in the United Arab Emirates that began after several of the children of the house were taken to hospital with high fevers and convulsions. Minnie, too, suffered from similar ill-health and "fits." Remember, too, the study from the chapter on poltergeists describing such people as repressing and denying hostility until they explode. I can't fathom what the mechanism might be, but there are centuries of reports about people with a mysterious talent for starting fires.

FOLLOWED BY FIRE
MYSTERIOUS FLAMES IN A HOUSEHOLD
AT SPRINGFIELD.
AN ORPHAN CHILD SUSPECTED OF BEING
THE FIRE-BUG.
FIRES IN RAPID SUCCESSION WHEREVER
THE GIRL APPEARS.
IN CONVULSIONS AT A HOSPITAL
AFTER THE LATEST BLAZE
NEIGHBORS BELIEVE HER BEWITCHED.

Springfield, Ohio, December 23. What is likely to become the most celebrated mystery in the history of the crimes of Springfield is developing. There is an uncanny air about it that the superstitious are using to good account. Last Saturday's *Enquirer* contained particulars of ten consecutive attempts in two days to fire the residence of Mrs. McGowen on Southern Avenue. There was a startling repetition of the experience to-day, and it certainly looks as though there were supernatural or devilish agencies at work against the safety of the life and property of the house. Miss Minnie Mackley, an orphan girl living in the house, is the only one suspected of the fifteen or more attempts at arson in the last few days, and detectives are at work....

Your correspondent visited the mysterious place and had a talk with all parties concerned. All denied knowing the origin and were indignant THAT THE GIRL SHOULD BE ACCUSED.

But a few minutes past 12 o'clock your representative had left and gone a few hundred feet, when he was called back by the excited exclamations. "Another fire!"

Going back he found that it was so. A lot of blankets, sheets, and dresses had been done up in a sheet so they could be easily handled in the case of serious fire. This bundle was in the hall upstairs on a chest, and at the time mentioned the Mackley girl again called attention to the smell of smoke and opened the door leading upstairs. The hall was filled with smoke. A bucket of water was thrown on the bundle of clothes, extinguishing the flames after the clothes had been ruined. The girl was seen to go upstairs and come down about three minutes before the fire was discovered, and

SUSPICION RESTS HEAVILY UPON HER

The girl will be taken to the Hospital tonight and watched by medical experts. There is a reign of actual terror in the neighborhood. This afternoon the girl was ironing and had a pile of folded linen in front of her a foot or more high. Suddenly a slow stream of fire burst from the pile of linen and scorched an upward streak, damaging each garment. At the same time the girl's apron strings caught fire and the garment dropped off of her.

The insurance agents canceled the policy on the house this evening, and the girl is raging in a series of strange and violent spasms. Certain of the neighbors affrightedly assert that she is bewitched and has the faculty of communicating combustion.

Cincinnati [OH] Enquirer 23 December 1890: p. 1

As I have said before, much poltergeist activity is symbolic, as in the episode above: Minnie Markle is ironing—she has a pile of dampened laundry at her feet. Not only does the linen blaze up, her apron strings catch fire and the apron, symbol of her domestic service, falls to the ground. Could the young servant's desire to be free be any more obvious?

THE MYSTERIOUS FIRES
THEIR ORIGIN STILL UNACCOUNTED FOR
INSURANCE CANCELLED

The mysterious fires at the McGowen residence on West Southern Ave., are still unaccounted for, although detectives, reporters, and neighbors swarmed over the place all day yesterday. No fires have broken out since yesterday noon, and the excitement has somewhat abated. The unfortunate girl, Miss Minnie Markley, toward whom suspicion was directed, was closely and rigorously questioned yesterday by Detective Wilson, but nothing criminating was found in her replies. She was then charged point blank with firing the clothing, and, although much frightened, she stoutly and bravely maintained her innocence, as did also Mrs. McGowen, when questioned and finally charged with the crime.

Officer Thompson remained at the house last evening but must have slept all night as he don't [sic] seem to know even that the girl slept in the house. When questioned this morning this officer, although knowing the interest taken in the matter by the public at large, exhibited surprising ignorance of what happened during the evening and peremptorily stopped inquiry by an ugly frown and monosyllabic answers.

Miss Merkley has not been taken to the hospital as at first proposed and is still at the house. Attempts were made yesterday to get her aunt to take her home, but she refused. Insurance agent Wallace cancelled his policies on the furniture, etc., belonging to Mrs. McGowen and the boarders, after paying $73.63 damages.

Springfield [OH] Republic Times 23 December 1890: p. 8

One has to feel sorry for Mrs. McGowen whose property was so extensively destroyed. Given what I know about Minnie's health and emotional instability, I have to admire the young woman, "although much frightened," standing up to the police. Some researchers believe that people who are the focus of poltergeist activity may sometimes perform actions in a dissociative state—and hotly deny that they are behind any of the events. Even if Minnie was physically behind any of the fires, but had set them in some sort of trance, she could truthfully say that she was not responsible. She would have no memory of the events.

There is one statement in the article above that is troublingly ambiguous. "Miss Merkley (still another misspelled last name) has not been taken to the hospital as at first proposed and is still at the house. Attempts were made yesterday to get her aunt to take her home, but she refused." Who refused? Minnie? Or the aunt?

I wish I knew more about Minnie's family relationships because Minnie's Aunt Dora Kirk lived only a third of a mile from the boarding house where Minnie lived. Why was she working in a boarding house and not living with family?

A few days later, the *Springfield Republic Times* dated 27 December 1890 contained lengthy reports of "firebugs at work" in St. Paul, Minnesota, where they caused a three-alarm fire. The article concluded, ominously, "The incendiaries will be hanged if caught."

Suddenly, as is the pattern with incendiary poltergeists, the fires subsided. But things were not well with Minnie.

THE FIRE MYSTERY

The McGowen fire mystery is still under cover. No fires have broken out for some days. The girl, Minnie Merkle, who was suspected of the crimes, is seriously ill at her aunt's in the east end.

Springfield [OH] Republic Times 29 December 1890

STILL UNDISCOVERED
THE ORIGIN OF THE MYSTERIOUS FIRES IN THE WEST END

The mysterious origin of the numerous fires at the residence of Mrs. Jane McGowen, on West Southern Avenue, is still unaccounted for.

The grave and causeless charge made by one of the papers last evening, that the fires have been started by an afflicted servant girl, Miss Minnie Markle, is indignantly and earnestly denied by not only Mrs. McGowen, but all the boarders in the house and in fact the entire neighborhood is up in arms at the cruel and utterly unfounded charges. [which the paper then kindly recapped...]

Detective Wilson was out at the house yesterday, and after thoroughly investigating the matter, think that there are no grounds for the charges.

The young lady was thrown into spasms last evening on reading the account and bitterly, tearfully denied the alleged report today.

Some of the boarders think someone has used chemicals to start the fires. Mrs. McGowen is still exceedingly nervous over the affairs.

Springfield [OH] Republic Times 30 December 1890

Note the suggestion about chemicals. Will Reeser, a boarder mentioned in previous articles, worked at the Innisfallen Greenhouse, about a mile from Mrs. McGowen's boarding house, as did two of the other boarders. Innisfallen Greenhouse was a world-famous center for growing roses; the owner, C.A. Reeser, had made a special study of soil preparation and fertilizers. It is interesting how often the notion of chemicals that cause spontaneous combustion arises in articles about incendiary poltergeists. In this case, there is at least a clear possibility that other persons in the household had access to combustible chemicals.

As I was reading through the newspaper accounts of the Markle case, I expected that at any moment one of several things would happen: The fires would stop; Minnie would be arrested and be brow-beaten into a confession; or the young woman would be caught in the act of starting a fire. Those are the "rules" of incendiary poltergeist outbreaks. They do not vary. So I was stunned at the following turn of events.

THE SAD SEQUEL
TO THE MYSTERIOUS FIRES OF A FEW WEEKS AGO AT
THE MCGOWEN BOARDING HOUSE
MINNIE MARKLE LYING IN A COMATOSE
CONDITION AT HER AUNT'S.

A sad sequel has just transpired to the McGowen boarding house fire mystery which so puzzled the authorities and excited the general public, early in December.

A young girl, the victim of cruel suspicion and unfounded slander, is lying at death's door, in a trance of a week's duration, from which all efforts to arouse her have been futile.

The young woman is Miss Minnie Markle, the person accused by some of being implicated in the origin of the mysterious fires. Since Sunday night she has been in an unconscious stupor, exhibiting only the smallest signs of life, at the residence of her aunt, Mrs. L. Carey Kirk, 357 West Liberty Street.

It will be remembered that at the time of the fire Miss Markle was accused by a police officer and one of the daily papers of being the incendiary. It seems that Mrs. William Moore, a daughter of Mrs. McGowen, weary of the delay of the police officers in ferreting out the instigator of the crime, consulted a "medium." She returned to McGowen's when the house was full of curious friends and in the presence of the young woman, threw up her hands and exclaimed, "My God! It's Minnie that has made the fires!"

It was all too much for the girl of a naturally hysterical disposition. She was seized with spasms and had to be taken to the hospital. Later she was removed to her aunt's, on West Liberty Street, where she has since been very ill. Friday, three weeks ago, her mind began to wander and she became entirely insane.

Monday morning, when the Kirk family arose, Minnie seemed to be sleeping. An effort was made to arouse her, but, proving unsuccessful, Dr. Brinkman was summoned, but still the entranced girl could not be awakened. The doctor pronounced it a case of hysterical coma. Yesterday electricity was tried to arouse her. A powerful battery was applied, the current being as strong as could be obtained, but it had no effect. This morning she was whipped with wet towels and the operation only succeeded in producing a few nervous twitchings of some of the muscles. Her tongue seems paralyzed and efforts to feed her result only in choking. The only nourishment she has had during the week has been by rectal injections.

It is a particularly sad case, and the sensational paper of the city is not blameless in the matter.

Springfield [OH] Republic Times 31 January 1891: p. 8

And reading this, if I could have gone back to that day in a time machine and slapped Mrs. William Moore, I would have willingly done so.

A *Cincinnati Enquirer* article of 3 February 1891 noted that "Application had been made to take her to the Hospital, but it was refused on the ground that she had been there before, and that it was impossible to treat her case successfully. The girl was in destitute circumstances." Another ambiguity: did her aunt think she could receive better treatment at the hospital? Or did she resent the medical bills, disruption of household routine, and the distasteful tasks of caring for an unconscious adult?

The *Enquirer* also commented that the girl had been "subject to fits since last July, having prior to the first fire, one about every three weeks" and "A strong proof of her innocence generally conceded is the fact that there have been no fires where she has been staying. There have also been no fires at Mrs. McGowen's since she left." *Cincinnati [OH] Enquirer* 3 February 1891: p. 1

Despite the desperate outlook, I still thought there might be hope of recovery. The history of such things is full of cataleptics making full recoveries; of girls in hysteric trances awakening rosy-cheeked and ravenous for breakfast.

But there was to be no awakening for Minnie Markle, as announced in a shocking headline:

RELIEVED BY DEATH
MINNIE MARKLE IS MERCIFULLY DELIVERED FROM HER PERSECUTORS

Poor Minnie Markle's long, consciousless sleep ended last evening in an eternal and wakeless trance. She died at 5 o'clock without any signs of returning consciousness and the McGowen fire mystery possibly will never be fathomed.

An autopsy will be held tomorrow morning. The time for the funeral has not been set.

Springfield [OH] Republic Times 3 February 1891: p. 8

The *Cincinnati Enquirer* recalled the episode for its readers in an article that both recapped the chronology of the fires and added some new details:

CATALEPTIC STRANGELY FOLLOWED BY FLAMES
FIRE MYSTERY DEEPENED
BY MINNIE MARKLE'S DEATH,
AFTER REMAINING IN A TRANCE FOR EIGHT DAYS.
FIRES UNACCOUNTABLY SPRANG UP IN EVERY ROOM,
SOMETIMES IN THE VERY PRESENCE
OF STARTLED INMATES
THE DEAD GIRL CHARGED
WITH BEING THE INCENDIARY,
WHEN SHE TAKES TO HER BED
AFFECTED BY COMA.
STILL WATCHING FOR SIGNS OF LIFE IN THE BODY.
SYMPTOMS WHICH STRONGLY RESEMBLED HYDROPHOBIA
ALLEGED CONFESSION THAT
THE GIRL KNEW THE REAL FIENDS,
BUT PASSED AWAY UNCONSCIOUS, AND
WITH HER LIPS SEALED
A MYSTERY NOT YET SOLVED.

Springfield, Ohio, February 3. The remains of Miss Minnie Markle, the orphan girl whose strange trance condition excited general interest in her case, lie to-night enclosed in a plain casket.

All signs of life disappeared last evening and a mirror applied to her mouth showed no moisture. On being removed a feeble pulsation of the heart had stopped.

Connected with her sad death is a remarkable and thrilling story. No one knows what the girl suffered. From the time she was accused of starting mysterious fires until death relieved her sufferings, life must have been a great burden. Her case mystified and baffled local physicians....

After a list of the first few fires, the *Enquirer* tells of the fear of the neighbors, the guards mounted, and the scope of the damage.

The news of the strange visitation of fire spread over the neighborhood and hundreds of people called at the house. It became an object of great curiosity.

A REIGN OF TERROR

Followed, and half the neighbors hourly expected to find their houses on fire.

Some of the superstitious and benighted claimed that Minnie Markle, the servant girl, was bewitched and were almost ready to inaugurate a Salem crusade against her.

But the fires did not stop, and occurred and all hours of the day and night, except early morning. Miss Markle discovered the larger number of them. She was constantly watched and searched, since the shafts of suspicion were first directed against her, and nothing tending to criminate her was discovered. The police were notified, and all efforts to discover the origin of the fires failed....In all about fifty-six fires broke out in the house in a few days. A singular fact about the mystery is that the fires occurred in every room but one, an upstairs room, occupied by two boarders, employees of the adjoining green houses. Nearly everything in the house, clothing, carpets, window curtains, books, &c., were partially destroyed....The state of affairs had become so alarming that the burned goods were carried into a yard and policemen detailed to watch the house. The fires immediately ceased as mysteriously as they had begun six weeks before. The last one reported occurred Monday, January 22.

A length of six weeks is a classic span for poltergeist outbreaks—typically they are reported as ceasing within either six weeks or six months.

The girl, whose sad death has caused so much excitement here, came to this city two years ago last December from Mendon, Mercer County. She was the daughter of Mr. and Mrs. James Markle. She was left an orphan at 11 years, and was left about $500, but it has all been spent. She was in the hospital last summer to receive treatment for a shoulder injured in a runaway [horse accident.] While there she tore the bed clothing to pieces, like one who was mad. Prior to the frequency of the fires she had fits

IN THEIR NATURE HYSTERICAL

About once every two weeks. Since then she had fits two or three times a day. On the night the fires stopped she had seventeen. They caused her to try to bite herself and anyone who approached. In fact, she acted like a person afflicted with hydrophobia, minus frothing at the mouth. The fits were caused by female complaint. On Christmas Day the girl was removed to the home of her aunt, Mrs. L. Carey Kirk, on Liberty Street.

Her relatives soon noticed signs of insanity. In walking about the house she would stop and look around to see if anyone was watching her. It grew rapidly, and she was subject to numerous fits. Three weeks ago Miss Markle was compelled to go to bed, from which she never arose.

During the first, she stated to *The Enquirer* correspondent that it would be folly for her to start the fires, as Mrs. McGowen's house was the only home she had, and when that was gone she would be cast upon the world to care for herself. Sunday, January 25, she went into a trance, from which she never awoke. Doctors pronounced it a

CASE OF HYSTERICAL COMA.

As has been stated in this paper, all efforts to arouse her failed, and she remained unconscious until the last. The unfortunate girl lay as one dead, and the only signs of life were feeble but rapid pulsations. She remained in the cataleptic condition eight cays and was not conscious one second. The only nourishment she received was by injections. The end, if such it is, came gradually and peacefully last evening. Her relatives watched her closely to-day

FOR ANY SIGNS OF LIFE.

The attending physicians will hold a post-mortem to-morrow morning and the funeral services will be held Thursday afternoon at 2 o'clock from the house. Before becoming so weak Miss Markle sent for Detective Wilson and told him she knew who started the fires, but refused to state until she was able to accompany him to the ill-fated house and furnish him with proof. But she made no ante-mortem confession of who the guilty party is. The authorities now make the startling statement that the fires were started with wax matches, and several were found in the house at the time of the fires. Suspicion now points to one of the boarders, and it is probable that an arrest will be made.

Cincinnati [OH] Enquirer 4 February 1891: p. 1

But no arrests were made. It was easier to bury the whole sad episode in that plain casket.

The doctors may have diagnosed a case of hysterical coma, but the autopsy told a different story.

THE MARKLE CASE
THE DOCTORS SAY DEATH WAS CAUSED BY THE STRAIN ON HER NERVES.

Dr. Brinkman, assisted by Drs. Kilgore, Baker, Randall and Lisle, held a postmortem examination on the body of Minnie Markle, who died yesterday after being in a trance for eight days. They found the brain, kidney, uterus and other organs normal.

They found a hypostatic congestion of the lungs, due to the weak action of the heart, but the most serious trouble, and what was the primary cause of death, was what is technically termed Hepatitis, or in plain language, vernacular inflammation of the liver.

The nervous system was in disorder and perceptibly weak and the shock and excitement brought on by the charge of being the cause of the McGowen fires hastened her death. The entranced condition was due to the condition of the nervous system.

The funeral will be held at the residence of her aunt, Mrs. L. Carey Kirk, 357 West Liberty Street, Thursday afternoon at 2:30 o'clock.
Springfield [OH] Republic Times 5 February 1891

A diagnosis of hepatitis, a viral infection of the liver, would certainly explain a lot. Mercer County, where Minnie had lived, was in the Great Black Swamp, which was not completely drained until late in the 19th century. Malaria and other fevers were common and long-term infection with malaria can lead to liver damage. One of the treatments for hepatitis was calomel, which contained mercury. Being dosed with something so toxic would offer yet another explanation for Minnie's ill-health and "fits."

Minnie remains a mystery to the end. Where was the girl from age 11 to 16? At an orphanage? At a relative's home? Did she have any siblings? The only relative we know of is her aunt. Where had Minnie lived until she arrived at the newly widowed Mrs. McGowen's home in December of 1888?

She had inherited $500, the equivalent of $11,628 in 2012 dollars. "It has all been spent." By whom? If it had been misspent by a guardian she must have been bitter that she'd had to go into service. She should have been the idol of her parents, had pretty clothes and smooth hands, not have to toil up and down stairs with bedding and hot water.

Did she think of Mrs. McGowen as a mother? The woman had been kind to her, but perhaps it was a limited kindness, one extended to an employee, not the wholehearted affection lavished on her daughter or nieces.

Minnie's aunt lived only a few blocks from the boarding house, yet she did not take in her niece. Was there a family feud, a lack of space or resources? Did her aunt simply feel that Minnie ought to be out, earning her own keep? Or was there something more sinister?

You get the sense from the articles of the boardinghouse as a place where you'd find women—friends, neighbors, and relatives—running in and out all day long. And, perhaps, an atmosphere of gossip and snubs and catty remarks about the help getting above themselves.

Yet, as she remarked pathetically to the Enquirer reporter, "Mrs. McGowen's house was the only home she had, and when that was gone she would be cast upon the world to care for herself." No wonder her heart broke when Mrs. McGowen's daughter turned on her.

In researching this case, I was hampered by the many different ways the newspapers spelled Minnie's last name. A final insult arose when I went to Springfield's Ferncliff Cemetery to find her grave. The clerk could not find any record of it. He worked the computer database several different ways and finally found her—listed as Minnie "Marble." Although her tombstone is correct, a hand-written Victorian internment card had been misread or carelessly transcribed. The clerk kindly wrote the right name on the card—at least she would be given back her proper name in *that* record.

Alone in life, she lies alone in death as well, in a single grave plot. There are no "Mother" or "Papa" or "Brother" stones to keep her company. Section K of Ferncliff Cemetery is filled with fine granite monuments, including those of the Reeser family, who owned the greenhouse where Will Reeser and the other boarders worked. The section where Minnie is buried was reserved for single adult burials as well as "3 tiers of infants, 22 graves per row." The infants' graves are unmarked. Minnie's small stone, obscured by dried leaves and bits of drought-pale grass, looks lonely in the large expanse of lawn.

Did those who buried her expect her grave to smoke and scorch? Did they mourn for one so young, doomed for her sins to eternal fire? At the end of her short, tormented life, I hope she found the *lux perpetua*, the Light at the end of the tunnel, a sunlit Summerland garden.

Anything but flames.

Appendix
Spook Squibs
Shavings from the Coffin of News

We can't whip anybody; don't want to murder any one; haven't the heart
to suggest suicide to a fellow and our stock of imagination is low, so if
you find no news in this item, don't blame us.

– *Richwood [OH] Gazette* 22 November 1877: p. 3 –

A feature of 19th century newspapers that I really enjoy are the squibs: very short news items, sometimes just a sentence or two long that we would call filler. Sometimes they are factual; sometimes they are meant as humor.

What is fascinating is the large variety of names used for these collections of squibs.

Chips from the News Log
Pith of the News
Queer Wrinkles
Cradle, Altar, Tomb
News Boiled Down
Lightning Splinters

And, most poignantly of all, Little Empty Cradles—for infant death announcements.

Here, in no particular order, is a collection of ghost-story squibs and very short articles. Think of this as the 19th-century version of the "Fright Bites: Mini-tales of the Macabre" chapters from *Haunted Ohio III, IV,* and *V.* If anyone has any more information about any of these stories, I'd love to hear it.

BY THE GHOST
OF A SOOTHSAYER, THEY SAID THEY WERE
DRIVEN FROM HOME.

Bellefontaine, Ohio, April 13. "Aunt" Mary Dixon, aged and eccentric for many years, lived alone in an old loghouse near Middleburg. She obtained an extensive reputation from the superstitious of this county as a soothsayer. She died a few days ago, and a well-known family moved into the vacant house. The family drove hurriedly into Middleburg the next day attired only in their night clothing, and excitedly stated that they were driven from their home by a ghost. The rattling of chains and deep groans disturbed them, and they claim that the old lady's ghost, wrapped in a table cloth, drove them from the place. The affair has caused great excitement. No one will go near the place, and the house will be destroyed.

Cincinnati [OH] Enquirer 16 April 1900: p. 4 LOGAN COUNTY

There is a rumor of a ghost having been seen at the Amanda graveyard. Can it be that in the nineteenth century a ghost will come about in Butler County, Ohio?

Hamilton [OH] Telegraph 24 March 1881: p. 1 BUTLER COUNTY

LOOKING FOR THE GHOST

Barnesville, December 7 Miss Sadie Dent, the young lady schoolteacher who was so badly frightened by the tall, ghost-like figure which accosted her on one of our secluded streets late last night, has recovered consciousness, but is under a physician's treatment. The excitement was intense, and the strong vigilance committee, which was the natural outgrowth of the affair, has its members stationed on our streets, and, should the mysterious object reappear, a liberal dose of lead pills will be freely administered.

Cincinnati [OH] Enquirer 8 December 1887: p. 2 BELMONT COUNTY

NOTE: I have not yet found the original article about the attack on Miss Dent.

PIONEER SEES GHOST
WHICH GIVES HIM MILITARY SALUTE AT SITE OF OLD FORT MEIGS

Toledo, Ohio. November 13. According to J.M. Wolcott, Trustee of Maumee Pioneers' Association and grandson of the famous Indian chief, Little Turtle, a ghost is in possession of the historic Ft. Meigs grounds and a thorough investigation of the matter is to be made by President D. K. Hollenbeck, of the Pioneers' Association. According to Wolcott's statement the ghost appeared one night three weeks ago about midnight.

The white object was in the form of a man, which gave Wolcott a military salute. He returned the salute, and the object then, according to Wolcott's story, vanished.

Cincinnati [OH] Enquirer 14 November 1910: pg. 5 WOOD COUNTY

NOTE: Wolcott was a descendent of the family who built Wolcott House, now part of the headquarters for the Maumee Valley Historical Society. At this time Fort Meigs was just open land, and not the elaborately restored fort we see today and which I wrote about in *Haunted Ohio V,* "Ghosts Along the Maumee."

An interesting ghost story is told that a widow at Findlay, O., is visited every evening by her deceased husband, who still clings to the old rocking chair, even though his bones lie in the cemetery. The chair begins to rock every evening, and the widow is sure her husband's spirit occupies it.
Xenia [OH] Daily Gazette 10 September 1886: p. 3 HANCOCK COUNTY

Mrs. Jonas Yoder, Millersburg, O., says she has been disturbed by the ghost of her husband who killed himself, and has had the remains taken up and buried four miles further away from her premises.
Massillon [OH] Independent 14 January 1887: p. 1 HOLMES COUNTY

NOTE: I don't know if the late husband was buried on the family farm or not. I found this note about his suicide:

Jonas Yoder, a wealthy old farmer and known to belong to the "Amish" sect, hung himself in his barn, near Millersburg, last Thursday.
Athens [OH] Messenger 30 December 1886: p. 1 HOLMES COUNTY

In a Hamilton church, the Bible is carried off every Sunday night, and it cannot be discovered by whom. Six Bibles have been taken, and some say the church is haunted by a ghost.
Athens [OH] Messenger 5 May 1881: p. 1 BUTLER COUNTY

An alleged ghost story on Spring Grove Avenue, near Lawler's Exchange, has been squelched by a proper course of investigation.
Cincinnati [OH] Enquirer 23 March 1883: p. 6 HAMILTON COUNTY

It is to be hoped that the residents of Presbyterian Flats [Cumminsville] will not persist in cooling off their piazzas these sultry evenings, clad in a single garment of the Mother Hubbard style. Although there may be nothing radically wrong about such a proceeding, the sight of these white ghost-like figures seriously disturbs the equanimity of lovers' moonlight promenades.
Cincinnati [OH] Enquirer 3 August 1884: p. 12 HAMILTON COUNTY

NOTE: A "Mother Hubbard" is a long loose gown.

NOT HAUNTED
THE CUMMINSVILLE GHOST STORY A MYTH.

Under the heading of "Cumminsville Chatter," there appeared in Sunday's issue a story of an apparition of a woman making its appearance in the dead of the night at the old fashioned frame house on the west side of the Cincinnati, Hamilton, and Dayton Railroad track, in South Cumminsville, adjoining the residence of Mr. Adam Steifel.

It is not for a moment supposed that there are any sensible persons who would take any stock in such a ghost story and only because there was absolutely no foundation on which to construct the story did those interested conclude to investigate and find out how it originated. This was easily accomplished. It seems that about a week ago one Caleb Canton, who lives about a mile from the South Cumminsville station, called upon Mr. Leahy, the agent for the house with a view of renting same. After being informed as to the price, terms and conditions on which the rent was to be paid, Mr. Leahy was astonished at the man's offer to take it at just one-half of the rent asked. This offer was promptly rejected and after a few words the applicant walked out, remarking "that it would not be many days before he could get the house for almost nothing."

An investigation reveals the fact that it was this same Mr. Canton who furnished the story to the correspondent, who in turn wrote it up, with the usual embellishments.

With these facts the reader can form his own conclusions as to whether the house is haunted or not.

Cincinnati [OH] Enquirer 26 October 1886: p. 4 HAMILTON COUNTY

CUMMINSVILLE GOSSIP.

The haunted house at South Cumminsville is again occupied and no trouble, as yet has been reported from the tenant.

Cincinnati [OH] Enquirer 2 January 1887: p 1 HAMILTON COUNTY

SEE GHOSTS.
SPRINGFIELD COLORED PEOPLE WHO RECOGNIZE THE SPIRIT OF A MURDERED RAIL-WAY CONDUCTOR.

Springfield, Ohio, August 2. Great excitement prevailed about 11 o'clock to-night on the levee among the colored residents. It was caused by the second appearance of the ghost of Christie Harris, a Big Four conductor, killed last Monday by Andy Farrell. The ghost was seen this time by several colored women and men, who claim that Harris visited the scene of the murder and afterward walked to Farrell's saloon. The ghost disappeared as the yard engine passed. The colored people fled into their houses and locked their doors.

A ridiculous report was circulated that the ghost was billed to appear to-night, and according to these people's statement it did. William Howard, a colored levee saloonist, claims that his business has decreased 25 per cent, since the ghost first appeared. Several fellows slept in his place Saturday night because they were afraid to go home, while two families have moved away.

Cincinnati [OH] Enquirer 3 August 1891: p. 1 CLARK COUNTY

NOTE: The Big Four was the Cleveland, Cincinnati, Chicago and St. Louis Railway. The levee was the "sporting district" of Springfield, full of saloons, gambling dens and brothels. It was also home to many African-Americans. Here is the backstory to the murder:

DISHONORED HIS HOME

Springfield, O., July 27 Andy Farrell, a saloonkeeper, shot Chris Harris, a railroad conductor at noon to-day with a charge of buckshot from a shot-gun, blowing the entire top of his head off and killing him instantly. Harris, it is alleged, has been intimate with Farrell's wife for several months. Deceased leaves a wife and two daughters, eminently respectable. The murderer, who is a low character, gave himself up, and is attempting the insanity dodge.

St. Paul [MN] Daily Globe 28 July 1891: p. 3 CLARK COUNTY

SPIRIT OF ENGINEER ROSS APPEARED AT SEANCE SAYS HE MET DEATH BY BEING STRUCK WITH A STONE

Readers will recall the tragic death of George Ross of Galion, engineer of the Erie road, who was killed about a year ago at the Old Forge by being struck on the head—with what remains a mystery. Considerable sensation was aroused, and it was rumored that arrests would be made of people suspicioned with the murder.

The matter has been forgotten until in Cleveland a few nights ago a great spiritualist meeting was being held. Prominent mediums were there and spirit after spirit was announced to be present, and messages were given.

Just when the meeting was closing a medium announced another spirit. "I am George Ross of Galion who was killed at Akron. I was struck on the head with a stone which was the cause of death," and then the spirit vanished.

This is considered strange from the fact that the medium who gave the reading had never heard of Ross. The incident has caused considerable stir at Galion.

Akron [OH] Daily Democrat 3 October 1899: p. 1 CRAWFORD/ CUYAHOGA COUNTY

FRIGHT CAUSED BY SEEING A "GHOST" BROUGHT ON HEMORRHAGES THAT KILLED YOUNG STEINLE

Toledo, Ohio May 5 Henry Steinle died at his parents' home on City Park Avenue last night of hemorrhage of the lungs, brought on by a fright he received nearly two weeks ago. Mr. Steinle was on his way home late one night, and when he reached a lonesome spot near a park he thought he observed some sort of an apparition that resembled a human being in form but was airy-like in composition. The shock to his nervous system was so great that he became prostrated after he reached home.

He tried to think nothing more of the incident, but it continued to prey on his mind. In a few days he was seized with hemorrhages, which continued until the time of his death.

The case was such a peculiar one that it baffled the physician.

Cincinnati [OH] Enquirer 16 May 1899: p. 1 LUCAS COUNTY

GHOST DOES STUNTS
TURNS THINGS TOPSY TURVY IN RAVENNA FARM HOUSE.

Ravenna, O., Oct. 15 A ghost at the farm house of Sidney Veon, south of here, is reported to play the piano, open and close windows, and move furniture. The family says the bed was turned squarely around at night and a hat hanging on a peg was whirled about like a buzz saw.

The Stark County Democrat [Canton, OH] 17 October 1905: p. 1 PORTAGE COUNTY

A MYSTERY
A MAN WHO ENTERS A HOUSE THROUGH
BOLTED DOORS

There is a mystery at the house of Joseph Boley, North Jackson Street, just north of Wayne; and one which causes some agitation to the inmates. It consists of the inexplicable appearance of a man in the house, at night. This startling apparition, says Mrs. Boley, "was first seen by Mr. Boley's son while he was sleeping on a lounge. The man came in, looked round, and disappeared again in a few moments, without speaking a word.

"Afterwards one of the little girls saw the man, in the same way. The queer part is how a man could get into the house as the door was bolted inside. There is no lock on it. Once we saw him as he was disappearing round the corner of the house. It makes me quite uneasy, and we have asked the police to watch the house.

"Yes, we have a revolver in the house but there has never been any chance to shoot at the strange intruder, as he slips away before anyone can get a fair sight at him."

Mrs. Boley speaks as though the strange visitor was not of flesh and blood, but an uneasy spirit.

Lima [OH] Daily Times 19 January 1891: p. 4 ALLEN COUNTY

SAW A GHOST.
THE SPIRIT OF A DEAD WOMAN EXCITES THE
COLORED PEOPLE

Springfield, Ohio, October 6. Considerable excitement exists among the colored residents of the levee to-night over the appearance of the ghost of Hattie Ward, who was found dead in her room Thursday. Quite a number swear they saw her ghost on the stairs and in the hall. Some became so excited that they ran from the building yelling, attracting the attention of the police.

Cincinnati [OH] Enquirer 7 October 1893: p. 1 CLARK COUNTY

"There is a legend associated with an old cemetery located near Damascus. It seems that a local farmer was plowing one of his fields near Damascus when he suddenly began to plow up tombstones. He told his neighbors about what he had done, and that he planned to continue his farming operation despite the fact that he would be plowing and planting a cemetery. His neighbors warned him that such actions would bring him back luck. The farmer scoffed at his neighbors' warnings and shortly afterwards he drove his tractor off a bluff into the Maumee River and he was drowned."

Ohio Ghost Towns No. 11 Henry County, Richard M. Helwig (Galena, OH: The Center for Ghost Town Research in Ohio, 1988) p. 31 HENRY COUNTY

ASKED FOR SHELTER
JOHN SAIGOT AT MASSILLON CAN FIND NO PLACE TO CALL HOME.

Massillon, April 16 John Saigot, the Hungarian who recently accidentally shot and killed his brother, called at police headquarters Monday and asked for food and shelter. He said that since the killing none of the Hungarian or Slavish boarding house keepers would permit him to live with them, and that none of the other boarding house men about the city would take him in. He said that his fellow countrymen believed him to be possessed of an evil spirit, which would cause ghosts, particularly that of his dead brother, to come into the house while he slept.

Some of the boarders at the Coshinski house say that they saw the ghost of Saigot's dead brother every night that he was in the place.

Marshal Markel, Policeman Gotz, and V.H. Morgan spent Saturday in the "haunted house," hoping that they might find some justification for the sights and noises that the Huns told about. But they never saw nor heard anything unusual.

The Stark County Democrat [Canton, OH] 19 April 1901: p. 6 STARK COUNTY

NOTE: Slavish means "Slavic." There was considerable prejudice against Eastern European immigrants at this time, hence the "Hun" nickname.

SALINEVILLE HAS A GENUINE GHOST
SPOOK HUNTERS ARE OUT IN FORCE
VISITOR HAS MANY QUEER DISGUISES

Salineville, O., Jan. 9 A ghost with striking peculiarities inhabits Schoolhouse Hill, in this town, according to several citizens of unimpeachable veracity. For the past two weeks it has been seen nightly by those who were out late.

The remarkable fact about this apparition is that it appears in a different guise each time. Tom Ellis, who has seen it twice, says the first night it appeared as a tall, old man, with a long beard, erect and walking briskly.

The next time it presented the same face, but seemed infirm, bent and decrepit and moved slowly, with tottering steps. He got a good look at it as it was bright moonlight, but when within ten feet of him, the specter vanished as if the earth had swallowed it.

John Edge also saw the "spook." It was clothed in white and moving fast. To him it appeared as a headless man. Others describe it as having a youthful face, with a singularly horrible leer.

A number of courageous young men have formed a "ghost hunters' league" and propose to solve the mystery.

The Stark County Democrat [Canton, OH] 13 January 1903: p. 6 COLUMBIANA COUNTY

The ghost of Mrs. Green, deceased, at Middleport, Pickaway County, O. is solicitous for the welfare of a ward of herself and husband, and suddenly appears and "blocks the game" whenever he visits the gambling table.

New Philadelphia [OH] Democrat 10 February 1871: p. 2 PICKAWAY COUNTY

A SINGULAR SPOOK

The household of Hiram Ruthless, of Mechanicsburg, O., is deeply distressed by the remarkable conduct of an "apparition." The spook has been in regulation style rapping on the walls, gliding through passage ways, and making general mischief. Recently the ghost has taken to such practical work as shoveling coal into the stove and setting the breakfast table and Mrs. Ruthless is thinking about dispensing with the services of the hired girl.

Lima [OH] Daily News 24 April 1891: p. 2 CHAMPAIGN COUNTY

There is a haunted hollow tree near Bethel, Clermont County, at which blood curdling hobgoblin sights are seen every New Year's night. So said.

Athens [OH] Messenger 18 January 1877: p. 1 CLERMONT COUNTY

This next article had five lines of headline that summed up the story—rather like the movie trailer that gives the plot away. I've given the citation, but, really, the headline tells you everything you need to know

A HEADLESS GHOST,
PERCHED ON A SYCAMORE STUMP
AND WITH BLOOD STREAMING DOWN HIS BODY,
IS EXCITING THE QUIET FOLKS
OF BUTLER COUNTY, OHIO.
A MAN'S REAPPEARANCE AFTER DEATH TO LOCATE
HIS REMAINS

Cincinnati [OH] Enquirer 14 September 1890: p. 10 BUTLER COUNTY

Squibs often had to do with strange deaths, ironic endings, or "funny" stories about death:

> Warning to wives: George W. Cram lately shot his wife because she nagged him.
> *Logansport [IN] Pharos* 23 October 1894: p. 2

> A little girl named Alice Brown died at Mt. Gilead, a week ago, from the effect of "skipping the rope." This is the second death at that place from the same cause.
> *Athens [OH] Messenger* 5 May 1881: p. 1 MORROW COUNTY

> Last year Bellaire burned more babies than were born in the town.
> *Marion [OH] Daily Star* 4 August 1882: p. 4 BELMONT COUNTY

NOTE: I assume this refers to accidental fire deaths and not human sacrifice!

CHILD'S BONES FOUND 'NEATH THE FLOORING
OF A MT. VERNON HOTEL.

Special Dispatch to *The Enquirer*

Mt. Vernon, Ohio, April 27 Workmen engaged in painting the St. James Hotel, in this city, made a horrible discovery this afternoon. One of them stepped on a board in the flooring of a room on the third floor, which tilted. Raising the board, he was horrified to see a skeleton. The bones were taken out and turned over to Coroner Scribner, who pronounced them to be those of an infant child. Rats had presumably carried away the head and eaten the flesh off the bones.

Cincinnati [OH] Enquirer 28 April 1897: p. 1 KNOX COUNTY

KILLED IN AN ATTEMPT TO SHOOT A CAT.

Cincinnati papers related that on Wednesday morning Louis Vollmer, a gardener employed at the suburban residence, Mount Airy, of Mr. W.T. Bishop, attempted, with the consent of his employer, to kill a cat which he believed to have eaten chickens. Loading both barrels of a double-barreled shot-gun, he discharged one, which only wounded the cat. Attempting to club her with the butt-end of his gun, the hammer of the remaining barrel caught in his clothing, and caused the discharge of the entire load through the upper and inner part of his right thigh. An artery was torn open, from the effects of which he bled to death in ten or fifteen minutes. Vollmer was married, about thirty-three years of age, and the father of a small family, the youngest of whom was born but a couple of hours before the accident.

New York Times 3 August 1883 HAMILTON COUNTY

KILLED WHILE PLAYING GHOST

Lima (O.) John Enulson, night watch at the Bluffton planing mill, has been troubled recently by seeing what he claimed to be the ghost of his dead wife at the mill. The other night he saw the apparition and decided to test its density by firing a revolver at it. The ghost dropped and then it was discovered to be Chas. Shelton, telegraph operator. He was killed.

Martinsville [IN] Morgan County Gazette 24 December 1892: p. 2 ALLEN COUNTY

Bibliography

The Anomalist, http://www.anomalist.com

Arment, Chad, *Boss Snakes: Stories and Sightings of Giant Snakes in North America*, Coachwhip Publications, 2008

_____*The Historical Bigfoot*, Coachwhip Publications, 2006

_____*Varmints: Mystery Carnivores of North America*, Coachwhip Publications, 2010

Dr Beachcombing's Bizarre History Blog http://www.strangehistory.net/

Bondeson, Jan, *Buried Alive: The Terrifying History of Our Most Primal Fear*, W.W. Norton, 2001

Brandon, Jim, *Weird America: A Guide to Places of Mystery in the United States*, E.P. Dutton, 1978

Citro, Joseph A., *Green Mountain Ghosts, Ghouls & Unsolved Mysteries*, Mariner Books, 2012

_____*Green Mountains, Dark Tales*, UPNE, 2001

_____*Joe Citro's Weird Vermont*, Bat Books, 2012

_____*Passing Strange: True Tales of New England Hauntings and Horrors*, Mariner Books, 2001

_____*The Vermont Ghost Guide*, UPNE, 2000 (with Stephen R. Bissette)

_____*The Vermont Monster Guide*, UPNE, 2009 (with Stephen R. Bissette)

_____*Vermont's Haunts: Tall Tales & True from the Green Mountains*, Bat Books, 2011

Clark, Jerome, *Unnatural Phenomena: A Guide to the Bizarre Wonders of North America*, ABC-CLIO, 2005

Coleman, Loren, *Mysterious America*, Pocket Books, 2007

Finucane, Ronald C., *Appearances of the Dead: A Cultural History of Ghosts*, Prometheus, 1984

Fort, Charles, Jim Steinmeyer, intro., *The Book of the Damned: The Collected Works of Charles Fort. Four Complete Volumes: The Book of the Damned, New Lands, Lo!, and Wild Talents*, Tarcher, 2008

Fortean Times http://www.forteantimes.com/

Frazier, Jeffrey R., *The Black Ghost of Scotia, and More Pennsylvania Fireside Tales Volume II*, Egg Hill Publications, 1997

Lesy, Michael, *Wisconsin Death Trip*, University of New Mexico Press, 2000

Maxwell-Stuart, P.G., *Ghosts: A History of Phantoms, Ghouls, and Other Spirits of the Dead*, The History Press, 2007

_____*Poltergeists: A History of Violent Ghostly Phenomena*, Amberley, 2012

Reiter, Nicholas A., *The Bridges of Avalon: Science, Spirit, and the Quest for*

Unity, iUniverse, 2005

Roll, Dr. William G., *Unleashed: Of Poltergeists and Murder: The Curious Story of Tina Resch*, Pocket Books, 2004

Woodyard, Chris, *Haunted Ohio: Ghostly Tales from the Buckeye State*, Kestrel Publications, 1991

_____*Haunted Ohio II: More Ghostly Tales from the Buckeye State*, Kestrel Publications, 1992

_____*Haunted Ohio III: Still More Ghostly Tales from the Buckeye State*, Kestrel Publications, 1994

_____*Haunted Ohio IV: Restless Spirits*, Kestrel Publications, 1997

_____*Haunted Ohio V: 200 Years of Ghosts*, Kestrel Publications, 2003

_____*Ghost Hunter's Guide to Haunted Ohio*, Kestrel Publications, 2000

_____*Spooky Ohio: 13 Traditional Tales*, Kestrel Publications, 1995

_____*The Headless Horror: More Haunting Ohio Tales*, Kestrel Publications, 2012

_____*The Ghost Wore Black: Ghastly Tales of the Past*, Kestrel Publications, 2013

General Index

Index by County

How to Purchase
Your Own Copies of
This and Other Books by
Chris Woodyard

You may purchase personally autographed books on our website:
www.hauntedohiobooks.com.

Or find Chris Woodyard's books at your local bookstore or library.

Visit us on Facebook at
Haunted Ohio by Chris Woodyard

Coming Soon, more books from Chris Woodyard:

The Headless Horror: More Haunting Ohio Tales
and
The Ghost Wore Black: Ghastly Tales from the Past